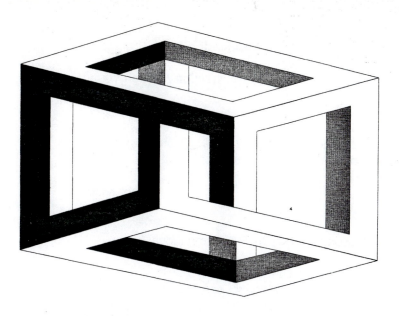

Case Studies in Building Design and Construction

Robert W. Dorsey
University of Cincinnati

Prentice Hall
Upper Saddle River, New Jersey   Columbus, Ohio

Library of Congress Cataloging-in-Publication Data

Dorsey, Robert W.
    Case studies in building design and construction / Robert w.
Dorsey.
      p.   cm.
    ISBN 0-13-079775-8
    1. Building—Superintendence—Case studies.   2. Building—Case
studies.   3. Building industry—Case studies.   I. Title.
    TH438.D65   1999
    690'.068—dc21
                                       98-8330
                                         CIP

Cover art/photo: © Mason Morfit, 1996. FPG International
Editor: Ed Francis
Production Coordinator: Christine M. Harrington
Production Editor: Custom Editorial Productions, Inc.
Design Coordinator: Karrie M. Converse
Cover Designer: Lisa Stark
Production Manager: Patricia A. Tonneman
Illustrations: Custom Editorial Productions, Inc.
Marketing Manager: Danny Hoyt

This book was set in Leawood by Custom Editorial Productions, Inc., and was printed and
bound by R.R. Donnelly and Sons Company. The cover was printed by Phoenix Color Corp.

© 1999 by Prentice-Hall, Inc.
Simon & Schuster/A Viacom Company
Upper Saddle River, New Jersey 07458

Printed in the United States of America

10 9 8 7 6 5 4 3 2 1

ISBN: 0-13-079775-8

Prentice-Hall International (UK) Limited, *London*
Prentice-Hall of Australia Pty. Limited, *Sydney*
Prentice-Hall of Canada, Inc., *Toronto*
Prentice-Hall Hispanoamericana, S. A., *Mexico*
Prentice-Hall of India Private Limited, *New Delhi*
Prentice-Hall of Japan, Inc., *Tokyo*
Simon & Schuster Asia Pte. Ltd., *Singapore*
Editora Prentice-Hall do Brasil, Ltda., *Rio de Janeiro*

Background of Author

Licensed architect, Ohio and Indiana; national certification, Member, American Institute of Architects; Past President and Fellow, American Institute of Constructors; 40 years experience in architecture, construction, teaching, and research.

Previous Publications

Project Delivery Systems for Building Construction

Guidebook for Architecture and Construction in Greater Cincinnati

Acquisition of Skills and Traits for Success in Management of Construction

Women in Construction

Evaluation of College Level Construction Education

Over 100 articles, conference proceedings, and book chapters

Preface and Introductory Comments

"The good old days are not coming back."

Fragmentation and Challenges

An academic veteran recalls one salient line from among many commencement addresses: "Prepare yourselves for a lifetime of increasing complexity; the good old days are not coming back." Thus spoke the late Francis Dale, newspaper publisher and World War II hero (submarine commander), in an address three decades ago, as the turbulent 1960s were coming to a close.

How right Mr. Dale was. Indeed our society has continually become more fragmented, rushed, and challenging in general, and its inherent complexities have certainly been manifested in the design and construction of our essential functional and aesthetic facilities—but the always-resilient architects, engineers, and constructors have regularly developed new ways of getting buildings designed, built, and utilized.

The innovations range from electronic design and document production to fledgling use of construction robots, to a whole wave of emerging project delivery systems. This book examines the intricacies of relationships, contractual and otherwise, among owners, designers, constructors, and other players in the fascinating drama of designing and building the arenas of human endeavor.

Glories, Problems, and Initiatives

When looking at cityscapes around the world, one can admire monuments to human endeavor. All parties to the construction process should feel immense pride in their accomplishments, but those individuals can just as readily look behind the marble, bricks, and glass to see arcane contract language, disputes, claims, and episodes of wasteful aggravation standing in the way of bringing projects to productive lives for their many users. There is no doubt that improvements must continue to be made in the whole process of working relationships among the parties. So, terms such as *partnering, total quality management,* and *alternative dispute resolution* have necessarily entered the construction lexicon. To quote many veteran constructors, "Let's get away from all this adversity and make construction fun again."

> **Can construction be fun? Yes, indeed, if we can remove much of the adversity.**

In fact, good strides in cooperation are being made. Design and construction associations, such as the American Institute of Architects (AIA) and the Associated General Contractors of America (AGC), are collaborating more closely than ever on forms of agreement, documentation processes, and other issues of mutual interest. All parties are attempting to cope with their changing responsibilities in the design/construct/maintain continuum, and are addressing the necessity of working together for the benefit of owners and ultimate users of buildings. Owners themselves, independently and through interest groups, are taking more active roles in determining how construction should be accomplished. The Business Roundtable, made up of the chief executive officers of 200 ranking corporations in the United States, published a series of booklets through the 1980s under the general title *Construction Industry Cost Effectiveness* (CICE), with the clear message that design and construction must become more efficient if the American economy is to remain competitive. CICE documents became standard reading for all serious designers and constructors, and for students of those professions. One of the outcomes of the CICE initiative is the Construction Industry Institute (CII), the first multimember private agency aimed specifically at researching issues that influence effectiveness in construction. CII combines the talents of owners, constructors, designers, and professors in pursuing problems relating to a range of construction topics, from productivity to safety and automation.

Author's Approach

As a professor, I urge my students to know the time and setting of any book, including "where the author is coming from." This author comes from the profession of architecture, but has devoted over a quarter century to construction and design education. As a design practitioner, I emphasize the relationship between design and construction, and am at least as comfortable with mud on my boots as bent over a drawing board or computer. As an educator, I espouse the thesis that construction should be a profession equal to and compatible with architecture and engineering, and that development of such professional status is dependent on high-quality education and performance. This segment of higher education has now grown into the distinct academic area of *construction*.

> **Construction should become a profession equal to architecture and engineering.**

One of my articles some years ago was "Construction, the Emerging Discipline," published by the American Institute of Constructors, the association established to promote professionalism in construction. The article examined requirements for the discipline to evolve, including strong academics, scholarship, research, and, above all, professional attitudes and ethical standards pervading both academe and practice. Indeed, the discipline of construction has emerged, and a range of texts has come forth to support both academics and practice. This book is intended to complement several that have been written on project delivery systems and contractual relations, from the points of view of both design and construction. The case studies can be used to explore concepts described in other books, or the cases can form the stand-alone basis of a course for aspiring designers, constructors, and facility managers.

My experience also includes constructor and owner roles. I have been an employee and consultant with several construction organizations. My owner role was in committee service to the University of Cincinnati and as a public official in a unit of local government that typically built one building per year. I was the person who guided that government's construction, dealing with designers and constructors—and stewarding the taxpayers' dollars. So, my background provides a balanced view of project delivery, representing the concerns of all principal interests. All parties are important, but the building users (sometimes owners, sometimes others) are central to the process. Other parties necessarily serve the owners and users in a variety of relationships. Part of the examination of any project or case study is to understand the varied relationships—and the responsibilities emanating from the owner's initiatives.

Case-Study Method

The case-study method has been employed in preparing professionals for many disciplines. The objective of cases is to present real-life situations with variable outcomes, through which teams of students (sometimes joined by practitioners) may examine cause-effect relationships and how various participants' actions may lead to different outcomes. Case studies typically do not have specific "correct answers" but several possible solutions. Team approaches work well, either with two to four persons working together comprehensively, or by team members taking on roles such as owner, designer, constructor, and building official. The model in Figure P-1 represents the process.

The case studies in this book are both factual and fictional, with none being identified by those categories. In the factual cases, details and personal identities have been changed to avoid any reflections on the individuals involved, and to avoid divulging the outcomes.

The book offers several illustrative case studies, with background information and outcomes, prior to presenting case problems designed for solutions. The intent is to first demonstrate relations and processes in various situations, and then for students to solve the case studies.

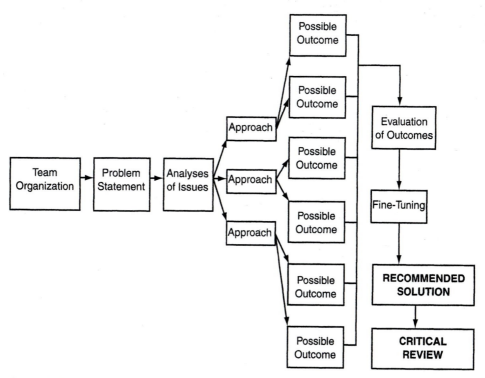

Figure P-1   Typical case-study problem-solving process. It is anticipated that a high level of dynamic interaction will take place among team members in moving to recommended solutions, as participants bring different experiences, perspectives, and research to the discussions. Critical review is important in all endeavors. "Right answers," particularly those quickly found, should be treated with healthy skepticism and examined to be sure that all parties are served equitably.

Acknowledgments

I wish to thank the following reviewers for their comments and suggestions: James S. Adrian, Bradley University; Flynn D. Auchey, Virginia Tech.; Jeff Burnett, Washington State University; and Richard Cole, Southern Polytechnic State University.

Contents

Chapter 1: The Organization of Design and Construction   1

Chapter 2: Contractual Relations Within Project Delivery Systems   37

Chapter 3: Illustrative Case Studies: General Contracting   49

Chapter 4: Illustrative Case Studies: Design-Build, Construction Management, and Program Management   77

Chapter 5: Case Studies Needing Solutions: Project Delivery Systems/Contractual Relationships; Public Sector Work   111

Chapter 6: Case Studies Needing Solutions: Project Delivery Systems/Contractual Relationships; Private Sector Work   139

Chapter 7: Case Studies Needing Solutions: Risk Distribution and Dispute Resolutions   163

Chapter 8: Government Regulations   195

xivContents

Chapter 9: Cases in Leadership 217

Chapter 10: Summary 231

References 237

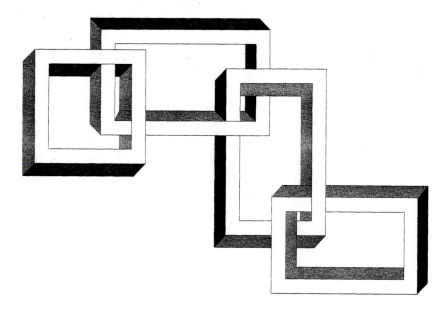

C H A P T E R   1

The Organization of Design and Construction

*"Men work together, I told him from the heart,
Whether they work together or apart."*
—Robert Frost, *The Tuft of Flowers*

It is important to understand the organization of design and construction to be able to deal with cases within the industry. A universal goal is to maximize effectiveness of built outcomes—a goal that can be enhanced by "working together." While necessarily being dynamic in order to keep up with constant changes, design and construction activities retain developmental patterns over time. As companies grow and expand operationally and geographically, their structures gradually change to allow continued efficiency and profitability. (Poorly planned growth is a leading cause of failure.) Business outlook and planning become crucial elements of growth, and organizations should regularly reexamine themselves, always seeking better performance professionally and in the marketplace. Broad construction organization and activity (including design) are, like most social phenomena, evolutionary.

Historical Perspective

Thousands of years ago, humankind ventured from caves and trees and began to shape the environment with crude platforms, dwellings, dams, and trenches. The early builders borrowed basic construction techniques from neighboring flora and fauna: the tree as structure, the beaver as reservoir builder, the finch as wattle-and-daub technician. But humans distinguished themselves through native ability to create various shelter types depending on materials available, climate, social patterns, cultural beliefs, and particular user needs. As with their animal counterparts, women and men worked together in shaping their habitat. It became evident that there is a basic human drive to build, experiment, and enhance well-being.

> **There is a basic human drive to build, experiment, and enhance the well-being of self, family, and community.**

Like all other activities in this early period, building skills were initially ubiquitous—everyone built, as everyone hunted, gathered, and carried on cultural traditions. With the growth of civilizations, building gradually became specialized, as governments, religions, and merchants needed functional and symbolic structures. Artisans arose to create buildings that became works of high craft as well as utilitarian structures, and the notions of architecture as building art, social art, and public art were gradually established (Figure 1-1).

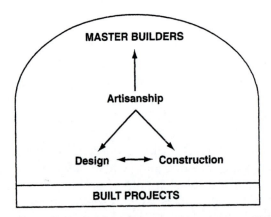

Figure 1-1 Historically, design and construction were merged through artisanship. Master builders were superior artisans with leadership abilities; they commanded the entire design/construction process.

Egyptian, Babylonian, and Assyrian cultures developed architecture that distinguished those early civilizations. The Greeks carried architecture and art (as well as literature and government) to levels of perfection never achieved before. The Romans were extraordinary engineers who built roads, aqueducts, fortifications, harbors, stadiums, baths, and circuses throughout the empire (despite a truly cumbersome numerical system). During the Middle Ages and the Renaissance, awesome cathedrals, libraries, and walled cities were carefully shaped by skilled artisans. The colonial movement spread Western civilization and architecture throughout the world and brought them face to face—and frequently in conflict with—other cultures and forms of architecture. Chinese and Indian traditional buildings were centuries old when Europeans first encountered them, and Islamic design developed unique characteristics as it blossomed in arid climes. Hybrid forms frequently grew out of these merging experiences, and the history of architecture is rich with the diversity of influences that shaped built form.

> **Every culture is identified with significant built works, thus establishing the importance of designers, constructors, artisans, and enlightened owners throughout history.**

What was the organization that brought thousands of historical landmarks into being? Allowing for variations across cultures, there was a fundamentally similar approach. Remarkable integration existed among the participants. No clear demarcation developed between design and construction. A continuum of activity existed around artisanship and the desire to create useful and beautiful objects for the well-being of the artisans' communities. Part of the well-being included community pride—and rivalry—with other communities.

Artisans chose their fields—or the fields were chosen for them—at early ages, and their knowledge and talents were developed deliberately through apprentice years, journeyman practice, and master status. One was an artisan for life, and the skill level and respect within the community grew to equally high levels. All artisans had artistic ability, and those with particular graphic skills became draftsmen and designers.

> **A person passing a construction site inquired of three masons what they were doing. The first answered "laying stone"; the second, "building a wall." The third stated enthusiastically, "I am creating a cathedral!" Who was the true artisan? Who would become the master builder?**

Architects were the premier graphic artisans—but all architects understood their materials and methods from having worked directly with them. Extraordinary craftsmen with leadership skills became the master builders, guiding the entire process, including design. The activities of design, construction, sculpture, and detailing were remarkably integrated. The separation of design and construction is largely a phenomenon of the past 150 years—since the flowering of the Industrial Revolution.

> **The Industrial Revolution changed everything, including building ownership, design, and construction.**

The Industrial Revolution, which evolved from the 18th-century English textile industry, and then impacted the entire world, influencing many phenomena related to design and construction:

- Industrialization and wealth generation gave rise to a new breed of owners: private individuals who contracted for design and construction of factories, mansions, hotels, and office buildings.
- Rapid development of cities generated huge construction markets where fortunes were made—and sometimes lost—by entrepreneurial builders.
- The ability of machines to manufacture materials in mass quantities reduced the need for artisans.
- The new age of specialization caused a breakdown of the integration of design and construction, as architects, engineers, and constructors began grouping into separate professions and trades, which then established separate societies and associations.
- Labor unions gained strength as a reaction to rampant industrialization and took on identities around craft skills, causing further specialization— and fragmentation.
- Trade contractors grew up around particular crafts, and subcontracting took on a major portion of the actual execution of construction.
- As formal education followed the paths of specialization, programs of study for architects and engineers arose in colleges and universities.
- Industrial innovation produced a vast array of building products that influenced design solutions and construction technology.
- Mass immigration, particularly to the Western Hemisphere, brought a diversity of cultures, ideas, skills, and workers.

○ Construction work was a great opportunity for many new citizens to gain employment, and this ready supply of inexpensive labor caused construction to remain labor intensive as manufacturing gradually automated.

○ The fusion of cultures and the variety of construction products caused architecture to become fragmented into an array of styles rather than following accepted design and detailing standards as during the days of artisanship.

○ Building and zoning codes evolved as governments saw fit to manifest their police powers to protect the health and safety of building occupants.

○ The specialization, fragmentation, legislation, and resulting breakdown of the integration of the parties to construction caused increasing disputes, producing claims and counterclaims and eventually giving rise to one more specialty—construction law.

The Industrial Revolution created vast wealth in countries that developed new technologies. It also generated air and water pollution, unsafe factories, and human exploitation. The salient outcome organizationally was that modern societies became both specialized and diverse. New design and construction specialties sprang forth to produce innovative facilities to reap the benefits of industrialization—while also seeking to rectify its excesses. Such specialties continue to evolve today, and they contribute to the evolution of project delivery systems to cope with increasingly complex relationships.

**A CONSTRUCTION SUCCESS STORY
THERE ARE THOUSANDS LIKE IT**

Dennis O'Brien was born in County Cork, Ireland, in 1849, into a family of brick masons. Despite his father's urgings to pursue a scholarly career, Dennis loved the family business and became a teenage apprentice. A skilled journeyman mason at age 22, he emigrated to Middletown, Connecticut, in 1871, where he contracted himself out to masonry companies. His skill and business acumen allowed O'Brien to quickly achieve master mason status and to build his own thriving business. Within a decade he was taking contracts for mid-size projects, first as a subcontractor and then as a general contractor. His company progressed to building major industrial, commercial, and institutional projects throughout Connecticut, including the Russell Manufacturing Company with16 acres of floor space. He also built the factories of the Royal Typewriter Company. In 1911 he formed a construction

Continued

corporation with his four children. He became one of Middletown's most respected citizens. O'Brien passed the business on to his sons and retired to enjoy his success and take part in civic activity. His heirs include contractors, engineers, an attorney, and an architect and professor at the Massachusetts Institute of Technology.

Bureaucratic Structure

Max Weber, the great 19th- and early-20th-century German social scientist who is considered the founder of sociology, coined the word *bureaucracy* to describe the organizational type that grew up around the Industrial Revolution. And, indeed, bureaucracy is alive and well as we enter a new millennium. Weber described bureaucracy as a hierarchical organization wherein a series of roles carry expectations of performance and are connected into decision-making networks and operational structures. The "coat-hanger" corporate chart is an artifact of bureaucracy, with the boxes not being people but roles that different people fill over time (Figure 1-2). Each role must be carried out effectively in regard to its expected responsibilities if the organization is to function efficiently—that is, to produce desired outcomes. Bureaucracies had become very efficient by the early 20th century. The rise of European and American manufacturing was largely due to sound bureaucratic organization. But, over time, bureaucracies can also be very cumbersome, particularly when people filling roles do not have the skills or motivation to carry out the expectations of their positions. This repeatedly happens in government, which gives bureaucracy a bad name. The most frequent criticism of bureaucracy is its resistance to change (inability to respond to dynamic environments) and discouragement of creativity among individuals.

> **Bureaucracies can be very efficient, but government has given them a bad name, and *bureaucrat* has become a pejorative term.**

Design and construction operate, to various degrees, under bureaucratic structures, but since the environment of construction continues to change, those organizations must be regularly monitored to avoid becoming too rigid in structure. Abundant studies in the social sciences have damned bureaucracies while encouraging new systems. However, it is apparent that this hierarchical organizational type is difficult to replace totally because, in various iterations, it has worked well in productive organizations. Invariably,

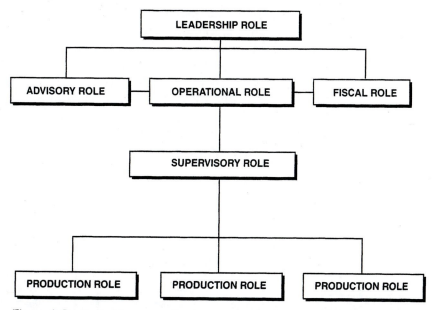

Figure 1-2 Typical bureaucratic structure for any business organization. Design and construction organizations both function in this basic alignment, with smaller companies having less rigid roles and larger ones having more hierarchy.

as small companies grow, some sort of multitiered structure emerges. The key is to recognize and avoid the demotivational deficiencies of bureaucracies and build on their structural strengths—sound organizations with clear, expected outcomes.

Line Versus Staff

The concept of line versus staff is important in bureaucracies and has reached its full application in the military services. The U.S. Navy, for instance, makes a clear distinction between line personnel and staff positions, the former being trained for and focused on direct military operations—the actual fighting—and the latter providing essential support for military activity. Examples of support services in the Navy are medical, supply, logistics, and intelligence. Officers of the line are the only ones who can command personnel in combat. This anecdote is told to young officers in training: "If a ship in combat loses its senior personnel, and the three remaining officers are a line ensign (lowest-ranking officer in the Navy), a supply lieutenant, and a medical captain, the ensign is in command of the ship." Thus the line drives and commands the organization; the staff supports line operations.

The issue of line versus staff also relates to construction company organization (Figure 1-3). Line personnel are responsible for operations—that is, the actual construction processes, or in financial terms, "making money for the company." (In fact, most employees help companies economically.) Staff roles are usually office based and support the operational line. Another duty of staff is "buffering" the line organization—in other words, performing miscellaneous duties to minimize external distractions to the line organization and to reduce the effects of peaks and valleys in the marketplace. Buffering includes government relations, marketing, accounting, and legal representation. In small- to medium-size companies, government relations and marketing (or development) may be parts of officers' roles. In larger companies they become distinct specialized roles.

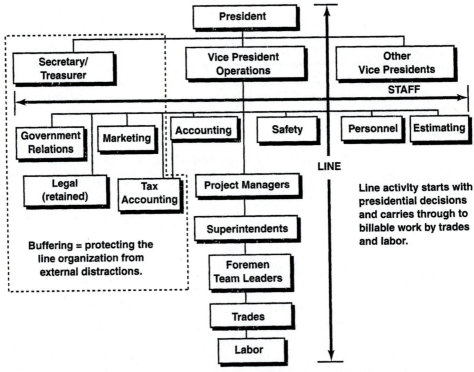

Figure 1-3   Line versus staff in construction organizations. The line duties are production and income related. Staff duties support the line and make it more efficient. Buffering, part of the staff function, deals with external factors that may influence the line. Such duties as government relations and marketing may be part of an officer's role. Legal counsel is ordinarily retained from practicing attorneys. Tax accounting may also be retained. Large organizations have total in-house accounting and may have an attorney on staff. *Note:* An objective of many companies is to better integrate line and staff into a functional whole.

Both line and staff roles are important. The challenge is to keep them balanced, so that adequate line energies are focused on rewarding productivity while staff roles effectively support the line, without becoming so abundant that "carrying the overhead" makes the organization non-competitive. It is easy for a growing organization to create new staff positions with the rationale of allowing line personnel to more fully perform their duties (most officers perceive the need for personal secretaries). However, new positions must be supported by increased income. A downturn in business activity may expose the flaw of organizational top-heaviness. Objectives of marketing, besides planned growth, are to weather fluctuating economic conditions by seeking a variety of customers and a range of contracts under different project delivery systems—to maintain the organization and to generate reliable profits.

> **The owner is always at the top of project organizational diagrams. The other salient parties, designers and constructors, necessarily serve the owner and each other to varying degrees.**

Project Organization

Construction is best described as quasi-bureaucratic. There are indeed roles to play and expectations to be fulfilled. But unlike manufacturing (involving continuous production operations), construction is necessarily more varied, which causes contractors to adapt to different projects in different settings under various contractual relations. However, from a project organization standpoint, there is one constant—the owner is always at the top of the chart. The owner, as initiator of the process, typically provides the land, funding, scope requirements, and basic program—and retains designers and constructors to carry out the project objectives. Design and construction, as performance roles, fall into place under the owner's authority. A generalized organizational chart for a construction project is shown in Figure 1-4.

Relationships change under various project delivery systems, and the number of participants varies by project types. On large hospital jobs it is typical to have several consultants, about 40 subcontractors, many sub-subcontractors (sometimes called *second-tier subcontractors*), and dozens of material suppliers. Project organization has steadily evolved through the decades. There once was more centralization of control in both design and construction and less use of consultants and subcontractors. Over time, business requirements, risk management, and project complexity have caused elaboration of organizations, resulting in many specialty roles and less-well-defined lines of authority.

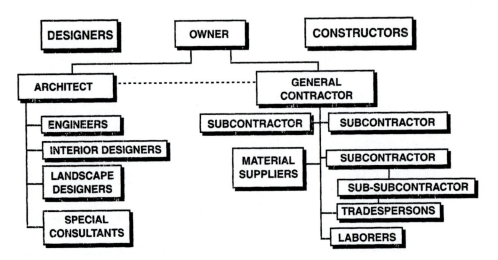

Figure 1-4 Generalized organizational chart for a construction project. The owner is always at the top of the organization. The architect and contractor are administratively related in several project delivery systems.

Use of Consultants and Subcontractors

Figures 1-5 and 1-6 indicate some of the specialties in design and construction, which can be performed by prime contractors or by subcontractors. The reasons for using consultants in design, and subcontractors in construction, include:

○ Individuals and firms become skilled and cost-effective when specializing in one or two particular areas of activity.

○ Segments of risk are distributed to subcontractors or consultants who take responsibility for pieces of the project and for the personnel involved, usually at known costs, allowing the prime design firm or general contractor to be more confident of the contractual price to the owner. (*Note:* Prime contractors still carry overall risk for performance relative to serving owners.)

○ Designers and contractors can take on larger volumes of work by distributing (outsourcing) segments of the work.

○ Several entities can work concurrently on a project, frequently in different locations, thus improving schedule efficiencies.

○ Large payrolls are avoided by design firms and contractors, thus reducing the unpleasantness of laying off workers during times of business reductions.

○ There is less requirement for capitalization by each entity, thus allowing many new entrants to the industry—and maintaining highly competitive conditions.

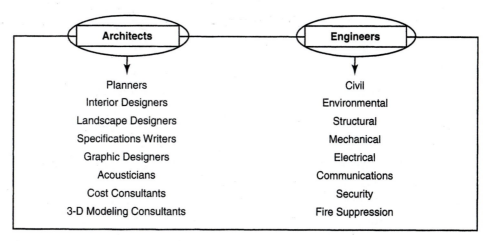

Figure 1-5   Design specialties may be in direct employment of design firms or may be retained as consultants (subcontractors).

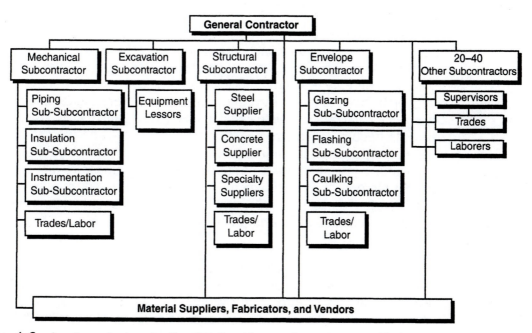

Figure 1-6   A pattern of subcontracting. Relationships vary by contract type. Trades and labor, material suppliers, fabricators, and vendors serve general contractors, subcontractors, and sub-subcontractors.

Subcontracting and use of consultants has several potential disadvantages:

○ There may be some loss of control by prime contractors (those who have contracts directly with owners). Subcontractors and consultants are more independent and thus more difficult to command and hold to a schedule than are direct employees.

○ General contractors and design firms need to invest time and energy in qualifying subcontractors and consultants.

○ Lead design firms must coordinate numerous design documents from various sources to avoid omissions, duplication, and ambiguity and to ensure proper coverage of all aspects of a project.

○ Subcontractors may not follow the same safety practices as general contractors.

○ Some subcontractors are very poorly capitalized, thus risking default and delay for their parts of the work.

○ Profit potential is distributed along with risk; the more contractors, subcontractors, and consultants involved, the less net profit for each.

Self-Performance Versus Subcontracting; Government Requirements

Designers and contractors make deliberate decisions regarding self-performance versus subcontracting on a job-by-job basis, unless regulations intervene. Some governments have requirements for particular levels of self-performance, typically on public works projects, to reduce outright brokering of the work of others by prime contractors. Several states require separate prime contracts for mechanical and electrical construction. Also, governments frequently have requirements for minority- and women-owned business participation in projects, which may dictate that certain percentages of total contract amounts be subcontracted to companies that are substantially minority or female owned. (A word on terminology may be helpful. *Minority business enterprise, MBE,* and *women's business enterprise, WBE,* are sometimes combined into *disadvantaged business enterprise, DBE.*)

Construction historically has been predominantly a white male enterprise. Regulations emerged in the 1960s to attempt to increase diversity and to allow access to public projects by previously disadvantaged segments of society. Thus MBE, WBE, and DBE became part of the industry lexicon.

Special requirements practiced by some governments, called *set-asides*, mean that segments of a project must be limited to bidding and performance by only minority or female contractors or suppliers. These regulations can influence the decision on self-performance versus subcontracting. Set-aside rules may cause a contractor to determine which trade or supply segments should have MBE or WBE participants and then, in fact, seek out only those parties for bids. If there are required employment levels (as distinguished from set-asides), the best strategy may be to self-perform work where minority tradespersons are available for hire. (The whole issue of required diversity participation is under review by legislatures and courts, and all parties need to know the current rules in the time and place of a particular project.)

Self-performance vs. subcontracting = profit potential vs. risk distribution. Government regulations may intervene.

While some private owners require DBE participation, most care less about who actually does the work than they care about safety, cost, quality, and completion time. Owners will hold prime contractors responsible for the work regardless of the degree and character of subcontracting. It is important to remember that owners do not have direct contracts with subcontractors.

Transportation, public works, and industrial projects tend to have relatively high levels of self-performance, partly due to the organization of construction companies that execute that work, partly due to government regulations, and partly due to involvement of fewer trades (particularly finish trades) than with habitable buildings. For instance, a school project will employ many trades not present on roads, sewage disposal plants, or factories.

The "bottom line" on self-performance versus subcontracting is, of course, economic. If a general contractor can perform a trade segment more cost effectively (which includes meeting a schedule) than a subcontractor, then that work will be self-performed. Another economic concern that has become more relevant in the litigious environment of construction is that construction employers carry liability risks for safety and other behaviors of employees. Many general contractors wish other employers to directly carry these risks, thus adding to the attractiveness of subcontracting.

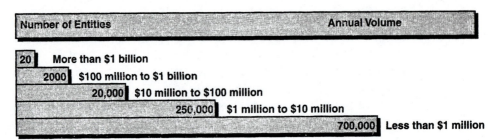

Figure 1-7 Representation of approximate number and sizes of construction entities in the United States, for a typical year in the 1990s, including all types of construction from road building to residential remodeling, and including general contractors and trade contractors. Numbers change regularly (not to scale).

Organization of Construction-Related Companies

There are really no typical construction companies. The size of the industry and diversity of contracting organizations make it difficult to identify archetypes. Also, the inherent fluidity of the industry causes each company to adjust regularly. About a million entities in the United States function in design or construction, from executing roads and bridges to casual remodeling. (*Note:* This number varies depending on the source of information, there being no truly reliable census of construction.) Most such companies are small; the national average size of construction entities is ten persons, and the average volume is less than $1 million per year. At the other end of the spectrum, a small number of companies contract for over $1 billion annually. Figure 1-7 indicates an approximate hierarchy of U.S. companies by annual volume.

Design and construction have been described as being easy to enter and easier to leave (voluntarily or involuntarily). Indeed, enthusiastic newcomers with power saws and pickup trucks, or with drawing boards and computers, are constantly setting themselves up in business, usually as specialty firms, subcontractors, or sub-subcontractors. They pick up bits and pieces of work, perhaps with a dream of being the next great success story, or with a short-term employment objective while seeking more permanent work. And every day many entities leave the industry. Construction has a high departure and failure rate.

Licensing, Qualifications, and Training

Licensing—and the lack thereof—influences entry into design and construction. While architects and engineers have licensing requirements, there are no such rules for designer/drafters and other office personnel. Contractors are required to be licensed in about half the states, and those states demand that only the principal (president or other key officer) of the construction company be licensed. Trade contractors (usually subcontractors) are typically not licensed, except for plumbing contractors, who are licensed in most states and municipalities, and heating/ventilation/air-conditioning (HVAC), electrical, fire suppression, and elevator contractors in some jurisdictions. Plumbers and plumbing contractors have historically been licensed because of their importance to public health. Designers who avoid use of the label architect or engineer and who limit their work to interior or residential design are not required to be licensed in most states.

> **Banner in a plumbing contractor's office in Milwaukee:**
> **"PLUMBERS—PROTECTING THE HEALTH OF AMERICA"**
> **A licensing issue: The plumbing industry has contributed greatly to American public health, and most states and municipalities require licenses of practitioners.**

While most design work and specialized construction trades, such as plumbing and HVAC, entail substantial training, many tasks in construction can be done with little experience, and these are inviting to ambitious dreamers. The entrepreneurial spirit and the openness of the marketplace carry advantages and disadvantages. New blood is vital, but the industry remains fragmented and, in many cases, poorly capitalized. This tends to inhibit technological development and training, which is usually affordable only by large organizations. New entries to construction may be proprietorships or partnerships, which are easy to establish though highly risky. Those planning to stay long in business usually incorporate.

Corporate Structures

Each state has laws on incorporation, usually requiring formal registration of articles of incorporation, a certain number of stockholders, and named officers. Most construction companies are closely held corporations, which entail a limited number of shares and shareholders and restrictions on exchange of shares, in order to maintain controlled ownership. A corporation creates a legal entity separate from the individual members and allows better management of risks, a partial shield from personal liability, and mechanisms for succession. Design firms have historically been partnerships, but most medium to large firms are now professional corporations, which typically improve business operations and continuity, but which have limited shielding of personal responsibility. An important requirement of any professional person is to take responsibility—and risks— for the service being delivered.

Individual Construction Company Characteristics

Individual construction companies take on their own particular characteristics, but several generalizations may be cited to compare large companies to small companies—*large* meaning those managing over $200 million annual volume, and *small* meaning those performing less than $20 million annually (Figure 1-8). These are somewhat arbitrary divisions and are intended only to differentiate organizational styles. In commercial parlance, 98 percent of all construction entities are small businesses, so "large" is relative only to the construction industry. Large construction companies (see Figures 1-9 and 1-10) usually:

○ Are better capitalized and can better endure fluctuations in the marketplace.
○ Are operated as true business corporations with financial strategies, structured roles and responsibilities, salary scales, employee benefits, and many formal procedures.
○ Have several organizational layers in a corporate structure.
○ Can perform large, complex projects profitably but may tend to avoid small projects (some large companies have smaller subsidiaries to take on "special projects").
○ Can take on the leadership of both design and construction for complex projects under program management, construction management, or design-build.
○ Adopt new technologies more quickly.
○ Have marketing divisions.
○ Are frequently multilocational and sometimes multinational.
○ Have ongoing education and training programs.

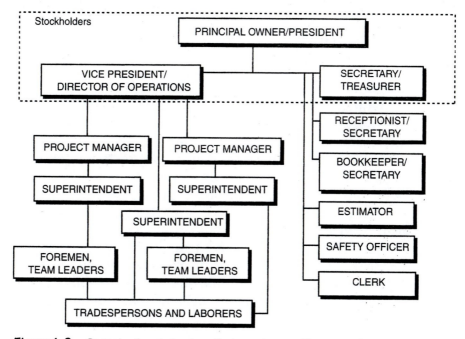

Figure 1-8 Organizational structure that may be used by general contractors or trade contractors performing annual volume of approximately $10 to $20 million, consisting of 5 to 15 projects per year. Most companies of this size are closely held corporations. It is important to control overhead—that is, to avoid overstaffing with personnel who do not contribute directly to producing income. For instance, the duties of safety officer may be part of one of the project manager's roles. All roles are flexible. The vice president for operations may act directly as project manager for some jobs. Project managers may assist in estimating. Subcontractors are not shown because they are separate business entities. The numbers of foremen, tradespersons, and laborers depend on the amount of self-performance. Many subcontractors have similar ogranizations.

Super-large companies, as shown in Figure 1-10, are likely to have the same characteristics plus the capabilities to handle dozens of projects at one time, literally all around the world.

Smaller construction companies (which may be general contractors or trade contractors) typically:

○ Are the results of individual ambition or the drive of two or three people.

○ Are more loosely organized, usually entrepreneurially led, with individuals taking on several different roles.

○ Are not well capitalized and frequently have cash-flow problems.

○ Tend to specialize in limited types of construction in limited geographic areas.

○ Can become highly efficient in their chosen skills.

○ Frequently are subcontractors rather than prime contractors.
○ Have relatively high failure rates.
○ May be quite agile in changing directions.
○ Can execute small work profitably but have limitations on project scope.

With just three prototypical companies shown here, obviously there are many more hybrid forms of organizations. Important objectives of any company are stability over time and successful growth. Growth is almost an "American virtue," but in construction it tends to complicate the inherent risks. Construction remains to a large degree cyclic (as differentiated from seasonal) and subject to the vagaries of the larger economy. Growth should be the result of a carefully drawn strategic plan, with a number of options. Erratic growth and decline can mean the loss of key personnel, problems with lenders and sureties, and an impaired reputation. Growth is frequently accomplished through mergers, where the objective is territorial diversity, operational breadth, or simply a stronger, more competitive organization. Carefully planned growth is to be encouraged.

> **Construction company growth tends to increase the risks of an already risky business. Ideally, growth should be part of a carefully planned business strategy with careful attention to cultivation or acquisition of adequate leadership personnel, marketplace expertise, and capital.**

Organization of Design Firms

Architects, engineers, and the many other design entities work in a variety of organizational types, including proprietorships, partnerships, and corporations. Also, they may be subsidiaries of government, industry, and construction companies (as in design-build). There is no attempt here to illustrate every variety; rather, prototypes are discussed and shown. First, here is a taxonomy of basic types:

○ "Pure" architectural firms concentrate on building design only, with no in-house engineering or other specialties.
○ Comprehensive architectural firms offer an array of design services, including master planning, building design, space design, interior finishes, and possibly landscape design and some engineering.

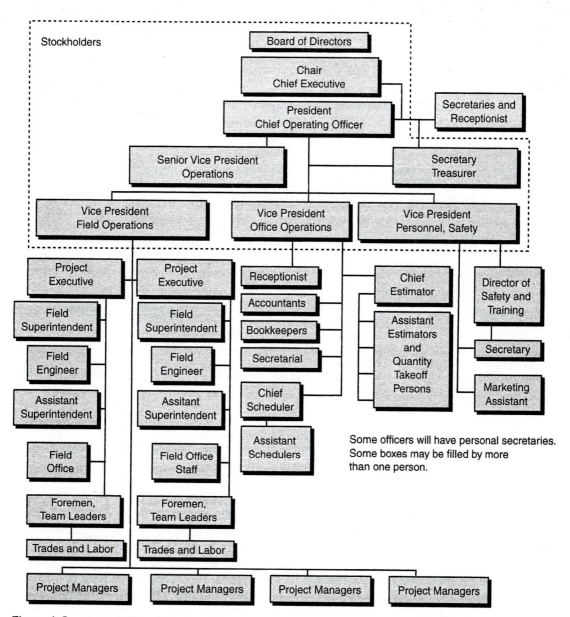

Figure 1-9   Organizational structure that may be used by a company performing annual volume of $100 to $200 million, consisting of 10 to 20 projects per year. The larger the company, the more structured the roles become. However, most construction companies retain sufficient flexibility to allow adaptation to projects of varying sizes. A company such as the one diagrammed will typically have jobs ranging from $500,000 to $50 million. Project managers have staffing depending on sizes of jobs being managed.

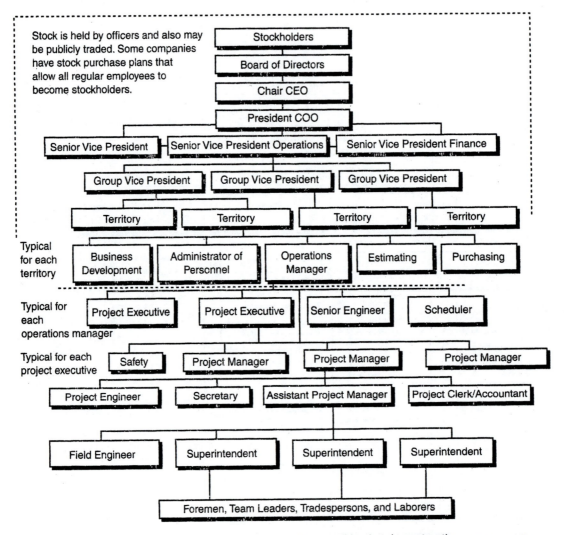

Figure 1-10 Organizational structure that may be used by a multinational construction company performing over $1 billion of work annually, with dozens of projects. The chart indicates a corporation with publicly held stock. Not shown are the many technical and administrative support positions. A company of this size is capable of performing all types of project delivery systems in a variety of settings. Each territory has similar structures under each territory general manager/vice president. Likewise, each project executive will command a similar array of roles.

○ Architecture and engineering (AE) firms or companies offer comprehensive services with relatively equal strengths in architecture and engineering, typically including structural and mechanical design and perhaps surveying, transportation, and environmental engineering.

○ EA companies are similar to AE, but engineering services take on a dominant role.

○ Engineering companies have one or more engineering disciplines, perhaps including design of building structures, mechanical systems or components, and land surveying.

○ Interior design or space design firms concentrate on interior planning, finishes, and materials, frequently completing the design of interiors of shell buildings for office and retail clients.

○ In-house design offices, in a variety of forms, are frequently employed by manufacturers, large retailers, some government agencies, and some design-build contractors. (*Note:* Sometimes these design units are set up as separate corporations, to distinguish design liability from the risk exposure associated with the principal enterprise.)

○ Landscape architecture, as the name implies, focuses on site planning and landscape design, but sometimes the practitioners engage major planning projects.

Most design firms of more than a few people are corporations. Many have evolved from proprietorships or partnerships to corporate status. Just as state laws regulate the licensing of design professionals, they also regulate the organization and identification of design entities. For a firm to identify itself as providing architecture or engineering services, most of the principals must be licensed professionals. Design corporations are called professional corporations, as distinguished from business corporations, and have the following characteristics in most states:

○ A majority of the stock must be held by professionals licensed in the respective disciplines in the state of corporate location.

○ The corporation cannot shield licensed individuals from liability for design decisions, the intent being that licensed practitioners must bear responsibility for the health and safety aspects of building design.

○ There is better capability for stable and continuous organization, business efficiency, succession, pension plans, tax advantages, and reward distribution than with proprietorships or partnerships.

The historic licensed professions of medicine, law, architecture, and engineering are increasingly operating under corporate structures, but these professional corporations do not completely shield practitioners from personal liability for their actions.

Design pursuits that are outside of architecture, engineering, and landscape architecture are not licensed in most states. Interior designers and landscape designers (as distinguished from landscape architects) are not regulated as professions, but rather as businesses. However, most states have laws precluding nonlicensed designers from doing the work of architects or engineers. These laws vary from state to state, but generally require that drawings for all buildings used by the public carry the official seal of an architect or engineer. This point is significant to contractors when owners may call on them to lead the construction team through design-build or other project delivery systems. They must be aware of state requirements for building design. In most cases, contractors should avoid becoming designers, or hiring unlicensed designers, because not only will they be taking on liability for which they are not insured, they may be violating state laws. (Home building and small remodeling work is usually not covered by state licensing laws.)

Design firms, like construction companies, are predominantly small businesses and are so diverse that showing typical organizations is difficult. Three prototypes are offered, a small to medium AE firm, an organization as a series of service nodes, and a large architectural firm with some engineering services (Figures 1-11 to 1-13). The American Institute of Architects (AIA) reports that the median size of firms headed by AIA members is six professional persons. While this statistic will probably remain valid over time, there is a continuing move toward large multinational firms with abilities to capture work in many locations, thus putting survival pressure on small to mid-size local firms.

The operative staffs in architectural and engineering design offices are mixtures of licensed and unlicensed personnel. As long as one or more principals are licensed—and accepting legal responsibility—there is no similar requirement for employees of the firm. Traditional employment patterns have been for new graduates of architectural and engineering schools to take positions as production employees (drafters or computer-aided drafting [CAD] operators for contract documents) while qualifying to complete licensing requirements. Once licensed, the young professionals anticipate moving into positions of greater responsibility with their employers, or moving on to other opportunities, possibly including establishing their own firms. There are a remarkable number of sole practitioners in building design, most of whom serve various stints of time with larger firms.

Another personnel tier in professional firms is made up of employees who are not professionally educated and who will never become licensed.

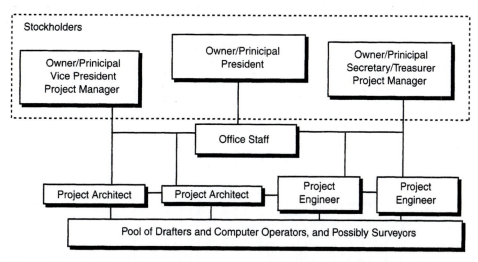

Figure 1-11   Small or medium architectural/engineering (AE) professional corporation, with 12–18 total personnel and the capability to handle approximately 20 projects per year with a total built value of $15–30 million. The term *medium* here relates to relative sizes of design firms, the average size of which is six professional persons, as reported by the American Institute of Architects. "Pure" architectural firms have a similar structure. Flexibility and open communications are important in a firm of this size. Even principals engage in the output of documents.

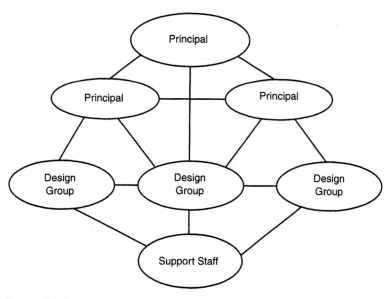

Figure 1-12   AE firm organized as a series of service nodes, which are organized around specific projects. Design and support personnel move from design group to design group as projects require staffing. The basic organizational ideas are based on a high degree of interaction among all individuals, and flexibility in team building. Such a structure allows for quick response to client needs and market conditions.

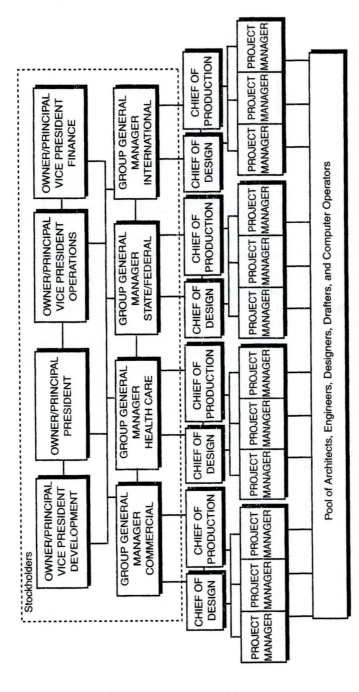

Figure 1-13 Organization of a large AE professional corporation, with over 200 personnel, and capable of performing 50 projects per year with a total built value of $500 million to $1 billion. (Not all administrative positions are shown.) Size of stockholder group is dependent on company policy. Most AE firms are closely held corporations.

They range from specialized production employees to support personnel for technical, marketing, financial, and secretarial duties. In fact, since many designers do not give sufficiently high priority to business operations, firms frequently hire nonlicensed business managers to guide marketing and financial aspects of professional practice.

> **Whatever the organization of design and construction companies, their successes will continuously depend on their abilities to provide value-adding services to an array of owners.**

The Information Age and Design

The information revolution is having a dramatic effect on design practice. Not only are computers and management information systems (MIS) changing office operations, they are allowing a relatively few highly skilled people to perform the work previously performed by many more employees. CAD is now routine. Firms are throwing off traditional organizational structure and are becoming flexible service nodes. Design firms—particularly small and mid-size ones—are among the most dynamic entities in the construction arena. They rarely settle into clear identifiable structures. This flexibility is also shown in a new willingness to participate in many different project delivery systems. Firms that once would not consider joint ventures with contractors are now working as co-venturers or subcontractors in design-build projects and collaborators in development ventures. There is no doubt that the relationships of designers to owners and to constructors are undergoing change, as the dynamics of the design/construct/maintain continuum evolve in the marketplace.

THE NEWLY FLEXIBLE ARCHITECT

Notes from a luncheon conversation with an architect with 40 years of practice, having assumed leadership of the firm from his father several years ago:

"Things are too exciting to even think about retirement. We now have 50 people in our firm, and most are adept at CAD and MIS. I'm the least computer oriented of the whole bunch, but I'm learning. We

Continued

plan to expand our practice, but not our staff—by becoming more efficient— primarily in computer use.

"We currently have projects in the field under seven different delivery systems, including design-build where we are a subcontractor. My dad is probably spinning in his grave.

"A problem we find is that few people really understand the nuances of some of the delivery systems. There is real confusion about design-build and construction management, particularly in regard to who is responsible for what. Architects and contractors need to iron out some of the misinterpretations. I know that things will keep changing."

Collaboration and Joint Ventures

It is becoming increasingly common for collaborations to occure among:

❍ Two or more design firms

❍ Two or more construction companies

❍ Design firms and construction companies

❍ Developers, design firms, and construction companies

The reasons for collaborative ventures include:

❍ Large national entities and smaller local firms collaborate when local governments or corporations desire the particular strengths of a large company but require local involvement for regulatory or civic reasons.

❍ Design firms known for expertise in specialized areas, such as laboratories or libraries, team up with local firms that are efficient in the production of contract documents.

❍ Relatively small firms known for aesthetic design excellence collaborate with production-oriented firms on large projects.

❍ Construction companies collaborate to:
   1. Engage particularly large projects beyond the capability of each company individually.
   2. Share bonding capacity.
   3. Meet DBE requirements.

Design and construction companies are increasingly collaborating in design-build and some types of construction management. The types of collaborations, from a business standpoint, may be:

○ Short term (one project), where temporary arrangements are reached regarding divisions of labor, responsibilities, and profit.

○ Alliances for several years or several projects wherein firms agree to work together on all projects or on particular types of projects.

○ Agreements wherein one party works as a subcontractor to another, such as a design firm having a subcontract with a construction company in a design-build project delivery system, or an interior architect working for a comprehensive design firm.

○ True joint ventures, where companies become corporately linked for one or more projects, usually with the new corporation being project specific or building-type specific.

○ New entities formed by design and construction companies to seek and perform particular types of work, such entities typically being limited liability companies drawing resources from the two collaborating corporations.

Joint Ventures and Limited Liability Companies

Joint ventures and limited liability companies have stricter legal requirements than most other types of collaborations. The joining entities (there may be more than two) become essentially one company for the project(s) at hand. They may establish new companies or definitive joint agreements for their working relationships. Usually there is a sharing of:

○ Resources, including capital
○ Risk and insurance responsibilities
○ Personnel at various levels
○ Preconstruction, construction, and postconstruction duties

It is important that other aspects and operations of a joint venture not be put at risk by the agreement at hand. Thus it is recommended to form separate companies just for the joint work. Design firms must be careful in joint ventures with construction companies because of the probable unequal capability to manage risk. For instance, most design firms cannot undertake:

○ Surety bonds
○ Liability insurance for construction
○ Levels of capitalization necessary for undertaking construction

It is obviously important for each entity to examine the balance of risks and opportunities prior to entering into joint ventures. Legal counsel and insurance advice are quite important.

Virtual Organizations— More a Concept Than a Reality

Virtual organizations are currently more conceptual than real, but with the rapidly changing environment of design and construction, the notion makes sense (see figure 3-15). Agility—that is, skill in moving quickly in several directions as the relevant marketplace demands—is becoming an important organizational concept. Evolution of project delivery systems, from traditional general contracting to design-build, construction management, and program management, has demanded agility in both design and construction companies. Virtual organizations, as described by S. Scott MacLeod (1995), are short-term mergers of the skills of two or more companies into highly interactive entities to produce one or more buildings, to create master plans, or to define business strategies. Roles are only sketchily developed; leadership emerges based on expertise and experience; and the overall objective is adding value for the sponsor of the collaboration, such as a building owner. An example could be a high-tech company wishing to develop a new electronic product concurrently with designing the production equipment and the built facility. (See Virtual Organizational Sample Case Study on page 31.) Operatives from different companies join talents while maintaining employment with their parent companies. They work in the "brain trust" as long as their contributions are relevant to the project at hand, and then return to their bases of employment.

Like all ideas, virtual organizations are not totally new. They are related to the old concept of task force and the latter-day trend of outsourcing. Task forces, by definition, are short-term bodies focusing on a specific task or tasks (as compared to committees, which tend toward formality and endurance). Outsourcing became prevalent in the 1980s and 1990s, and, coupled with downsizing, caused companies to reduce workforces and related overhead, in part by shifting work to consultants and subcontractors.

Virtual organization as a term is trendy, uses current popular language (*virtual*, meaning "simulated" or "representational"), and will take on various meanings over time. The relevance in this discussion is to illustrate the need for any company to avoid being locked into a semirigid organization, but rather to be ready for any opportunity to provide services. (See Figure 1-14 and the sample case study titled "A Virtual Organization" on page 31.)

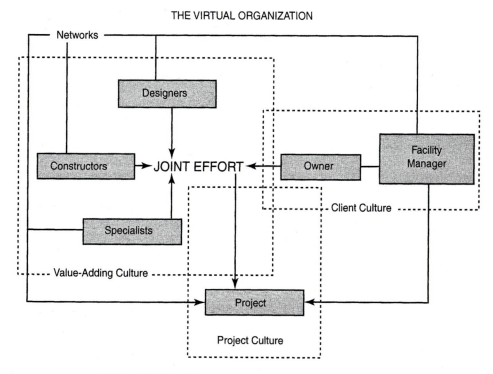

THE VIRTUAL ORGANIZATION

DESIGN-CONSTRUCT-MAINTAIN
The virtual organization is:
• Value adding/client oriented
• Flexible
• Nimble/quick responding
• Networked/information rich
• Culturally aware

Figure 1-14 The virtual organization is based on an idea presented by S. Scott MacLeod (1995). MacLeod suggests that in the future, design and construction organizations must be highly adaptable to serve owners in a variety of settings and project organizational types. Owners outsource more responsibility and depend on design and construction companies to provide both reliable information and superior performance. A project culture results. Successful service providers are those that can quickly adjust to new expectations of owners and that can guide owners through optimal project delivery systems.

Sample Case Study on Organization: Evolution of a Construction Company

When they were laid off by a general contractor who had lost an important project, two carpenter brothers decided to start a framing business. They offered their skills to homebuilders, small general contractors, and developers, and provided labor to erect wood, and occasionally metal, framing supplied by the contractors or owners. They functioned as subcontractors and sub-subcontractors. Though enjoying wood, they developed a specialty in light metal framing and soon became a preferred team for metal stud work. After several months of 70-hour weeks, no formal organization, few detailed agreements, and no insurance (except state-required workers' compensation coverage), they hired a retired vice president of a mid-size general construction company to take over the business aspects of their operation. The new member advised the following:

○ They needed to incorporate for better operation and continuity, and to improve their shield from personal risk.
○ They needed to make a key decision on whether to remain small—and overworked—or to expand their workforce and become more supervisors than mechanics.
○ They needed to acquire proper insurance coverages.
○ They needed to lay out a business plan.
○ They needed to invest in the business for its continuity.

The brothers took the advice and sought a few other like-minded mechanics. Employment grew by twos and threes as their reputation for good work and reliability spread. Soon they had 20 field employees and 3 office employees. They took on drywall work as well as framing. Then they hired two graduates of a university construction management program to help them manage the business and to improve scheduling, resource allocation, and overall operation—and in anticipation of the retirement of their valued first employee. They made the careful decision to outsource most of the staff needs, such as accounting, safety training and safety documentation, and various reporting requirements. They emphasized line positions over staff roles, and kept control on overhead. The good business planning paid off in continued growth and caused the brothers and their professional managers to face other decisions a few years later:

○ Should they expand beyond the current 50-mile radius?
○ Should they expand their work to full interior contracts?

○ Should they consider general contracting, to build on their successes?

○ Should they establish a stock distribution plan to key employees?

As his final package of recommendations, the retiring vice president suggested deliberate growth into total interior contracting, but to avoid full general contracting (which might alienate sources of work), and to gradually expand geographically but to be sure that they had competent, trustworthy superintendents to place on all the projects. He also recommended both a formal training program and a stock distribution program and that the two initiatives should be linked. As leaders emerged, they should be attracted to remain with the company through stock ownership.

At their fifth anniversary celebration, the 32 employees spoke with pride about their accomplishments and about their dreams for the future. Five employees were given stock certificates, and all employees received bonuses and company jackets and caps. The path forward looked bright.

Sample Case Study: A Virtual Organization

A producer of electronic products anticipated marketing a dramatic new device to access the Internet inexpensively in private homes throughout the world. Knowing that other companies were pursuing the same idea, it became important to have production facilities ready as soon as the prototype devices were "debugged" and ready for production. It had been ten years since the company had built a structure, and no one aboard had the time or ability to manage the construction from an owner's point of view. It was decided to assemble a special team to design and build the facility on a fast track. Two individuals from the company were designated as project coordinators with extensive responsibilities. One was very knowledgeable about production of electronic devices; the other was in charge of overall facilities management. Their charge was to quickly:

○ Draft a basic program of needs, including:
  1. Spaces and amenities
  2. Schedule
  3. Ergonomic issues related to worker comfort and productivity
  4. Life-cycle considerations
  5. Approximate budget
○ Prepare a short list of design firms and construction companies
○ Seek a qualified workplace psychologist

○ Interview the several parties to be retained

○ Establish a work area for collaboration to take place

After selecting a workplace psychologist who had ample experience in management relations, physical environments, and ergonomics, the trio interviewed short-listed architects, engineers, production specialists, and contractors. The objectives were to:

○ Identify firms that would be fully committed to engaging the processes of:
  1. Adding value to the owner's operation through their skills and quick performance
  2. Assigning key personnel to a special team to pursue the design/construct/maintain continuum, and dedicating those personnel from final programming through commissioning of the built facility
  3. Full integration of the many players into the process to optimize the construction efficiency and life-cycle value of the production facilities
  4. Allowing team members to work in a location where all prime players were to be assembled

○ Determine optimal schedule

○ Scope the costs of consultation and design

○ Select actual participants

○ Determine project delivery system

The three-person team expedited interviews, selected design and construction companies, and assembled a ten-person team consisting of:

○ In-house production person (original company team member)

○ In-house facilities manager (original company team member)

○ Workplace psychologist, who had helped evaluate the other consultants

○ Consulting industrial production specialist

○ Two members of the selected architectural firm

○ Mechanical engineer from a firm that specialized in high-tech manufacturing facilities

○ Electrical engineer, a self-employed specialist with skills in both electronics and power installations

○ Project manager from the selected construction company

○ All-purpose executive secretary from the electronics (owner) company

○ Other personnel who were added from the firms as the project progressed

Consulting contracts were on a per diem (hourly rate) basis throughout the design phase. Overall agreements were negotiated by the company duo and company attorney, with emphasis on regular consultant availability and dedication to the process. These would not be 9-to-5 positions. Long weeks were anticipated early in the process, but the remuneration was attractive. The actual project delivery system was cost–plus a fixed fee, with additional reimbursement based on a multiple of cost of management placed on the project. The contractor would be paid actual costs of personnel, including burden and benefits, plus a factor to cover overhead and profit. It was anticipated that the management staff for construction would grow to eight people at peak activity.

Special office space, adjacent to an owner's existing production facility, was created for the newly assembled ten-person team, with space to expand as new personnel were added. The total later became 20. Fully equipped workstations included drawing boards, computers, modems, faxes, and Internet connections. Huddle spaces for up to ten people were available at either end of the space. Team members would be in regular contact with their home offices but would perform their duties in the integrated office—as a short-term virtual organization linked directly to the client. Team building was initiated by a two-day partnering session with an outside facilitator. The early expectations were that:

○ All members of the team would fully understand the owner's goals.

○ A true team spirit would prevail, with no private agendas.

○ All members would focus on the objectives of providing the best possible manufacturing workplace in the shortest possible time at reasonable costs.

○ Safety would be a high priority during construction and plant operation, and should be a prime consideration during design.

○ An accelerated, phased construction schedule would be developed, with all parties committing to adhere to its milestones:
   1. The company facilities manager set the occupancy date.
   2. The construction project manager established schedule phases and determined bid packages and document deliverables for each phase.
   3. All parties identified long-lead-time items and the contractor would order, same with direct payment by owner.
   4. The architects and engineers committed to delivering the necessary documents for each phase—without superfluous or overlapping details.

○ Local building authorities would be invited regularly to review document preparation to ensure code compliance, and to be ready to issue a series of conditional permits as the project progressed in phases of bid packages.

○ Value engineering, constructability, and cost control were ongoing activities throughout, with full integration of all participants.

○ Ergonomics of the manufacturing work areas were regularly evaluated.

○ All parties searched for components and systems readily available in the marketplace that would expedite completion of the facility.

○ The construction project manager sought and qualified reliable trade contractors to perform most of the actual work under subcontractors.

A highly modular building was conceived consisting of prefabricated steel structure and light metal envelope, sufficiently reinforced to allow production equipment to be suspended from roof and walls. A large shell would be erected initially, and spaces would be equipped and made operational as dictated by market acceptance of the products, and as the capabilities for automated manufacturing improved. The idea was to begin manufacturing with a basic workforce and then increase the productivity of that cadre by gradually improved automated processes. The components for the products would be stored on mezzanines and be transported to fabrication suites by conveyors. Fabrication suites were capable of being highly individualized in regard to ergonomics, colors, lighting, tempered air flow, and music. The interior was bright, colorful, and easily maintained for cleanliness. The workplace psychologist assisted in design of the interiors. Several parties would collaborate on commissioning all the systems.

Within nine months of hiring the full team, the first new electronic devices were being shipped from one third of the structure, while another third was being equipped for production. The virtual team had been gradually reduced as progress allowed. The construction project manager stayed on to coordinate the outfitting of production space. The owner was sufficiently impressed with the skill of the construction company that a maintenance contract was signed to keep the new building in a high state of operation.

On fully disbanding the virtual organization, the original company management duo debriefed all participants through an evaluative process, using company standards and the team's own measures of successes versus needs for improvement. Their report to upper management included the following points:

○ Overall the process was successful.

○ A well-designed building was delivered on a short schedule.

○ Economical space was available for immediate expansion.

○ Workspaces were designed for superior ergonomics, quick reconfiguration, and easy maintenance.

○ Production employees enjoyed their abilities to individualize their spaces.

○ Building costs were 8 percent higher than with similar facilities.

○ This expense would be won back within two years through optimal productivity.

○ The building was designed and built more quickly and was more employee friendly than similar production facilities.

○ Most of the team members collaborated very well, but two were regularly distracted by other projects in their home offices.

○ One architect had difficulty working with the workplace psychologist, particularly on several interior design issues. The company duo intervened as required.

○ The level of intensity of activity wore down several team members. Most planned vacations as soon as the team was disbanded.

○ There was some disagreement between the designers and the construction project manager on the definitions of deliverables for each phase:
   1. On the one hand, the designers felt pressed to meet deadlines.
   2. On the other hand, the designers wished to provide adequate details to guide the project.
   3. The project manager was adamant that many detail decisions could be made more efficiently in the field.
   4. The disagreements, at least in part, were about who should control the project.
   5. The owner's duo forced compromises to stay on schedule.

○ Because of acceleration, the number of field problems was slightly more than on a conventional project, but the problems were solved quickly because all participants were close at hand.

○ Overall project communications were excellent based on the tight organization and networks provided by the owner, consisting of:
   1. Several video cameras on the jobsite linked to monitors in the team office
   2. Interlinked computer terminals
   3. Daily printouts of project status including work accomplished, inventories, and anticipated needs for upcoming time periods

○ Safety on the project was excellent because of:
   1. Early priority during design
   2. Careful prequalification of trade contractors

3. Regular jobsite monitoring and reporting
4. Attention to safety in constructability planning
5. Considerable use of prefabricated components, thus reducing site personnel

In summary, the virtual organization was sufficiently successful to cause the owner to consider similar systems for future projects.

> ***Virtual organization* is a trendy name for a highly integrated effort by owner representatives, designers, constructors, and special consultants to improve efficiency in the design/construct/maintain continuum.**

CHAPTER 2

Contractual Relations Within Project Delivery Systems

"Construction is a dynamic industry with a dynamic language."

Design and construction form a dynamic industry with a dynamic language. Terms and definitions vary regionally, by occupation, and over time. Any study of construction by means of case studies requires clarity of terms, particularly as they refer to contractual relations—the glue that binds parties together for participation in constructive endeavors. Contractual relations are contained within (and are made operational by) project delivery systems, the term defining the comprehensive set of dynamics by which projects move from ideas to built facilities, or from vision to reality (Figure 2-1).

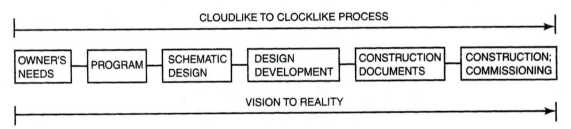

Figure 2-1   Design and construction embrace cloudlike to clocklike process, bringing a vision to reality. The overall process is a project delivery system, which can take on a variety of contractual relations.

Basic Definitions

Following are numerous definitions of terms that are prevalent in modern construction and that will be used in this chapter and in the case studies to follow:

○ Project delivery system (PDS): a set of procedures and relationships by which a project is delivered to an owner. The PDS includes the design/construct continuum and can be extended to building maintenance. The PDS determines which parties are responsible for all activities. Various forms of agreement describe the relationships and responsibilities. Salient PDSs include:

1. Lump sum general contracting, which is also called *design-bid-build* to designate the linear process of completing design documents prior to competitive bidding, and which is used to select the contractor who offers the best responsive price. Lump sum is used predominantly in the public sector (and is also called *stipulated sum* in some forms of agreement). A few states require separate contracts for mechanical and electrical work.

2. Negotiated general contracting, which may be based on either a fixed price (lump sum) or a cost–plus a fee, the latter frequently including a guaranteed maximum price; used predominantly in the private sector where negotiations cover a number of issues besides price, such as safety, schedule, construction quality, and performance incentives in any of those or other criteria (Figure 2-2).

3. Design-build, wherein the design and construction activity are contractually linked, to offer the owner a single point of responsibility for delivering the entire project. Design may be provided by in-house employees, or by one or more consulting firms under subcontract to or in joint venture with the design-build contractor. Subsets of design-build are:

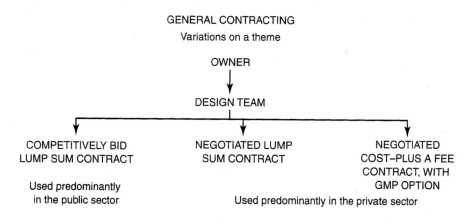

Figure 2-2 Options in general contracting. Typically the owner first selects a design team. Then the project delivery system is determined, and a general contractor is selected accordingly.

    a. Turnkey, in which the contractor provides a complete package of land, design, financing, and construction and then "turns the key" over to the owner on completion, for a previously agreed-on price.

    b. Design-build-lease and build-own-transfer (BOT), the latter also called *design-build-lease-to-operate,* both of which are extensions of turnkey wherein the owner delays capitalizing the project permanently or to some future date.

    c. Bridging, which entails traditional owner/designer relationships followed by competitive proposals by design-build contractors to complete documents and execute construction.

    d. Subcontractor design-build, where a trade or specialty contractor performs both design and installation of particular systems such as HVAC, curtainwall, or roofing.

4. Construction management (CM), which places the construction entity in an agency relationship with the owner for preconstruction services (costs, schedules, value engineering), followed by construction execution in one of several fashions, as designated by the types of contractual relations:

    a. Agency CM, wherein the construction manager is retained in an agency relationship throughout the project and administers a number of trade contractors who have prime contracts directly with the owner.

    b. At-risk CM, wherein the construction manager takes on direct responsibility for construction means and methods, and trade contractors become subcontractors to the construction manager, who frequently works under a guaranteed maximum price agreement with the owner. This general arrangement is sometimes called CM/GC because the construction entity provides agency CM preconstruction services and then performs much like a general contractor during construction.

c. CM hybrids of agency and at-risk construction management tailored to particular needs of owners. (Some states are statutorially defining CM and CM/GC.)

5. Program management (PM), which is usually not considered a project delivery system per se, but rather an overarching management umbrella for a number of services beginning with programming and then carrying that programming intent through design and construction to start-up of the completed building, and possibly including initial management of the completed facility. The program manager works as agent to the owner, who outsources many responsibilities to the PM to guide overall design, construction, and commissioning of the completed facility or facilities. (See Figure 2-3 for comparisons to design-build and CM.)

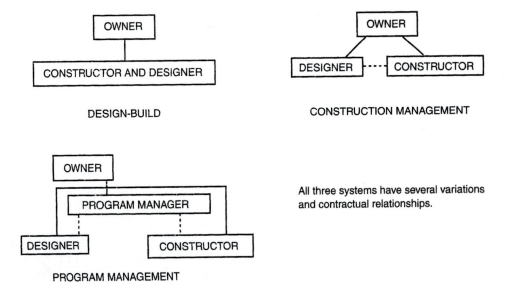

Figure 2-3 Simplified organizational relationships of design-build, construction management, and program management. Solid lines are contractual; dashed lines are administrative.

○ Contract: any formal agreement to do work, provide services, or deliver materials or products. A contractual agreement may be spoken but is recommended to be written if for significant monetary sums. A prime contract is between two principal parties. A subcontract is between a principal party and a subsidiary party (see later definitions). Offer, acceptance, and consideration (money) are viewed as the key elements in a legally binding contract.

○ Form of agreement: a written instrument that defines terms of a contract and that establishes contractual relations between two or more parties. Detailed forms are typically used to bind principal parties together for construction projects. Sources of standard forms for prime and subsidiary agreements include:
1. American Institute of Architects
2. Associate General Contractors of America
3. Engineers' Joint Contract Document Committee, with input from:
    National Society of Professional Engineers
    Consulting Engineers Council
    American Society of Civil Engineers
    Construction Specifications Institute

4. Parties who produce special or nonstandard forms, which may be project specific or written for particular types of jobs, sometimes by owners (assisted by attorneys), and which display language peculiar to the projects or owners' needs; examples:
    a. Owners who build enough projects to generate their own forms
    b. General contractors, who write their own:
        Subcontract forms
        Supply contract forms
        Purchase orders
        Letters of agreement, authorization, or intent

○ General contract: agreement for total project construction; to deliver the building as described in the contract documents.

○ Prime construction contract: an agreement directly between a contractor and an owner. General contracts typically are prime contracts. Sometimes mechanical contracts and specialty trade contracts are also prime, depending on PDSs and requirements of states or municipalities.

○ Separate prime contracts: a condition (sometimes statutory) required by owners in certain PDSs. The number of primes can range from three or four, with mechanical and electrical contractors typically being separated, to dozens of primes under agency construction management.

○ Subcontract: an agreement between a prime contractor and a trade or specialty contractor.

○ Sub-subcontract: an agreement between a subcontractor and another specialty contractor (sometimes called a *second-tier subcontractor*).

○ Contract documents: the set of information, including drawings, specifications, conditions, instructions, and forms of agreement, which details the basis of an agreement for construction (sometimes called *construction documents* while under preparation, but they become contract documents once an agreement is signed).

○ Contract bonds: instruments of assurance sometimes required by owners from contractors, or by contractors from subcontractors, and provided, for fees, by third parties called *sureties*. Typical construction contract bonds are:

1. Bid bond, used to assure the validity of a proposal, and usually covering a portion (such as 10 percent) of the bid amount, which may be payable to the owner if a selected contractor does not sign a contract.

2. Performance bond, used to guarantee performance of a contract; causes the surety to assume responsibility for the work if the original contractor defaults (usually for 100 percent of the contract amount).

3. Labor and material payment bond, which provides funds to pay for labor, material, and equipment if the contractor fails to pay for these (usually for 100 percent of the contract amount, and under some circumstances may be combined with a performance bond in one "contract bond").

○ Guaranteed Maximum Price (GMP): a proposal given by a contractor to an owner, with the stipulation that the overall cost will not exceed the stated sum, but with an expectation that the cost may accrue to less than the stated amount. Savings within the GMP may stay with the owner or be shared with the contractor as an incentive for controlling costs. GMPs are used predominantly in negotiated private contracts, such as cost–plus a fee, at-risk construction management, and design-build. If GMPs are given prior to completion of construction documents, *contingency funds* are recommended to "cushion" the cost growth that frequently occurs as documents are brought to detailed conclusion.

BASIC PROJECT DELIVERY SYSTEMS

Lump sum general contracting, based on the design-bid-build process (competitively bid or negotiated).

Cost–plus a fee general contracting, based on negotiations that frequently include a guaranteed maximum price.

Design-build, based on one agreement between on owner and a design-build contractor, who then achieves design either from in-house personnel or design firms; or between an owner and a joint venture of a designer and a contractor.

Construction management, based on an agency relationship between owner and contractor, which may then become at-risk CM (CM/GC) if the contractor takes on responsibility for means and methods, possibly including a guaranteed maximun price.

Program management, based on comprehensive agency services aimed at delivering a project to the owner as programmed. PM is not ordinarily considered a project delivery system per se, but an umbrella of services under which one or more PDSs may be used.

There are many other elements of contracts and bonds, some of which will be discussed as required in particular case studies to further explain relationships among the parties. Relevant points may also be researched in other sources. The aforementioned dynamics of construction language means that terminology continues to change; therefore, practitioners need to stay abreast of evolving definitions and vernacular meanings.

Choosing the Appropriate Project Delivery System

An important early decision, made by an owner in consultation with design and construction consultants—and possibly lawyers and financiers—is what PDS to use for a proposed building. It is a relatively open selection in the private sector, but in the public sector, statutory guidelines limit the decision. Besides regulations, other factors include time, cost control, marketplace conditions, and quality expectations. Among those variables, time has arisen as a crucial factor in making most PDS decisions.

Traditional general contracting, using a design-bid-build approach leading to a lump sum agreement, has proven to take too much time for most private owners and for some public owners. Thus the evolution of alternative delivery systems has been driven largely by pursuit of ways to compress schedules.

> *Speed to market* is a term favored by industrial owners for acceleration of the design-construct process. *Fast-tracking* is now an "old" term (1960s) for schedule compression, and *phased construction* is currently a preferred term for overlap of design and construction, which is then divided into segments by bid packages.

Lump sum general contracting remains the preferred way to deliver most projects in the public sector, where the overriding considerations should be stewardship of the taxpayers' money and objectivity in selection of contractors. Public owners need to have firm prices in hand prior to signing construction contracts, and this requires a bidding process based on complete contract documents. One of the great disappointments of public owners, however, is the "bid-day surprise" of having all construction proposals exceed their budgets by significant amounts. Early cost assurance has thus become another important determinant of selection of PDSs. This control is possible only by having the contractors involved and committed early, so that cost studies can be made while design is underway, and then relatively firm prices are actually known prior to completion of documents.

Public owners have employed both design-build and CM as ways to achieve better cost prediction in the design stage, and thus better assurance of early budgets being adequate for construction. Owners may further wish to guarantee the adequacy of their budgets by including guaranteed maximum prices in agreements with construction companies under design-build or CM. If a GMP is set during design, the contractor must become integrated into the design process to protect against cost overruns. The contractor regularly reviews design documents to be assured that the building can be completed within the GMP—and the contractor must have the authority to veto certain design elements or material selections to maintain cost control, or gain owner authorization to increase the GMP. A triangular relationship is developed whereby the designer, constructor, and owner regularly interact to be sure that most of their priorities are being met within a budget—or they may need some flexibility to allow growth in a GMP. Such flexibility may be in the form of contingency funds, amounts set aside to absorb limited cost overruns. Public owners frequently do not have much financial flexibility, so the reliability of early cost studies by contractors becomes crucial. In design-build, if the designer is literally working for the contractor, cost control during design can be dictated by the contractor. In joint venture design-build or in CM, where designers and constructors are in co-agency relationships with owners, a more collaborative approach is required.

To employ construction entities during the design stage, public owners need to follow all relevant statutory requirements. Most states allow CM so long as the construction manager selection process can be demonstrated to be objective, and the construction manager is precluded from any self-performance of work on the project (which could be construed as a conflict of interest). Thus practically all public CM contracts are agency CM, wherein the construction entity is administering trade contracts held by the owner, and the CM is employed on a fee basis, similar to a designer. In rare cases, agency CMs provide guaranteed maximum prices.

Design-build, while gaining a foothold at the federal level, currently enjoys only limited use at the state and local levels, because of the difficulty of meeting the requirements of objectivity of contractor selection. Nonetheless it is becoming quite attractive to boards of education and town councils, who have been stung by bid-day cost overruns and who wish to have price assurances early in their design phases. State regulations continue to evolve to allow broader use of design-build.

PM is gradually gaining acceptance in both the public and private sectors for large, complex projects, particularly those with multiple buildings or multiple sites. Universities, prison systems, and public school districts have used PM effectively. Program managers evolve from construction companies or design firms and manage the entire process. Self-performance is rarely an issue because all design and construction are contracted out to others.

> **The essential difference between public and private construction is the level of regulation. Use of taxpayers' money is guided by extensive statutes, which influence the selection of project delivery systems. The true owners of all public projects are the taxpayers.**

Flexibility in the Private Sector

Being less regulated than public owners, private owners can readily select PDSs tailored to their particular needs. Without the statutory tests of objectivity, private owners can select contractors and establish contractual relationships in almost any manner, short of fraud. Thus almost all private construction work is done under some form of negotiated contract. Negotiations allow many selection criteria beyond lowest cost, including:

○ Safety
○ Optimal schedules
○ Quality of work
○ Prior mutually rewarding relationships between the parties
○ Experience of key personnel
○ Financial stability
○ Overall track record of the contractor
○ Proposed subcontractors to be used on a project

Negotiations can lead to lump sum contracts, usually after screening (prequalifying) candidate contractors and then receiving competitive proposals from those selected. The proposals are evaluated on the several criteria important to the particular owner, including price. Then the contractor who presents the most attractive overall proposal will be awarded a fixed-price contract. There is no obligation in the private sector to select the low bidder. Obviously the contract documents must be complete or substantially developed to allow a fixed-price contract. In the absence of complete drawings and specifications, a contingency fund may be included in the contract to allow for cost growth during completion of documents. Of course, change orders, the traditional mechanisms for amending contracts, may alter prices when construction is underway.

Typically, negotiated contracts are more frequently used for PDSs other than lump sum, including:

○ Cost–plus a fee, with or without a guaranteed maximum price
○ Design-build in its many iterations
○ CM, either agency, at-risk, or hybrids

All three of these delivery systems allow extensive preconstruction services, which have become popular with private owners. Under cost–plus a fee contracts, construction entities frequently negotiate with owners after schematic drawings are complete and design development is underway, wherein part of the negotiations concern the contractors' abilities to collaborate with the designers on value engineering (VE), constructability, and cost control. Normally a guaranteed maximum price is agreed on when the documents are sufficiently complete to allow adequate project definition. Nonetheless, a contingency fund is recommended to allow for some inevitable cost growth as further design decisions are made, and to address inevitable design-related exigencies during construction. Even with contingency funds, change orders are used to increase the contract amounts for work involving a change in project scope or considered to be within design-related cost growth. An important goal in negotiating contracts is to define and resolve all potentially disputable items early in the relationship.

> **Prequalification (qualification) is done frequently in both the public and private sectors as a quasi-objective way to limit the number of contractor candidates. The public sector process is usually more formal, using standard forms from the AIA or AGC.**

Design-build contracts are usually negotiated based on scope descriptions supplied by owners. Since the designers are contractually linked to the contractor, the construction entity is automatically involved in preconstruction services. Design-build negotiations usually begin with target prices and schedules, then refinements, and finally agreed-on cost limits, as sufficient information is generated during the design stage. A contract can be based on a fixed price or on a cost–plus agreement, with or without a GMP and with or without a contingency fund, all dependent on owner needs or objectives.

> **For optimal employment of design-build, an owner should provide a comprehensive scope statement of needs and objectives.**

CM works best when negotiations are carried on between owner and constructors concurrently or immediately after negotiations between owner and designers. The design and construction teams can then immediately begin collaborating in a co-agency relationship to provide best services and value to the owner. CM preconstruction services include cost studies, VE/constructability, scheduling, bid package determination, and dealing with public officials. In the private sector (and somtimes in the public sector), at-risk CM is frequently used for project control and cost containment, particularly if a GMP is used. Also, in the private sector, there is no constraint on the CM self-performing some of the work.

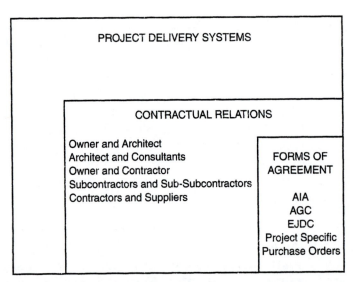

Figure 2-4 Comparative terms and their relationships. *Project delivery system* is a holistic term embracing all the dynamics of a project. Contractual relations describe how the parties are bound together. Forms of agreement provide details for the contractual relations. Designers and constructors should advise owners on the various options.

Project Delivery Systems: Summary

The earlier the delivery system is selected for a project, the sooner other salient decisions can be made. Owners are advised to evaluate delivery systems and related forms of agreement essentially at the same time as deciding that new space is needed (Figure 2-4). Designers and constructors are quite willing to discuss their points of view on various systems, as are attorneys who specialize in construction law. Other owners with construction experience are also sources of useful information. But, contractually, the owner must make the decision based on time, safety, costs, quality, risks, and other pertinent factors important to that owner.

> **The selection of a project delivery system sets the stage for a whole series of decisions to follow. It is an important early strategic decision by an owner.**

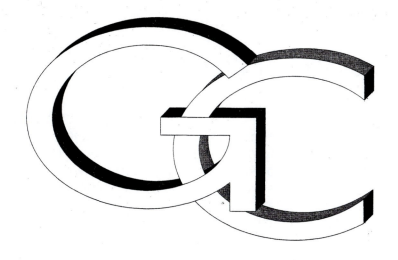

C H A P T E R   3

Illustrative Case Studies: General Contracting

"In the face of evolving project delivery systems, general contracting remains a proven way to produce buildings."

General contracting is the "traditional" way of delivering projects in 20th-century America. Design-build enthusiasts claim their delivery system is rooted in the medieval master builder tradition, but by any measure, more significant buildings have been built through general contracting in the past 100 years in the United States than by any other delivery system. Only in recent times have other PDSs challenged its supremacy. General contracting has sufficient flexibility to continue to adapt to many situations.

The Objectives of Illustrative Case Studies

The case studies in Chapters 3 and 4 are offered to illustrate various approaches to carrying out design and construction. The objectives are to spotlight typical procedures and cause-effect relationships—how actions of particular parties will cause reactions by other parties. The idea is to use these "solved" cases to prepare teams to engage the cases needing solutions in later chapters.

Case studies in this chapter illustrate the applicability of a particular set of delivery systems for design and construction: traditional general contracting in various iterations. The intent is to show how characteristics of projects and objectives of owners influence PDS selection and execution. Also, the case studies introduce issues that occur frequently, such as different interpretations of agreements, disputes, cost overruns, and schedule problems—and show how adroit practitioners work their way through these challenges to produce completed buildings.

Beyond the issues directly related to design and construction, external factors frequently influence the success of projects. Such factors include government regulations, interest rates, and a variety of activities in the broader economy.

Case 3-1   The Job That Went Right

Project:	New combination city hall, community building, and police station
Location:	Mayfield, a midwestern town of 9500
Budget:	$2,575,000 (expanded to $2,600,000 including all costs except site)
Project delivery system:	Traditional lump sum general contracting

Mayfield needed a new combination city hall, community center, and police station. Careful planning ensued over a two-year period, entailing site selection, programming, and budgeting. All affected city personnel were allowed input to the program. Some departments produced diagrams showing optimal space layouts. The professional town manager guided the process through several meetings. A working budget for design and construction was set at $2,575,000, based on prospective needs, a reserve fund of $1,220,000, and anticipated issuance of general obligation bonds for the remainder. When all departmental and individual requests were converted to square feet, it became obvious that either the budget would need to be increased or space constraints invoked—not an unusual problem when planning a building. The town manager, having had previous experience in corporate facilities management, made comparative evaluations of requests and needs and adjusted accordingly, in consultation with salient parties. She then produced a schedule of spaces and spatial relationships for review by all participants. After further negotiations with department heads—and quelling a few disputes—she finalized a design program statement, which included:

○ The schedule of spaces with their particular requirements, including preferred dimensions, finishes, and amenities
○ Relationships of the spaces, ranging from desired adjacency to distinct separations
○ Special needs of departments
○ Support system characteristics, including all mechanical and electrical distribution plus security and various levels of public access
○ Requirements for a user-friendly facility to satisfy staff and citizens
○ Architectural statement; blending with the town but displaying an up-to-date image

Next, discussions ensued regarding PDSs. In the past, the town had always used competitively bid lump sum general contracts, following state statutes and traditional guidelines. Since this was a deliberately planned project without a tight schedule, it was decided to continue in that mode with the proposed building (Figure 3-1).

Four architectural firms were interviewed by a selection team composed of the mayor, the town manager, one council member, and two department heads. Two of the design firms had principals living in Mayfield. Besides the typical issues of design credentials, experience, and capability to perform this project, the firms were also asked to respond to the owner's program, with possible suggestions for improvement, and to preliminarily evaluate the site already owned by the town. The intent was to gain an understanding of how each firm would approach the project and develop dialogue with the owner, while not requesting any up-front free design or planning services. After evenly balanced interviews and evaluation of qualifications, the selection committee recommended the firm of Hollander and Smith to the town council. The factors that gave this firm a slight edge over the closest competitor were that their office was just 16

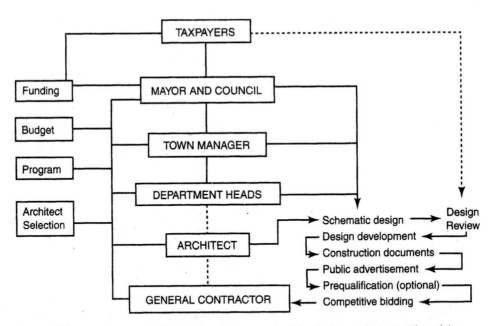

Figure 3-1 Simplified organizational and process chart for design and construction of the Mayfield City Building. Taxpayers are the funders and ultimate owners of the facility. Their representatives and appointed staff guide the process while necessarily following regulations imposed by state and local legislation. Both the design and construction contracts are held by the town council, which delegates day-to-day authority to the town manager and department

miles away in a nearby city and that Mr. Smith lived in Mayfield and would take direct responsibility for the project. After entering into a $175,000 contract for design services, using an AIA B141 form of agreement, Hollander and Smith amplified the owner's program in consultation with the town manager and department heads, and then began schematics. The agreed-on programmatic goals included a highly functional building with good life-cycle costs and a public architectural statement, which blended with the scale of the town but which clearly identified the product as an important community building. All furnishings and landscaping were to be included in the contract documents, so that a true overall cost would be known on bid day. No particular style was stated. The owner was open to design recommendations.

> It is not an extraordinary condition that the first schematic design estimate exceeds the owner's budget. In trying to satisfy an array of needs and desires—particularly with a

> **multifaceted public client—architects tend to show optimal design solutions. The important point is to be as honest and accurate as possible with projected costs and have open dialogue in finalizing design.**

Through a series of sketch studies and regular meetings, agreement was reached on design, and the schematics were completed along with outline specifications and a preliminary estimate of $2,500,000, exclusive of design fees. Since the total estimated costs including design were obviously above the stated budget, the owner was faced with agreeing to more money or to cost cutting. A compromise was reached on several room sizes and on some finishes, and the overall budget was increased to $2,600,000. It was also determined to place some of the desired items and finishes in alternates to allow purchasing upgrades if bids permitted such. A model of the proposed building was displayed in the existing town hall to give the true owners, the taxpayers, a preview of their building, and to allow public feedback. A few comments were generated, which the town manager discussed with pertinent officials and then with the architects. From the public commentary, it was decided to enhance the main entrance and lobby and to relocate the flagpole onto a small plaza.

> **Opportunity for public review gives taxpayers a sense of ownership of their project. Obviously officials should take the input seriously.**

Design development and construction documents were achieved in a timely manner, and a public advertisement, 30-day bid period, and bid date were scheduled, all following state requirements. The architect submitted a set of documents to the county building department, which had code enforcement authority. The town council decided not to go through a prequalification process, since most of the anticipated bidders were known, reliable general contractors—and since full bonding of contractors (bid, performance and labor and material bonds) would be required. (*Note:* Bonding may or may not be adequate prequalification.) Instruction to bidders requested base bids plus prices on eight alternates, with the explanation that the contractor would be selected on the base bid, and then alternates could be added to that price at the discretion of the owner.

Sets of documents were picked up by seven general contractors for a deposit fee of $100 per set. Other sets were sent to the county contractors' association office, where they could be reviewed by interested subcontractors and suppliers. (Of course, subcontractors and suppliers could also buy plans or do their cost estimate takeoffs in the general contractors' offices.) Two addenda were issued during the bid period based on findings by the code official, omissions discovered by the architects, and clarifications requested by contractors. Five bids were submitted on the due date and were opened in a public meeting. All bids were read aloud. The proposed costs ranged as follows:

Contractor	Base Bids		Alternates		Total
A	$2,348,000	+	178,200	=	2,526,200
B	$2,600,215	+	201,115	=	2,801,330
C	$2,401,017	+	182,500	=	2,583,517
D	$2,377,100	+	175,850	=	2,552,950
E	$2,312,115	+	172,550	=	2,484,665

All bids were declared to be responsive—that is, they included all requirements of the bid documents and instructions to the bidders. A meeting was held with contractor E to confirm some issues important to the owner, including alternates, and to ensure the contractual submission of a list of subcontractors, time schedule, and a schedule of values, all within 72 hours of signing a contract. Several, but not all, of the alternates were agreed on, and a lump sum was set at $2,392,315, within the modified budget, allowing for a small number of inevitable changes during construction. A standard form AIA A101 stipulated sum contract was signed a few days later. By prearrangement, a one-day partnering session was held, which included the contractor's project manager and superintendent, architect, town manager, public works director, key subcontractors, county building official, and local fire marshal. The partnering facilitator (retained by the owner) led all parties through an interactive session wherein:

○ Project goals and objectives were clarified for all parties—and accepted by those parties.

○ Participant responsibilities were understood.

○ Potential problem areas were identified and approaches determined in advance.

○ Dispute resolution was agreed on, with mediation and then arbitration, if required.

○ Benefits to all parties were made clear.

○ Mutual support was gained on all key issues.

All parties signed the partnering charter, which was drawn up near the end of the session. Later, most participants agreed that it was a good beginning to the project.

Construction proceeded on a 12-month schedule. Liquidated damages had been set at $500 per day in the contract documents. Work ensued in a normal fashion, with remarkably few problems. The architectural firm provided contract administration as per AIA B141 and AIA A201, *General Conditions of the Contract Between Owner and Contractor*, which was included by reference in A101. Thus, Mr. Smith, the architect who resided in the town, visited the site regularly, as did Mayfield's public works director. They interpreted documents, monitored progress, ensured contract compliance, approved quality issues, reviewed material samples, and answered questions. The architect also processed and certified payment applications, various submittals, and change orders, all being forwarded through the public works director to the town manager for final approvals. Monthly payment checks, signed by the mayor and town clerk, were sent to the general contractor within two weeks of submittals of applications to the architect. The project had typical disagreements, but the good contract documents and partnering guided the job well. The contractor's superintendent was also a resident of the town and took extraordinary pride in the project.

An ordinary array of change orders added 2 percent to the final costs, and the architects' reimbursables (printing, special travel, and so on) added $8252, making the grand total $2,623,413. Mayfield was able to cover the excess in current funds. Substantial completion was eight days early. A punch list of 21 items was concluded within two weeks, in time for a brief ceremony and open house for the taxpayers to inspect their new asset. Aspects of the success of the project included:

○ The owner allowed adequate time for preconstruction planning and design.
○ The architect was selected on a basis including both qualifications and particular interest in the project.
○ Budgets were carefully and reasonably established, with no self-deception.
○ The public owners (taxpayers) were allowed a degree of design input.
○ The contractor selection process was open and objective.
○ Surety bonds protected the taxpayers' investment.
○ The architect and owner provided good contract administration.
○ The contractor executed the work in a timely and quality manner.

○ The owner made prompt payments for work completed.

○ A high degree of harmony was established by the partnering process and continued throughout the project, due to key parties adopting "enlightened self-interest" in producing a good building.

However, even with all the positive aspects of the project, there were normal minor problems within the client group and a small cost overrun—not unusual occurrences, even on good jobs.

> **The design and construction of buildings is never problem free, and all parties must be willing to engage and solve problems with minimal diversion from successful conclusions of projects.**

Amplification of Issues to Enhance Understanding of This Case

While this is an idealized case, it does illustrate that when parties faithfully carry out their responsibilities, satisfactory outcomes occur. The case also emphasizes that all public work is owned by taxpayers, and that there is a fiduciary obligation for public officials to provide value to those citizens. Project partnering is advisable to address potential problems before they happen and to establish harmonious relationships early. Standard forms of agreement are preferred for most projects. They are updated typically every decade and remain abreast of changing relationships, legal decisions, and dispute resolution.

Discussion Questions

○ What other delivery systems might have been used as alternatives to lump sum general contracting?

○ Would you characterize this as a cost-driven project or a time-driven project?

○ Did the public officials fulfill their fiduciary obligation—might they have done so better?

Exercise

Draw a chart showing the relationships of the parties to the Mayfield project, including subcontractors and material suppliers.

Sources and Issues to Investigate to Maximize Learning From This Case

○ AIA forms B141, A101, and A201 (most recent iterations)

○ Surety bonds; talk to an agent if possible

○ Partnering as a concept and a process; seek advice of a facilitator

○ Management of change orders, architect's view versus contractor's view

○ Efficacy of including furnishings and landscaping in contract documents versus making those, and perhaps other items, direct owner purchases

○ Liquidated damages, their function and application

○ Substantial completion and final completion; check general conditions

○ Project close-out and item list (punch list)

○ Structure of local government and how decisions are made, including hiring architects and contractors

○ How public projects are funded, using various revenue streams and issuance of bonds

Case 3-2   Jefferson County Justice Center

Project:	New jail and administrative facilities
Location:	Jefferson County, an urban node on the northern Great Plains
Budget:	$40 million
Project delivery system:	Traditional lump sum general contracting

A federal judge ruled that the antiquated county workhouse, a relic from the Civil War period, was in violation of the U.S. Constitution because the facility constituted "cruel and unusual punishment" for the 1225 inhabitants jailed there, and she ordered Jefferson County to replace the facility within five years. Thus another costly federal mandate was handed down to local government. After some preliminary programming, it was estimated that a new jail would cost $40 million. The county commissioners considered a number of financing alternatives:

○ A special bond issue to be placed before the voters

○ Increased court costs for all litigated cases

○ Federal and state criminal justice grants

○ Increased sales tax
○ Sale of revenue bonds to be financed through increased fees for a variety of county services ranging from building permits to auto inspections

It was determined that the voters would not approve a bond issue for a jail, particularly since some preliminary programming statements had been picked up by the media, and the project became known as the "Jefferson County Hilton." Also, a non-voter-approved sales tax increase was considered to be political suicide for the county commissioners. An impassioned appeal was made to state and federal governments, which led to $20,000,000 in grants. The remainder would be financed with general obligation bonds, to spread the cost over 25 years and allow payback by anticipated steadily increasing revenues from an array of taxes already in place. The county had a very good bond rating based on a diversified tax base plus gradual continued growth in real property development. However, by spreading the $20,000,000 local investment over 25 years, it would nearly triple the amount ultimately paid by county taxpayers, due to interest paid on the bonds.

Lump sum general contracting was selected for the project because of its traditional use in that county and state, and because past legal opinions had indicated that competitive bidding for projects could not be circumvented. While the state had used agency CM in some prison projects (with competitive bidding of all trade contracts), the county commissioners viewed the Justice Center as a cost-driven project rather than a time-driven project (even though the judge had set a time limit on providing new space). It was crucial to know accurate costs prior to commencement of construction. Given the controversy regarding the overall project, the elected officials could not risk a legal challenge of nontraditional contracts, nor could they tolerate cost overruns. A very deliberate process was dictated.

A special criminal justice expert was retained to guide further programming, and all relevant public officials were consulted. Hearing rooms, offices, and extensive ancillary space needs were identified, and a large "wish list" was generated. Fearing cost problems, the commissioners directed that a "basic building" be designed, and that many alternates be included to allow them to purchase desired amenities up to the budget limit of $40 million dollars (Figure 3-2). A design team consisting of local architects and engineers was retained, with consultation from a national architectural firm that specialized in prisons. Fourteen months were scheduled to produce the required documents and for the various required approvals. The design was funded with county reserves, so as not to invade the $40 million construction budget. Numerous reviews were required by the county and state officials and by the representative of the federal judge who had issued the mandate.

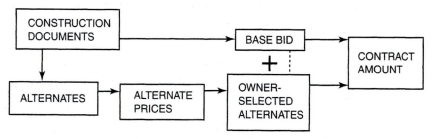

Figure 3-2 The process of using alternates to control project costs, as used in the Jefferson County Justice Center. Owners are cautioned against overuse of alternates, which may complicate bidding and actually drive up costs. Also, it must be clear whether bidders are selected on base bids or on bids plus alternate prices.

As directed by the program, a basic construction package was described in the documents, and 24 alternates were used to price added space, extra equipment, better finishes, and special amenities. Although the designers were wary of so many alternates and knew that contractors disliked them, the county commissioners persisted. It was made clear in the documents that the general contractor would be selected on the base bid, and that alternates would be determined following the contractor selection. Also, bidders were requested to state on their proposal forms any requested time extension for each alternate. However, it was not clarified whether contractors were required to price all alternates in order to have responsive bids. The designers recommended that the owner have all interested general contractors submit prequalification forms at the beginning of the bid period, but the commissioners decided against this because of fear that a disqualified contractor would sue the county, based on perceived discrimination. Further, the commissioners believed that bonding requirements were adequate prequalification (though their legal counsel suggested that such was not completely reliable, since bonding companies also may default).

The county had a disadvantaged business enterprise (DBE) resolution calling for at least 10 percent contractual participation, half minority (MBE) and half women (WBE). Also, the state required prevailing wages to be paid on all publicly financed work above a threshold of $100,000. All such issues were stipulated in the contract documents. Because of the extensive alternates, a 45-day bid period was allowed. But the large number of calls for clarification by contractors led to 27 addenda items, primarily concerning the alternates, and the bid period was thus extended to 50 days. Sealed bids were received from six general contractors by noon on the appointed day. Four of the contractors had priced all alternates, and two had left some blanks. While this caused some surprise to the architects and owners, it did not become a problem because the low bidder, a well-established local company, had priced all alternates. The bids were publicly announced, and the low bid was carefully checked by a county attorney for responsiveness. The proposal was indeed responsive to all requirements, including minority and female participation. Following the bid opening, the county commissioners, key officials, and consultants met for the remainder of the afternoon to determine which alternates to accept. The numbers were as follows:

○ Base bid = $36,472,550.
○ All alternates = $7,215,842.
○ Total time extension for all alternates = 44 calendar days. The construction documents had stated 600 calendar days for work covered by the base bid, and liquidated damages had been set at $1000 per day.

It actually took several days for the owner's team to select alternates, given the desires of the many users of the building. A public defender appointed by the federal judge to represent the prisoners' interests even offered advice. Finally, alternates equaling $2,754,200 and 18 days were accepted, making the contract amount $39,226,750, leaving $773,250 as a reserve against change orders.

The execution of the project was relatively smooth except for some interesting management issues. Legal counsel determined that the state prevailing wage law was superseded by the U.S. Davis-Bacon Act because federal funds were involved. This was not a large problem since the rates were similar, but it did require a different reporting system by the contractor. What became even more of a management challenge, however, was the awarding of the plumbing subcontract of $2,552,702 to an open-shop company from another city. The general contractor and most of the other subcontractors were signatory to union labor agreements. The local union officials complained to the owner and general contractor about the plumbing contractor. However, they actually had no recourse under law. While prevailing wages essentially equaled union wages, an open-shop contractor could not legally be precluded from bidding; if the low bid was in compliance with the law, it must be accepted. Of course, all contractors were required to document their wage rates. The following drama ensued:

○ Legal counsel to the general contractor advised that to bypass this plumbing contractor could result in a lawsuit as well as added costs to the contractor, who had already committed to a lump sum contract, and delays could lead to liquidated damages.

○ Further legal advice was to prepare for turmoil on the site when the plumbing contractor first arrived to begin underground installations. The general contractor and attorney made appropriate preparations.

○ Dual gates were provided at the site, one for union workers and one for open-shop workers.

○ An injunction was prepared, and a judge agreed to sign it if work stoppages or picketing occurred. These would be declared secondary boycotts, which are illegal under federal labor law, and courts could enjoin workers or union officials from exercising such boycotts. (*Note:* It would be a secondary boycott because the picketers would technically be boycotting other contractors with whom they had no agreements or business arrangements.)

○ If they picketed the open-shop gate, it could be further illegal by interfering with those workers' rights.

○ The general contractor's staff prepared in advance for the probable sequence of actions.

As anticipated, as soon as the plumbing contractor's crew arrived at the site, all union workers, by prearrangement of union officials, stopped work and picketed the entire job perimeter. The site superintendent immediately called the GC's attorney, who walked the three blocks to the courthouse and presented a writ of injunction to the judge, who signed it after verifying by phone that the picketing was indeed in progress. The attorney then walked the two additional blocks to the site, where he met the lawyer for the local combined unions and presented him with the writ. After some routine questions and challenges, the unions' attorney advised his clients—four local presidents—that if the picketing was not stopped, the four of them would be arrested, found in contempt of court, and fined—and, depending on the judge's ire, could possibly even be sent to the old condemned jail. After some fussing and fuming, the presidents called off the picketing. The workers grumbled and, after various insults directed at the plumbing crew, resumed their activity. The job progressed to conclusion with no major labor conflicts.

> **Contractors should know labor law to protect their interests, and they should seek legal advice on particular procedures.**

One lesson learned is that construction executives need to know "the playing field" and basic law. Further, they must know when to seek legal advice, and they should not be intimidated by those whose priorities may impinge on successful projects. Another lesson is that public regulations can impact good project management. The time and energy spent on resolving the labor dispute were resources not expended on actual construction. On the other hand, the up-front planning greatly minimized the distraction when the dispute occurred.

Amplification of Issues to Enhance Understanding of This Case

Alternates are devices used by designers and owners to control costs. Only contractors, agreeing to perform designated work for a certain amount of money, can provide actual true construction costs. While designers provide cost guidelines, "bid-day surprises" are too frequent. Thus the idea of a basic building package plus add-ons has appeal. The problem occurs in the cumbersome process of pricing alternates, and with the possible result that the overall building cost might be greater with alternates than without. This may be caused by contractor tactics of being highly competitive on base bids but less so on alternates—or simply the frustration of sorting out so many issues, and the possible resultant errors.

The other key issue in this case is labor law and labor relations. This is a good example of construction being *regulated capitalism*. To fully utilize capital, a contractor must be able to navigate through the myriad labor laws. While unions are not as strong as they once were, a significant amount of public work is still being done using union labor. In any case, how a contractor deals with labor has a great impact on productivity, quality, cost, and schedule. Contractors must work out the best processes for utilization of labor, and employ good leadership and motivation, while avoiding labor's interfering with management's right to manage. (*Note:* There is no intent here to cast labor unions as being obstructions to project management. The history of unions is rich with efforts to improve safety, training, and benefits. It is important that contractors understand unions.)

Discussion Questions

○ What are the advantages and disadvantages of using union labor?
○ What are the historical achievements of American labor unions, and why has the unionized segment of construction labor declined?

○ What are some items in a typical building that might be cast as alternates?

○ Is it appropriate for contractors or contractor associations to lobby for changes in labor law?

Sources and Issues to Investigate to Maximize Learning From This Case

○ The U.S. Constitution: cruel and unusual punishment

○ Federal (Davis-Bacon) and state prevailing wage laws; rates and threshold determinations

○ U.S. Hobbs Act regarding labor

○ Labor union organization and contracts between unions and contractors

○ Open-shop organization: see Associated General Contractors of America and the Associated Builders and Contractors

○ AIA A401, Standard Agreement Between General Contractors and Subcontractors

○ Contractor prequalification: see AIA A305

○ Secondary boycotts, U.S. Taft-Hartley Law, 1947

○ Efficacy of using alternates as a way of controlling construction costs

○ Potential advantages and disadvantages of using agency construction management as a PDS for the justice center

○ The concepts of time-driven jobs versus cost-driven jobs

○ How bonded debt (and mortgage loans) spread construction costs over time, but greatly add to the ultimate expense

---

MINI–CASE EXAMPLES OF REGULATORY RISK

The Jefferson County case study showed the importance of understanding regulations, which can work for or against a contractor. The following examples demonstrate dangers that may lurk within seemingly positive regulations:

A painting contractor received a record $5 million fine from the U.S. Occupational Safety and Health Administration (OSHA) for alleged egregious, willful violations of the OSHA lead hazard standard for exposure of workers to products, particularly paint, which contain lead. OSHA's case against the firm was based on the charge that the contractor failed to provide appropriate engineering controls,

Continued

training, respiratory protection, and medical surveillance for workers who were blast cleaning and repainting a bridge. The maximum penalty was imposed for each of the 20 exposed workers. The fine was 20 times greater than the expected profit on the project.

The Americans With Disabilities Act (ADA) was passed by Congress with the aim of removing barriers for physically impaired persons. In one year there were over 1000 employee complaints in construction based on the ADA, including:

- Discriminatory discharge
- Failure to make reasonable accommodations
- Discrimination in hiring and job placement

Thirty different employee disabilities were cited, including alcoholism, mental illness, arthritis, and hypertension. Was this the intent of the law?

Case 3-3   The Monday Morning Deadline

Project:	Parking garage
Location:	A Rocky Mountain city
Budget:	$8,900,000
Project delivery system:	General contract with two-stage bidding

A publicly held (through stock ownership) private hospital programmed a 1600-car parking garage for a site adjacent to its main health services building. An $8.9 million private bond issue was devised while documents were being prepared by an engineering architectural firm that specialized in parking garages. A public-like design-bid-build lump sum process was selected as the PDS because the hospital executives were familiar with the guidelines, and, with a broad constituency, they wished to demonstrate objectivity and marketplace competitiveness in contractor selection (Figure 3-3). During the process of preparing the documents and the bond issue, the U.S. Federal Reserve Board raised its discount rate by a full percent (in two steps), thus raising the interest payable on bonds a similar amount and adding hundreds of thousands of dollars to the overall life-cycle cost of the garage. While several options were explored, three months elapsed before the hospital board determined to proceed with the project and the bond sale. The construction documents, which had been placed on hold, were expedited during autumn with the hope of beginning construction prior to the onset of winter.

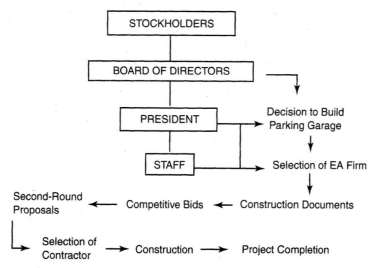

Figure 3-3   Decision process leading to construction of a parking garage for a private hospital. Second-round proposals would typically not be allowed in the public sector as not meeting requirements of objectivity in contractor selection.

The typical delays in finishing any set of documents pushed the bid period into December, and a bid date of December 28 was set, with the full knowledge that it was not an ideal time. But, to add to the problem, the 28th was a Monday. Contractors complained, but the date had already been published, and the hospital was reluctant to change. The contractors proceeded to price the job and urged subs to submit bids on Thursday (Christmas Eve). Most of them did not submit, so the general contractors bidding the job were unsure what they would have on hand for the Monday submittal. Most of the generals priced the entire job to be sure of having a comprehensive bid.

> **Ideal bid submittal times are midday, Tuesdays through Thursdays.**

Five general contractors, out of eight who took out documents, submitted sealed proposals, which were opened privately. One bid was substantially below the others and below the estimate. Three contractors were closely grouped around the estimate. One was quite high. The hospital board and EA consultants huddled on the matter. Although the low bidder apparently had all parts of the project covered, there was doubt about the company's accuracy. It was determined to negotiate with the three closely grouped contractors. Since this was private work, there was no prohibition of such a procedure. Also, in its request for proposals, the hospital had stated that "the Hospital Board retains the right to accept any proposal tendered, or to reject any and all proposals, or to negotiate with one or more contractors as such actions may be in the best interests of the Board, staff, and stockholders of this institution." Each of the three contractors was given two weeks to prepare second proposals, consisting of:

○ Value engineering/constructability/cost-reduction recommendations
○ Adjusted prices based on acceptance of some or all of those recommendations
○ Proposed time schedule
○ Proposed procedures for winter construction

The three contractors, all veteran building companies with ample experience in parking garages, provided a number of attractive recommendations, prices, and schedules. The decision remained difficult, but the owner, pressed to get the project underway, selected the CXT company at a price of $8,885,000 and a schedule of 11 months.

CXT reviewed the few subcontractor bids it had received and determined to self-perform 80 percent of the job, subcontracting only the plumbing, elevators, and electrical and signaling work. Of course, most parking garages are primarily structural, but nonetheless, it is not unusual to sub out 50 percent of overall work. The awkwardness of the Monday bid date had caused CXT to prepare to perform the entire project, if need be. Further, since CXT had good management staff and tradespersons available, the company executives decided that for time and cost control, and managing through the exigencies of winter weather, they would do more than usual self-performance. January was fortunately sufficiently mild to allow the project to "come out of the ground," and then preplanned cold weather practices allowed the job to move ahead on schedule. The project ensued with typical problems but concluded successfully. The CXT president said to the president of the hospital board at the dedication of the garage: "Let's not have any more bid dates on Christmas Monday."

Amplification of Issues to Enhance Understanding of This Case

Private work is always less regulated than public work. Private owners can use any means short of fraud to select contractors. Nonetheless, it is in the best interests of all parties to be as objective as possible, with clear decision-making criteria. While lump sum bidding has marketplace objectivity, it does not necessarily provide the best quality, safety, and schedule performance. Also, the timing of bidding influences its efficiency.

It is important to understand the effect of the greater economy on design and construction. The raising of interest rates by the Federal Reserve Board ripples through the economy and makes borrowing more expensive, causing owners to defer projects. Rising interest rates usually have a dampering effect on construction spending.

Discussion Questions

○ How could the owner have improved the bid timing?
○ Was there a better overall approach to the project?
○ What other PDSs would be valid here?

Sources and Issues to Investigate to Maximize Learning From This Case

○ Optimal bid times by hour and day of the week in your area
○ General contractor decision making regarding self-performance versus subcontracting
○ Special planning and operations for cold weather construction
○ Value engineering and constructability issues, including using precast members for the garage structure
○ How and why the Federal Reserve Board sets interest rates

Case Study 3-4   Shenandoah Paint Company

Project:	Auto paint production plant
Location:	Central Tennessee
Budget:	$70 million (exclusive of design)
Project delivery system:	Negotiated cost–plus a fee general contract

The Shenandoah Paint Company received a long-term contract to supply automobile coatings to manufacturers in Tennessee. Initially Shenandoah planned to ship paint from its Virginia plant, but in recognition of capacity

problems and shipping costs, it determined to build a $70 million pro-
duction facility in central Tennessee. An architectural engineering (AE)
firm employed on previous work by Shenandoah was interviewed and
selected, with the advice to staff-up and to seek a specialty consulting
firm skilled in complex automated industrial facilities, in order to produce design documents for a bigger, faster job than the AE had ever
done before. A principal of the AE firm then began reviewing a list of
mid-South construction companies to determine if a suitable regional
contractor could be found, or if national companies should be invited to
give proposals for a negotiated cost–plus a fee general contract. It was
decided to seek proposals from three construction companies, from
Chattanooga, Memphis, and Norfolk. A ten-page scope statement/pre-
liminary program was sent to each with a request for a preliminary response
(statement of interest and basic qualifications) to that program within
ten days. All three sent responses indicating strong interest, state-of-
the-art knowledge, and industrial experience adequate to perform the
work. The owner's objective was to expedite the design and construction
process by overlapping the responsibilities, ensuring collaboration, and
clarifying the duties of AE and contractor (Figure 3-4).

> **Prequalification in the private sector is done rather informally—
> by developing a contractor candidate list of known performers.**

    In the meantime, the AE firm and retained consultant were preparing a
schematic design, while Shenandoah purchased a 200-acre farm in
Tennessee that had ample relatively flat terrain. Local officials offered
assurances that a zone change could be expedited and that necessary
infrastructure would be provided. No special tax advantages were
sought by Shenandoah.
    One month after the hiring of the AE firm, the three construction
candidate companies were invited to the AE offices on three consecutive
days to review the documents in progress and to interview with representatives of Shenandoah and the AE. The objective was for the constructors
to spend several hours with the designers and owner representatives and
to engage in comprehensive dialogue regarding overall approaches to
the project, but not yet to discuss definite information on costs and
schedule. Also, all contractors were expected to assure the owner that,
if selected, they could take on the project immediately and complete it
satisfactorily.

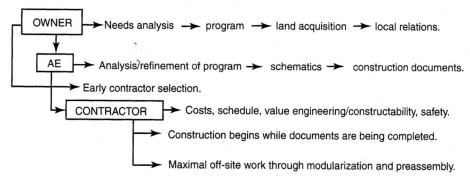

Figure 3-4   Model for expediting design and construction of the Shenandoah Paint Company plant in Tennessee, under a cost–plus a fee general contract with a guaranteed maximum price.

At the end of three days of project reviews and interviews, the owner and AE determined to solicit proposals from the Chattanooga and Memphis companies. The AE was to submit early schematics and outline specifications to them within a month, and the contractors were to return to the AE's offices three weeks later for a second round of interviews, during which the following would be discussed:

○ Updated overall approach to the project

○ Time schedules considering several exigencies

○ Ideas for schedule compression

○ Cost projections considering several design approaches and options

○ Thoughts on the site, including new roads, local traffic, and impact on the surroundings

○ Projected self-performance versus subcontracting

○ Methods of qualifying, selecting, and controlling subcontractors

○ Approaches to hiring local subcontractors, suppliers, and workers

○ Preliminary value engineering and constructability ideas, and any other thoughts on cost containment

○ Proposals on modularization and preassembly

○ Approaches to safety

○ Partnering and total quality management (TQM)

○ Participation by women and minorities

○ Orientation of new employees

○ Approach to dealing with local officials, neighbors, and potential adversaries

○ "Chemistry" and teamwork of owner/designer/contractor; particularly how the contractor would mesh resources with the designers for optimal efficiency

> **The "chemistry of collaboration" is crucial to expedited projects. Owners expect that all energies will be focused on project objectives and that harmony will prevail. They have particular disdain for disputes, accidents, and other events that distract from successful return on their investments.**

Shenandoah wished to be a responsible corporate citizen in Tennessee, and emphasized to the two candidate contractors the importance of having construction done with a minimal degree of disruption to local patterns. They planned to have an orientation program for all interested people in the county where the construction would be located. Further, all construction employees would go through a one-day owner-paid orientation to understand:

○ The overall objectives of Shenandoah in Tennessee

○ The economic impact on the region

○ The operations of the finished facility

○ A good-neighbor policy

○ Expectations of employment:
  1. Reliable attendance
  2. Safety on and off the job
  3. Drug and alcohol prohibition on the job and prior to coming to work
  4. Training opportunities
  5. Requirements for motivation and productivity
  6. The first day of deer season would be a paid holiday

○ Long-term plant employment opportunities with Shenandoah

○ An introductory video explaining operations and safety requirements

Also, Shenandoah would pay for a two-day partnering session for all major project participants and local officials. The company wanted assurances from the candidate contractors that they were sympathetic to their corporate goals. In the contractor selection process, Shenandoah did not wish to cause each candidate to go to extraordinary amounts of work prior to selection; thus the discussions were kept in a semiformal context, rather than in complete detail. Nonetheless, the two construction companies were thoroughly prepared for the next stage of discussions.

At the conclusion of the second round of interviews, Shenandoah selected the Chattanooga company for the project—if a final proposal could be assembled within two weeks, such proposal having firm costs (with contingencies), schedule, and overall management approach, including identification of project leaders. The Memphis company was told that if for any reason the Chattanooga company did not comply satisfactorily, Shenandoah would give them the same opportunity. Within 12 days the Chattanooga company proposed the following:

○ A target price was set at $65.15 million plus a $2.5 million contingency fund, half of which was under the contractor's control, and half of which could be committed only on permission of the owner. The contingency amount would be used to cover cost growth during document completion and design-related changes during construction.

○ A $3.15 million fixed fee to be adjusted only as a result of owner-driven changes or constructive changes. (The term *constructive change* means alterations in design caused by unanticipated site conditions, such as soil problems.)

○ Reimbursibles would not exceed $100,000.

○ Thus a guaranteed maximum price of $70.9 million was proposed, including contingency fund and fee—expandable only by bona fide change orders.

○ A 15-month phased construction schedule was set, with the first phase of the facility to be in paint production in 11 months, and the third and final phase ready by the 16th month.

○ A $5000-per-day penalty clause and a $5000-per-day incentive clause were included on each phase.

○ Mobilization would start as soon as a contract was signed.

○ The contractor would work closely with the AE in completion of documents, particularly in regard to schedule and cost control.

○ Self-performance would be used on all site preparation, foundations, and concrete work, and subcontracts would be used on all other trade work, with the option to self-perform certain trades if it became necessary.

○ There would be maximal feasible use of local trade contractors and personnel.

○ The owner had previously prescribed a two-day partnering session that would be held for all principal construction participants, designers, owner personnel, and local officials.

○ An ongoing training program would be instituted, including safety and drug and alcohol abuse prevention.

○ A strict drug policy would be enforced.

○ Several ideas were proposed for modularization, preassembly, and acceleration:
  1. Building several steel towers horizontally on grade and then lifting them into place, to reduce safety risks
  2. Using a preengineered timber building as a temporary office during construction and then as a permanent facilities management headquarters afterward
  3. Specifying all exterior walls to be precast concrete, using a plant in Knoxville
  4. Using totally preassembled toilet and shower units
  5. Using a sloping metal roof rather than a membrane, such roof to be similar to those used on prefabricated metal buildings
  6. Placing all concrete slabs and driveways prior to the erection of structural steel, to improve site conditions, with the understanding that later, driveways would be blacktopped over the concrete, and the interior floors would be ground down with terrazzo grinders, filled, and epoxy sealed, all prior to occupancy
  7. Several other component assemblies and off-site-fabricated units

○ All documents were computer generated and were to be transferred on diskettes from the AE to the site regularly by overnight delivery.

○ Day-to-day liaison would be maintained between the construction site and AE offices on the Internet, regarding completion of documents, scheduling of bid packages and document deliverables, and discussion of fabrication details.

○ The contractor would assist the owner with commissioning and start-up, including ensuring that all systems were working properly and that plant personnel were adequately oriented to everyday operations.

An AIA A111 form of agreement, with several modifications, was signed, and mobilization began the next week. The job progressed well and all foundations, slabs, and paving were placed ahead of schedule. Then a week of rain ensued, justifying the decision to install the slabs early. Conventional steel framing had been chosen for most of the building to speed delivery. Its erection began soon after the rain stopped. Then, just after the metal roof was in place, setting of permanent modern paint manufacturing equipment was begun, before the walls were in place, to allow maximal access to the work areas.

The schedule was updated weekly. Miscellaneous problems occurred, but the construction company's best project manager and superintendent were on the site and quickly addressed issues. Weekly meetings kept the spirit of partnering alive. Shenandoah's public relations paid off through excellent cooperation from local officials, contractors, and utility company personnel. Worker absenteeism and turnover were remarkably low. However, local contractors complained that their best people were being drawn away from their projects by the better pay and working conditions at the plant site. Shenandoah officials and general contractor personnel attended a meeting of the local contractor association and explained that they understood the problem, that the project was short-lived, and that they anticipated awarding maintenance contracts at the conclusion of the project.

The first paint line was commissioned as scheduled. The subsequent lines followed on three-month intervals to meet the overall schedule. There were 15 change orders overall, raising the GMP by $785,600, but the contingency was invaded only by the sum of $1,520,600. The contractor's fee was raised by $42,000 based on changes. The final cost, exclusive of design fees, became $70,748,200. Substantial completion was achieved five days late, but the owner waived the penalty because of overall satisfaction with the project. Rolling punch lists were employed throughout the project; thus, just a few items remained to be done, along with wrap-up commissioning, to reach final completion. A ceremony was held to celebrate the conclusion of a successful project. Hundreds of people toured the plant. Shenandoah was happy with the cost–plus a fee general contract and soon began interviewing local contractors regarding maintenance contracts. Lessons learned include:

○ A properly managed cost–plus a fee contract can serve all parties well.
○ Cost–plus allows early start of construction and acceleration without the contractor taking on extraordinary risk.
○ Preconstruction planning should involve all parties, including the local entities impacted by construction.
○ Safety can be improved through comprehensive planning.
○ Partnering once again proved to be a good investment (Figure 3-5).
○ Weather patterns should be anticipated—even unusual patterns—and preparations made accordingly.
○ Prudent prefabrication and componentization can help compress a schedule, improve safety, and reduce site staffing.

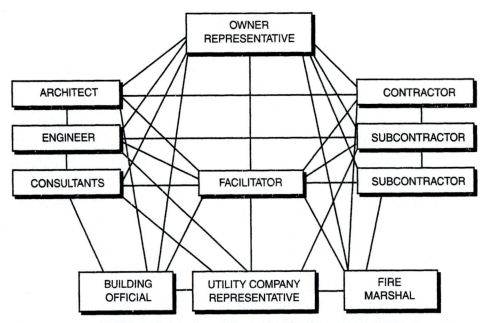

Figure 3-5 The project partnering process, as employed on the Shenandoah Paint project, kicks off with a two- to three-day intensive session to establish communications and relationships among the parties. More than one person typically represent the key stakeholders. An "all points" communications model is developed through the facilitator. The objectives are to establish trust and communications, to identify future problems and their solutions, and to reach consensus on dispute resolution.

Amplification of Issues to Enhance Understanding of This Case

Cost–plus a fee general contracts are also sometimes called *time and materials*, denoting the fundamental basis of costs. These agreements are disliked by some owners because of the mythology surrounding perceived flaws of cost–plus a fee contracts. These include:

○ Contractors are not motivated to be efficient.
○ Designers must watch contractors more closely than in lump sum contracting.
○ Contractors are freer in spending on materials and equipment.
○ The spirit of competition is lost, thus affecting the price.

In fact, the industrial sector, which has led the way in the evolution of PDSs, relies heavily on cost–plus a fee contracting. The motivation of contractors to perform well is contained within the prospect of receiving ongoing work from satisfied owners. This can lead to alliances, also called *continuous partnering* or *preferred suppliers*, which have proven to be good business relations for owners and contractors.

As contractors have sought to broaden their domains, commissioning has become a frequently added set of activities. It entails responsibilities (usually shared with owner personnel and possibly designer personnel) to ensure that all parts of the building and equipment are working properly—and that operators are properly trained. Also, maintenance contracts are attractive to some owners and contractors. This is a type of outsourcing designed to control direct personnel costs by owners, and it allows ongoing work by contractors, though at limited profit margins.

Discussion Questions

○ Is it wise for owners to agree to savings splits with contractors of any money saved within a guaranteed maximum price?

○ Should contractors design their business plans based heavily on negotiated work, heavily on lump sum bidding, or a combination, including other delivery systems? What are the determinants?

○ What are the pros and cons of contractors taking on maintenance contracts for industrial owners, institutions, and government agencies?

Sources and Issues to Investigate to Maximize Learning From This Case

○ AIA A111, Standard Form of Agreement for Cost–Plus a Fee Contracts

○ Value engineering and constructability; procedures, measures, and outcomes

○ Commissioning new facilities; responsibilities, transfer of information, and warranties

○ Close-out procedures; punch lists; substantial completion, certificates of occupancy, and final completion

○ Modularization and preassembly to improve schedule and safety

○ Change orders versus contingency funds; similarities, differences, and overlaps, and how they affect contractors' fees

MINI-CASE ON PUBLIC COST–PLUS A FEE

A rare use of cost–plus a fee in the public sector was a negotiated contract to rehabilitate a state governor's mansion following a fire. The governor was eager to return to his living and work quarters, and thus the legislature (of the same political party) passed a special bill for this project. The governor quickly signed the bill to allow an accelerated selection process whereby several contractors were interviewed; one was selected while design was underway. By integrating the skills of designers and constructors, the project was executed with time and cost efficiencies, without a guaranteed maximum price. All parties were satisfied, and there were no complaints from contractors not selected, because of the openness and objectivity of the process. Nonetheless, the state does not plan to use negotiated cost–plus on future projects, despite strong evidence that this job was done less expensively than a lump sum contract would have been. When bidding remodeling projects on a lump sum basis, contractors tend to include factors representing the "unknowns" in the existing building.

C H A P T E R   4

Illustrative Case Studies: Design-Build, Construction Management, and Program Management

*"Schedule compression or project complexities
frequently call for alternative delivery systems."*

Like those in Chapter 3, these case studies are designed to illustrate phenomena relevant to design and construction within particular delivery systems, preparatory to moving to cases needing solutions in later chapters. Whereas the previous chapter focused on traditional general contracting, Chapter 4 describes systems growing in popularity as alternatives to general contracting. These case studies discuss issues in both the public and private sectors. They are sufficiently varied to encourage research and discussion that will amplify the nuances and idiosyncrasies of each delivery system.

Case 4-1   Lakeside Ball Park

Project:	Minor league baseball stadium
Location:	City on the Great Lakes
Budget:	$11,500,000 (including design and construction)
Project delivery system:	Design-build

A small city on the Great Lakes needed a new stadium to retain its minor league baseball team, the Lakers. The project became known as the Lakeside Ball Park, after the city funded a site selection process that led to the purchase of an old junkyard near the lake. A combination public-private campaign generated $11.5 million for infrastructure, site preparation, design, construction, and start-up. The city would be official owner, with several private parties buying box lounges, long-term concession rights, and parking lot control. It was further determined that the basic program should include:

○ Seating for 6500 people
○ Ten corporate semiluxury lounge boxes
○ Picnic and play area
○ Traditional "cozy" ballpark feeling
○ Real grass field
○ Semianimated scoreboard
○ A progressive MBE program included in design and construction (current political "hot potato" in the city) (Figure 4-1)
○ A target construction budget of $10.5 million, excluding site and preliminary design fees

Design-build was selected as the best PDS to exercise good cost control and to expedite the design/construction process toward opening day 17 months away. A local AE firm was chosen to prepare preliminary site studies and diagrammatic layouts of the stadium. This firm would remain in the employment of the city throughout the design-build process, to coordinate the interests of the owners. It was recognized that the selected contractor would have in-house design capability or would retain, or joint venture with, a design firm.

> **Design-build can function well with in-house design, or by using retained designers as subcontractors, or through joint ventures between designers and contractors.**

A preliminary request for qualifications (RFQ) was publicly advertised and was mailed to 40 construction companies to seek their interest in entering into a design-build contract. They were invited to contact design firms if the project fit their plans. Twenty-seven companies responded affirmatively with statements regarding capability, experience, financial resources, and MBE programs. A client team reduced the list to five apparently best-qualified contractors, which were sent more detailed programs, the diagrammatic drawings prepared by the AE firm, and a prescriptive request for proposals (RFP). All five were instructed to submit formal proposals and to present the following in an interview to be held one month later:

○ Commentary on the early sketches from a design standpoint
○ Suggested overall approach to design and construction
○ New diagrammatic sketches illustrating their ideas:
   1. Graphics limited to three sheets accommodating 12 square feet total
   2. Line diagrams only
   3. A similar display could be shown in 3-D on a computer screen or video

○ General approach to life-cycle costing
○ Description of the design/construct team and credentials of key personnel
○ MBE track record and current strategy
○ Suggested fee

The submittals were kept to a minimum because the city would not pay stipends and did not wish the candidates to spend extraordinary amounts on their presentations.

The interview client team consisted of representatives of the city, private stakeholders, the original AE firm, and the local president of the National Association for the Advancement of Colored People (NAACP). One design-build team chose not to submit. The other four were interviewed during one day to allow comprehensive review and comparative analysis. The C. H. Hall company, which had in-house design capability, was chosen. In addition to the company's own designers, Hall retained a national sports design firm for consultation. Their recommended scheme was relatively close to that composed by the original AE firm, with a few notable exceptions to give the park a distinctive look. Hall's proposal included other key features:

○ Target schedule of 15 months, with liquidated damages of $1500 per day to begin after 16 months
○ Basic construction budget of $9.55 million
○ $695,000 for design and construction fees, which, when added to the construction budget, produced a guaranteed maximum price of $10.335 million
○ Contingency fund of $300,000, over and above the GMP, for extra design and construction costs beyond the control of the contractor
○ Several VE, constructability, and acceleration ideas
○ Inclusion of a minority-owned (67 percent) plumbing company, which would be responsible for both design and construction of related systems
○ Direct craft and management employment by Hall to be maintained at 8 percent minorities

This proposal totaled $10.635 million, slightly above the target construction budget but within the overall $11.5 million budget, still allowing the city to perform site preparation and basic infrastructure improvements. An important part of the site preparation was an environmental cleanup. A survey by a team of specialists had identified a number of toxic conditions. The city employed a company that was 50 percent minority owned to remove junk, debris, and 200 truckloads of soil at an expense of $82,400.

While the environmental cleanup was underway, C. H. Hall worked to finalize design and to move into final document preparation. The city solicitor's interpretation of state regulations was that a substantial portion of the project must be competitively bid by trade contractors, but that if C. H. Hall could demonstrate conclusively that its prices for any parts of the work were lower than those of trade contractors, or if no bids were available from trade contractors, then Hall could self-perform the work with standard preagreed overhead and profit markups. In fact, Hall wished to let subcontracts for all the trade work, while performing overall management and supervision with company personnel. A schedule was laid out based on 7 bid packages, with 22 trade subcontractors. Additional site preparation and painting were set aside for bidding by MBE contractors only (in addition to the plumbing contractor). Most other subcontractors were required to have at least 8 percent minority participation in their workforces. The Hall project manager continued to carefully monitor completion of design, so that the budget would be adhered to.

Construction work began soon after completion of the environmental cleanup, when the contract documents were 75 percent complete. The first bid package resulted in a site preparation contract to be awarded to a company listed as being 51 percent minority owned. This contract covered additional site alteration (beyond the essentially completed cleanup), plus excavation and grading, all preparatory to placement of foundations and surface paving. The company that had earlier performed the site environmental cleanup—and had sought the site preparation contract—lodged a protest with the city, stating that the selected contractor was really a "front" for a majority-owned company. Picketing by the complaining contractor ensued, and the project was halted for six days. The media played the issue to the hilt. Fortunately, the project manager for C. H. Hall was skilled in communications and human relations and quickly met with city leaders and members of the NAACP. Although no irregularities were found in the ownership of the site preparation contractor, Hall's project manager agreed to participate with the city to attempt amelioration of distrust. Site preparation resumed, and a special program was inaugurated to attract black youths to construction generally and to this job in particular. Further, the project manager generated a program with the local public schools to inform the students about careers in construction. The program would include "hard hat tours" of the site, with the hard hats bearing the C. H. Hall logo, of course.

Further problems were averted and the project proceeded on schedule. C. H. Hall and city officials persuaded the rather conservative city building department to give conditional permits to allow acceleration. Bids came in generally as expected, with the exception of structural steel erection, for which only one "high ball" bid was received. Hall, with the blessing of the city council, proceeded to self-perform that work by directly purchasing the steel from a fabricator and hiring tradespeople to erect it. The total cost of the steel erection was less than budgeted; savings were credited to the owner's account for possible later use or for outright overall savings. The schedule was kept on track.

The structure was sufficiently out of the ground to allow work to continue during a stormy lakeside winter. The delay of a week due to the early misunderstanding on site preparation stretched to four weeks due to weather. Thus the schedule became exactly the anticipated 16 months. No liquidated damages were assessed. A grand parade and ceremony opened the Lakeside Ball Park. The NAACP president delivered the opening pitch to the C. H. Hall project manager behind the plate. Then they all retired to watch the home team Lakers—lose.

A final accounting on the project showed:

- ○ Total paid to C. H. Hall = $ 10,592,418
    — Broken down as follows:

    GMP (including fee)   10,335,000
    Contingency invasion   205,008
    Net change orders   52,410
    (an additional $9875 was offset by savings on steel erection)

- ○ Liquidated damages   - 0 -

- ○ Total minority participation   11.8%

Final payments were made by the city within 45 days of the ballpark opening date, after several miscellaneous punch list and warranty items were resolved. All parties were satisfied with the outcome. The Lakers went on to win the league championship and to set all-time attendance records for the franchise.

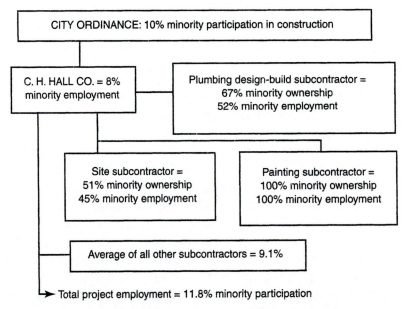

Figure 4-1   Minority participation in the Lakeside Ball Park. Through careful planning and recruitment, C. H. Hall was able to meet city MBE requirements and complete the project within budget and on schedule.

Amplification of Issues to Enhance Understanding of This Case

Two salient issues are interwoven here: public use of design-build and minority business enterprise. A public-private collaboration is a secondary issue. Early controls on time and cost were the primary objectives in causing the city to adopt design-build, but it was also seen as a way to satisfy the MBE problem, which had become a political issue in the city. One of the criteria for contractor selection was a track record in employing minority trade contractors and mechanics. This criterion could not be used in competitive bidding, although the city could attempt to coerce a lump sum contractor into using minorities. The national track record on these tactics is not good. Excessive public expense in monitoring employment leads to alienation, delays, and lawsuits. Retaining a cooperative contractor is far preferable.

   Public-private ventures are not uncommon, but they tend to become predominantly public projects, with all the regulatory requirements that accompany "pure" public work. Normally, "arms-length agreements" between public and private entities are made "in the light of day," with particulars spelled out in regard to payments, obligations, and potential rewards.

Discussion Questions

○ Is the concept of special employment of previously disadvantaged groups currently valid? If so, what is the fairest way to implement DBE?
○ Is design-build appropriate in any project where taxpayers' money is at risk?
○ In what other projects might public-private ventures be valid?

Sources and Issues to Investigate to Maximize Learning From This Case

○ AIA set of contracts covering design-build
○ AGC family of documents on design-build
○ Local government MBE programs; their efficacy and the effects of the U.S. Supreme Court decision *Croson v. The City of Richmond* and similar cases
○ Sample RFQs and RFPs
○ Peculiarities of public-private clients in construction; how decisions are made, responsibilities are allocated, and risks are shared

AN ARCHITECT'S CRITICAL REVIEW OF DESIGN-BUILD

James R. McGranahan, FAIA, president and chief executive officer of the McGranahan Partnership of Seattle, and a former national director of AIA, published a series of articles about design-build in "Issues in Architecture" for the *Daily Journal of Commerce*. He based his observations and experiences on being involved in several design-build projects. Significant points from the articles:

- Design-build is a complex alternative project delivery system that modifies the traditional roles and responsibilities of owner, contractor, and design team, but is not a panacea for anything.
- It should be used with extreme care by parties who first fully understand the roles and responsibilities of all the parties.
- Owners should not assume that a single-point responsibility reduces their roles as clients. Many important decisions still have to be made.
- Design-build has not proven to save much overall time in public sector work because of lengthy selection processes.
- This delivery system can lead to an excellent team spirit in the design-build group when all parties cooperate and work to reduce conflicts. It fosters a "can-do" spirit and brings out the best in team players.
- The competitive selection process is similar to gambling, with the losers losing big, potentially over $100,000 in direct costs, time, and lost opportunities.
- Despite his own reservations about the process, his firm won four of six competitions, and he recognizes that design-build is here to stay.
- A drawback of the competitive process is the inability of competing design teams to participate in the programming process.
- A public agency that decides to use design-build should:
    1. Employ an experienced administrator to manage the overall process and resolve a number of decisions and conflicts
    2. Develop a well-conceived request for proposals, including a comprehensive program and outline specification
    3. Thoroughly outline the selection procedure to be used
    4. Provide honorariums or stipends to all finalists
    5. Allow a reasonable time frame for design and construction

McGranahan emphazied these points at a public AGC/AIA-sponsored seminar on project delivery systems in Salt Lake City, Utah.

MINI–CASE STUDY ON PUBLIC SECTOR DESIGN-BUILD

The Harold Washington Library in Chicago was a classic design-build competition wherein five teams of developers, designers, and constructors were paid stipends of $50,000 each, in the late 1980s, to produce proposals for the $140 million building. The competition developed great local interest and became the subject of a public television program in the Nova series, called "Design Wars" because of the five highly competitive, stimulating designs that were illustrated in superbly crafted models and drawings. Each team spent over double the stipend amount in creating the proposals, however, and even the winning firm of Charles Beebe and Associates had difficulty achieving adequate remuneration for the total effort.

Case 4-2   Fountain of Youth Center

Project:	Cosmetic research and production facility
Location:	Mid-Atlantic region
Budget:	$100 million (for building and equipment)
Project delivery system:	Agency construction management

A major producer of food and tobacco products, after six months of intensive strategic planning and market research, determined to make a bold move into a new consumer area, cosmetics for mature men and women. The company was cash rich but feared declining markets in its current product mix, particularly tobacco. Cosmetic products have high markups of retail prices compared to actual production costs, and sales are driven by astute marketing, a skill that the company had in abundance. Given the highly competitive nature of the cosmetic industry and the continuous flow of new products to the market, the owner recognized the need to be quick and nimble in its new undertaking. Some initial chemical research produced high-quality skin creams and makeup that had dramatic effects on appearances of older people. The products could be easily tinted to enhance the facial appearances of people of all skin hues. The market plan was to promote the products under the name "Fountain of Youth," and an advertising agency began organizing a campaign even before the product was perfected.

The challenge to the owner was to have an "instant" laboratory, pilot plant, and support facilities to finalize the product development and to begin making medium-quantity batches for test marketing. A budget of $100 million was set for the project, including an array of sophisticated production equipment. A real estate team was immediately charged with finding a large site where rigid security could be enforced and future growth could be accommodated. An AE firm that specialized in aesthetically pleasing, highly functional, and ergonomically advanced laboratory design was retained at the same time as a CM company known for its ability to handle complex projects on an accelerated basis. Both the AE and CM signed contracts with the owner with fees based on reimbursement of personnel on a multiple of 2.1 of salary and base burden, with no cap on compensation (fees). The owner was willing to pay for high-quality performance. This was definitely a "speed-to-market" project—but a handsome, employee-friendly building was an equally high priority.

The owner agreed to absorb most of the risk of construction and purchased wrap-up insurance accordingly. The owner had excellent risk management and could acquire insurance coverage more economically than could the CM. Thus the entire construction project was covered by one insurance contract, including workers' compensation.

An intense two weeks of negotiating, programming, partnering, planning, preliminary design, and value engineering/constructability studies were held with key personnel from owners, designers, construction manager, process equipment suppliers, and key trade contractors. Four trade contractors had been selected early based on their design-build capability in HVAC systems, fire protection, electrical, and elevators and conveying systems. Thus there were elements of design-build within the overall construction management agreement. The design-build trade contractors were required to have licensed engineers take responsibility for all design aspects of their work. A site was purchased during the first week, and public officials from the community were invited to sessions during the second week to discuss the project generally, plus utility and roadway improvements, fire protection requirements, and conditional building permits. The public officials became stakeholders in the project, quickly seeing tax benefits to local government, and they pledged full cooperation and public investment in infrastructure upgrades.

At the conclusion of the two weeks, the CM agreement was modified into a hybrid of agency CM. The construction manager remained an agent of the owner, with the latter technically holding the contracts with a series of prime trade contractors. But the owner would assign the contracts to the CM for optimal project control. Thus, while actually having agreements directly with the owner, the trade contractors would function operationally very much like subcontractors to the construction manager, as in at-risk CM. There was a target price but no guaranteed maximum price. The owner identified many important aspects of the project beyond the physical realities:

○ Safety was absolutely critical—as important as schedule.

○ Environmental protection was important—full measures should be taken to avoid erosion, unreasonable damage to the site, or impact to surrounding property.

○ Stormwater control should include attractive ponds.

○ TQM and partnering sessions should be held with all trade contractors, emphasizing full cooperation, quick dispute resolution, and meeting the owner's requirements.

○ All workers on the job would participate in a half-day orientation session involving:
  1. Project goals
  2. Work rules
  3. Safety expectations
  4. Drug and alcohol policy to consist of prehire testing for cause, and posthire random testing
  5. Recognition and rewards to be given for extraordinary performance

○ Training of workers would be provided through a $.07 per work hour contribution by the owner (where not already provided for by labor contracts).

○ Minority participation was required, with a goal of 15 percent for trade contractors and suppliers. This was based to some degree on "doing the right thing," but also on good business principles. Fountain of Youth products would be sold to a wide range of customers, and the owner wished to take the initiative in establishing good market relations.

○ Commissioning, occupancy, and start-up would be on a phased schedule, with the laboratories being the highest priority, pilot plant next, and then offices. The CM would handle commissioning, all operations training, start-up, warranty documentation, and assurances of all systems.

○ Each prospective trade contractor (beyond the four initially selected), prior to being considered for bidding, would be prequalified via an information questionnaire including:
  1. Performance history
  2. Safety records, with insurance modifiers and OSHA citations

3. Financial condition
4. Record of arbitration and litigation
5. MBE practice
6. Quality assurance program
7. Innovative construction approaches used in the past
8. Drug testing policy
9. Key personnel who would be assigned to this project

The AE and CM jointly produced a schedule that determined bid packages and dates for document deliverables to match each package. Eighteen bid packages were planned, containing 48 trade and supply contracts, many for specialized equipment. Each trade and specialty contractor had an individual contract with the owner, assigned to the CM, who scheduled and coordinated all the work and processed progress payments. The owner fed new information constantly to the AE and CM. Processing equipment was being modified as the buildings were being designed. Redrawing by CAD was constant. Simulation and 3-D modeling were used extensively to match production machinery to building systems and to test the fit of equipment and people in various spaces. A computerized document control system was established to ensure that the most up-to-date documents were being used. The schedule was developed around 6000 activities and 30 milestones. A series of two-week look-ahead schedules were issued, and weekly job meetings were held to review all exigencies (Figure 4-2).

The quality assurance program was maintained at a high level. A master control system was established. All vendors were required to expedite shop drawings and samples, and the CM managed the turnaround process expeditiously. On delivery, no materials entered the site until they were checked by a representative of the receiving contractor and a representative of the CM. All trucks were literally stopped at the gate for a thorough inspection. Consequently the need to return unsuitable materials or equipment was essentially eliminated. After a few early rejections of deliveries, vendors quickly learned the rules. The quality assurance program was made a part of all contracts. TQM was encouraged of all trade contractors, and a high level of cooperation was achieved. The CM was quick to reject unsatisfactory work; thus quality standards stayed high. Unfortunately, two trade contractors were dismissed from the project for quality problems after adequate warnings. Though the whole process was being accelerated, neither the owner, AE, or CM would tolerate poor-quality work.

Mock-ups were built of a section of the laboratory and a section of the pilot plant to establish quality and to coordinate the many elements,

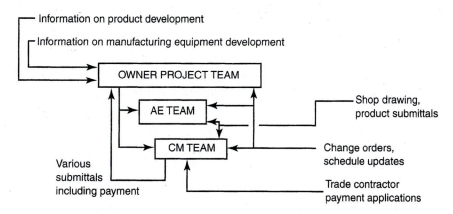

Figure 4-2   On an accelerated project, such as the Fountain of Youth facility, quick decisions and communications are crucial. The three salient teams must work closely together.

including utilities. The mock-ups were done on a cost–plus basis, in a metal building on site. They were "tinkered with" several times to achieve satisfaction.

The CM team grew to 12 people on site during the peak of construction activity. Work weeks for the trade contractors were typically six 9-hour days. The owner was well aware of the effects of overtime on productivity and sought a balance of straight time and overtime. All workers were required to take at least one whole weekend off per month. The CM team occasionally worked on Sundays to maintain control of the work.

The fast pace of the job and the regular upgrading of laboratory and production equipment caused 720 documented changes by the conclusion of the job and numerous other alterations. The traditional change-order process was expedited. Special forms were designed specifically for the job, and CM representatives walked through most changes. Three owner staffpersons were on the project regularly to manage the owner's responsibilities, including signing change orders. The outcomes of the change orders were to amend trade contracts in regard to costs and sometimes schedule.

The laboratory wing was ready for occupancy 17 months after the owner retained the AE and CM. Total project occupancy was achieved 6 months later. Marketable products were coming out of the pilot plant 20 months after design began. Following the well-earned celebration and a few days of reduced activity, the many participants had a two-day project evaluation session, paid for by the owner, to document "lessons learned." Some key lessons were:

○ The intensive two-week initial planning period should have been longer. Many issues came up on the job that should have been subject to more preplanning, such as designing larger, lighter-weight wall panels for quicker enclosure while allowing openings big enough to receive (and replace) production equipment, and making utilities more accessible for life-cycle maintenance.

○ Better overall management of the fire protection system was needed. It was a highly sophisticated array and beyond the capability of the local fire marshal. The owner should have agreed early to pay for consultants to assist the local personnel.

○ Better resource leveling was needed. At mid-construction, the site population reached 800; serious congestion occurred and productivity lagged. More preassembly and modularization could have been used.

○ While overall safety was good, there were four lost-time accidents, all avoidable. Three workers were discharged for testing positive on random drug screening.

○ Thirteen percent minority participation was achieved, and ways were identified to increase that in the future.

○ Total project costs were $108 million, 8 percent over the original target but acceptable given the adherence to schedule.

Many other less salient items were identified and carefully placed in a computer database. The owner anticipated building full-scale manufacturing plants for Fountain of Youth in the near future and planned to use the same professional team.

Amplification of Issues to Enhance Understanding of This Case

Accelerated projects, whether they are called fast-tracking, phased, or simply "quick," require extraordinary cooperation by all parties. The owner sets the tone by rendering early decisions to design and construction parties aboard at the outset of planning. If construction management is to be used as the PDS, one of the important decisions concerns which basic model should be employed, agency or at-risk—or a hybrid suited to the particular project. The PDS choice has implications for managing the project and for responsibilities in regard to approvals, quality control, cash flow, and schedule.

Processing of submittals is also crucial. Since most building components are fabricated from shop drawings, which are adapted from contract documents, quick reviews and approvals are necessary to avoid delays in delivery of critical components.

The issues of bid packages and "deliverables" demand coordination between designers and CM personnel, who tend to have differing opinions on what deliverables (drawings, specifications, and instructions) are necessary at various points in a project. Superior communications are essential.

Discussion Questions

○ Was a hybrid construction management PDS the best choice for this project, or could it have been at-risk CM? How about PM or design-build?

○ Is it good practice for private companies to insist on minority participation on projects?

○ Should there be rigid rules on drug and alcohol use on a project? If so, who should enforce the policies—owner, contractor, or third party?

Sources and Issues to Investigate to Maximize Learning From This Case

○ AIA/AGC forms of agreement for CM:
  1. AIA 121/CMc—AGC 565, for guaranteed maximum price contracts.
  2. AIA 131/CMc—AGC 566, for various pricing arrangements.
  3. Determine which is most appropriate for the project at hand. Clarify the meaning and implications of "holding the contracts."

○ Interview a local construction company that specializes in CM. Seek comparisons between agency and at-risk CM—and the various hybrids.

○ Interview an architect who has had CM experience. Seek comparisons with general contracting operations from the architect's point of view.

○ Seek advice from an insurance agent regarding optimal ways to insure a project such as this. Would a wrap-up policy be appropriate?

○ Draw an organizational chart for the project.

MINI–CASE STUDY OF A CM JOINT VENTURE

The city on the prairie had a 12 percent requirement for minority business participation on all city contracts, including construction. There was extreme difficulty in achieving this on lump sum jobs, so it was decided to try agency construction management on the $20 million renovation of the city hospital. Scheduling and cost control were also reasons for CM. There was one minority general construction company in the city with a good performance record, but it had never done any CM work. The city architect interviewed the minority company president and was impressed that the company had sufficient management potential to make it part of a CM team. Further, the minority company was in a good network to find minority trade contractors and workers. In RFPs to five construction companies, a stated requirement was that the minority company become a joint venturer with the selected construction manager. One candidate company withdrew from consideration, but the other firms agreed to the stipulation and proceeded to prepare proposals and to interview for the project. The selected CM formed the joint venture and proceeded on the project. A number of anticipated problems occurred, such as merging different management styles, dealing with some duplication of effort, and doing more reporting to the city architect than had previously been done. The selected CM company president later confided that the joint venture probably added some cost to the job, compared to having done it with just his own forces. Nonetheless, it was overall a good experience, and he would look forward to another joint venture with the minority company. The 12 percent MBE goal was reached with generally good results.

Case 4-3   Harradge County Exposition Center

Project:	Exposition and Convention Center
Location:	Southwestern United States
Budget:	$240 million (for construction)
Project delivery system:	Joint venture agency construction management

Because of outstanding success and high demand for the facility, the Harradge County government decided to proceed with Phase III, based on an earlier master plan for the Exposition and Convention Center. Two design firms were chosen by the County Exposition Board, partly to spread the workload and partly because of complex program requirements, including a variety of high-tech adjustable spaces, a theater, a parking garage, a very large exhibit hall, meeting rooms, and special utilities that included capability for future expansion. A comprehensive CM team was selected to provide CM services in a joint venture. The team was made up of:

○ A regional company that had built convention centers and conference facilities in several states
○ A local company that knew the area idiosyncrasies and labor markets, and that had part minority ownership

Both entities were required to meet contractor licensing requirements in the state, and their joint venture agreement was subject to the approval of the state attorney general. Between them they needed to fully bond both their performance and payments to subcontractors and material suppliers.

The CM team was brought aboard early in the schematic design phase. The owner had a target price of $240 million for the 2.3 million square feet of space, but recognized some probable cost growth, particularly since the budget had been set in 1996 dollars. The CM contract was agency in form, with the county holding the contracts. But the CM team was to commit to a guaranteed maximum price at the conclusion of schematics. Also, somewhat unusual for public work was the allowance of the construction manager to self-perform work if satisfactory contracts could not be gained with trade contractors. The immediate challenge to the CM team was to verify the budget and establish a strategy of cost control. The strategy included three contingency funds:

○ Design contingency, to be used to handle cost growth during completion of construction documents.
○ Construction manager's contingency, to be used for cost growth during construction.
○ Owner's contingency, to be used for both owner's desired changes and unforeseen conditions. If the owner's changes exceeded the contingency amount, additional costs would be handled as change orders, thus adding to project costs and CM fee.

Review of early schematics by the CM team indicated probable cost overruns. Extensive value engineering, constructability, and cost review were done during the remainder of document preparation to keep the price within $240 million. As bid packages were issued and trade contracts procured, continuous cost studies were done. A series of mock-ups were built on site to review integration of mechanical and architectural elements. These were valuable for coordination of trades and for ultimate productivity. At the conclusion of design documents, and as construction was underway, over a million dollars was left in the design contingency, and this was transferred to the owner's contingency. By the time all parts of the project were procured and underway, an estimated $15 million had been saved from original design proposals through careful cost monitoring—and the project was $2 million under budget. One cost control and coordination technique was monthly audits by personnel of both CM firms, wherein a number of progress items were reviewed. The audits covered schedule compliance, productivity, expenditures compared to estimates, change orders, problems to date, watchouts (anticipated problems to be avoided), and profit projections for both companies.

The CM team members were quite proud of their joint management and cost control and of their ability to bridge differences within their team and between the two design firms. The two construction companies maintained good working relationships through regular meetings of executives and managers, by the monthly job audits, and by a careful structuring of the combined team. The project organization is shown in Figure 4-3. The audits were particularly important for the business relations between the companies. Given the management challenges and risks involved, it was crucial to regularly review the financial status of the project.

The CM team exceeded a 14 percent DBE requirement, primarily through the relations of the local contractor with the trades community, plus a team commitment to meaningful participation. The project had a typical number of problems but no extraordinary delays or disputes. The most significant changes were for owner-directed enhancements using funds made available through savings in efficient design and procurement. Principal upgrades were in outfitting of meeting rooms and installation of a large bridge structure to facilitate circulation to a future phase.

Amplification of Issues to Enhance Understanding of This Case

Joint ventures are common in large projects. Besides the merger of resources, particularly management personnel, other advantages are

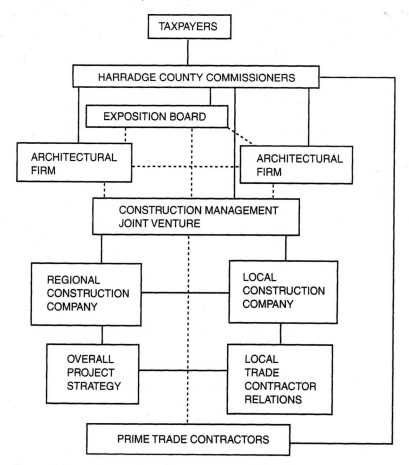

Figure 4-3   Project organization for Harradge County Exposition Center. Solid lines indicate direct or contractual responsibilities. Dashed lines indicate administrative responsibilities.

capitalization of the project (it may be two months prior to the first payments by the owner) and bonding. All construction companies have bonding capacities—that is, limits on amounts of backing provided by surety companies. Joint ventures expand that capacity. Also, joint ventures are done for political reasons, where, for instance, local officials desire the involvement of a local contractor who may not have the total capacity for an entire project. And, as in this case, joint ventures are ways to achieve substantive minority participation. All such ventures have serious legal implications, and participants are advised to seek experienced legal counsel in regard to shared liability and related factors.

Discussion Questions

○ What items should be spelled out in a joint venture document?

○ In value engineering procedures, what are the roles of owner? Design team? Construction team?

○ Should the owner have shared with the construction management team some of the savings they helped to generate? What are the pros and cons of savings splits?

Sources and Issues to Investigate to Maximize Learning From This Case

○ Review legal aspects of joint ventures. Interview a lawyer who has drawn up such agreements.

○ Study state licensing laws to learn requirements to practice construction in various states. Some states have very comprehensive laws on licensure, while other states have no requirements.

○ Review value engineering and constructability as concepts and how they are employed relative to building costs.

○ Review contingency funds and how they are employed in guaranteed maximum price contracts, with particular attention to how cost growth is handled by these funds as compared to change orders.

○ Investigate mock-ups, how they are designed, built, evaluated, and used for quality assurance and productivity.

MINI–CASE STUDY ON COST OVERRUNS

The civic auditorium was a long-time dream for the small city on the "Mighty Mississippi." Thirteen million dollars had been generated through fiscal reserves, a state grant, and a generous bequest to name the building for a deceased local citizen. There were no additional funds available so the budget was fixed. City council decided to use agency construction management as the project delivery system, and a construction company and architect were hired simultaneously. The team dynamics were good, and ground was broken when contract documents were 70 percent complete, with a "comfort level" that the budget would be met (but no guaranteed maximum price). However, the site, overlooking the river, was soon inundated by record flooding, which caused delay, cleanup, and rework to site and foundation, at a cost of $37,000. It was then decided to raise the floor level by 5 feet. Later, some other unanticipated expenses arose, making the extra costs, at the midpoint milestone of construction, $112,000. City council stood firm on the budget, so it was determined to delete the granite floors in the lobby, special exterior lighting, and decorative ceiling panels in the auditorium, as well as to modify stage amenities and seating quality. These components were all in later bid packages, so changes were made in the documents and prices taken accordingly. The budget was met, but with the loss of several desired features. The lesson is that when under a firm price, cost overruns must be offset in some manner by savings in other areas.

Case 4-4   Metropolitan City School System

Project:	Multibuilding program
Location:	Mid-size city in the Midwest
Budget:	$130 million (for all building fees)
Project delivery system:	Program management

Metropolitan City schools were deteriorating. The 82 buildings in the system ranged from 10 to 95 years old. Some were majestic Romanesque monuments; others were sleek International Style "machines." Most had received additions or remodeling sometime during their lives. Roofs were leaking, windows were broken, and heating systems were failing regularly. Federally mandated handicap access posed major problems. A cursory review suggested $60 million would be needed just to bring the buildings up to suitable functional and regulatory status. The Board of Education had no in-house expertise, unlike the period in the 1950s and 1960s when schools were being built continually under coordination of construction experts directly hired by the board.

It was decided to retain a program manager to evaluate all the facilities and to estimate and prioritize costs of improvements. Three construction companies were interviewed based on their documented estimating skills and proven abilities to manage multibuilding, multiphase projects. The interview committee was composed of one board member, one maintenance supervisor, a local businessperson, and an architect who had already been retained by the board to help manage the overall program process. A scoring matrix was developed to help make the evaluation as objective as possible. Objectivity is always important when selecting construction companies for public projects, even for program management. It was determined prior to the interview that the selected program management company would not be allowed to perform any ensuing actual work on any buildings, but rather all trade contracts would be competitively bid as required by state statutes. It was anticipated that a variety of PDSs would be used on the several schools, once the Board of Education had adopted an overall improvement program.

Each box on the evaluation matrix was to be scored from 10 (high) to 0 by each member of the interview committee, based on a combination of written submissions and interviews (Figure 4-4). The highest possible cumulative score was 400 (four committee members times ten points

Criteria	The Garn Company	Riverside Construction	Ferguson Building Co.
Familiarity with the Metropolitan City School District			
Familiarity with a variety of types of school construction			
Proven ability to manage complex projects			
Proven accuracy in estimating			
Experience and number of personnel who would be assigned to the project			
Proven ability to manage an array of general contractors and trade contractors			
Fairness of fee recommendation			
Proposed schedule for school evaluation and estimating			
Exhibited professionalism			
Public relations—to help present findings to interested citizens			
Total scores			

Figure 4-4 Evaluation matrix used for selecting program management company for the Metropolitan City Schools. Each evaluator should score each prospective program management team for each criterion.

times ten items). In letters to the three candidate companies, they were given the criteria and other aspects of the selection procedure, including the actual interview process, so that their preparation would address the expectations of the selection committee. They were cautioned not to attempt to lobby any committee members prior to the interview. Written proposals were to be received ten days prior to the interview date. The proposals would be the basis of the initial matrix scoring, but the scoring could be changed following the interview. The matrix would not be the absolute determinant of selection but would form the basis for final discussion and selection. Each interview lasted two hours and became quite detailed. The final matrix scoring was as follows:

The Garn Company   352 points
Riverside Construction   341 points
Ferguson Building Co.   313 points

Ferguson was dropped from further consideration, and discussion continued regarding Garn and Riverside. All criteria in the matrix were reviewed, and the strengths of each company were reevaluated. By a final vote of three to one, Garn was selected as program manager. No questions were raised later about the objectivity of the process.

An agreement was signed, wherein the building evaluation and strategic report would be delivered in eight months. The report would contain an outline program for the overall system, priorities, milestone schedule, estimates, and contracting recommendations. A fixed fee plus reimbursables was set for this first phase, and it was agreed that Garn would be retained for an additional fee to manage the comprehensive construction program as it unfolded over the next several years. Either party could terminate the contract with sufficient cause—that is, lack of performance or response by the other party. Four persons in the Garn Company were assigned to the task, including a project executive, and they immediately began in-depth analyses of all buildings. Faculty and staff were interviewed, and an extensive database and photo file were developed. The bound, illustrated report was delivered on time, and the Board of Education accepted its main premises:

○ Four schools should be decommissioned as being not suitable for upgrading.
○ Major rehabilitation should be done on 27 schools, in phases, involving their partial closures for an average of one year each.
○ Moderate improvements should be made on 32 schools, during summer recesses.

○ Cosmetic improvements should be made on 19 schools.

○ Four new elementary schools and two new high schools were recommended, all to be built prior to the partial closures of the 27 existing schools.

○ Total cost was estimated at $137 million.

○ Total duration was estimated at six years.

○ Lump sum contracts were recommended on those buildings where the improvements could be readily scoped and defined in contract documents.

○ Cost–plus a fee was recommended on buildings that involved substantial removal of existing material (it was further recommended that the board request special legislation at the state level to allow cost–plus contracts).

○ CM was recommended for the new schools and for ten others that required extensive remodeling (the state allowed CM if all trade contracts were competitively bid).

The Board of Education had $22 million in budgeted funds plus reserves to begin the construction. Sale of the four decommissioned schools would bring in about a million dollars. Discussions were held with leaders of the teachers' union, city government, and the business and civic communities on how to proceed. The PM team was an important ingredient in the several public meetings that followed—to present the information and to clarify the importance of proceeding with all deliberate speed. All attendees at the meetings were impressed with the quality of the study and the communications skills of the PM personnel.

The Board of Education determined that a special bond issue should be submitted to the voters at the next general election. The report by Garn would be the central information for the campaign. Though not without controversy (one newspaper was critical of the process), the bond issue was successful at the ballot box, and the program was begun as scheduled by the program manager. A revised PM agreement was signed with Garn, with a number of variables based on the actual path forward. A basic fixed fee was set for services, over and above all reimbursable expenses, including personnel, with a cap on the overall cost of services. Clauses allowed the fee to expand if there were scope or time increases.

Two of the new schools were begun under CM, one with Garn as construction manager and one with Riverside Construction as construction manager. The board felt the need to "spread the glory," even though it probably would have been more efficient to place both projects with Garn as CM. Garn remained as program manager for both jobs and represented the board in many decisions aimed at gaining efficiencies by contracting the two jobs simultaneously. Garn received a separate fee for the CM responsibilities. This is not unusual. Program managers will move into construction manager roles for more direct administration of projects.

Several cost-plus remodelings were also scheduled for the upcoming summer. The additional new schools were scheduled for the following year. The overall program ensued without extraordinary problems. The Garn project executive stayed with the program throughout its six-year duration. At the conclusion of the program, it was considered a success by all parties.

Amplification of Issues to Enhance Understanding of This Case

Program management is sometimes called *project management, professional project management*, and perhaps other names, representing the relatively recent development of this process and the dynamics of language in construction. It has grown with the increasing tendencies throughout industry to outsource activity. Companies that once did accounting, training, and safety management in-house—and perhaps design and construction, or at least the coordination of construction in-house—are now finding economies in contracting such services to others. Thus ongoing payrolls and benefits are reduced and replaced with consultants hired only when needed. Companies that once had executives coordinating construction projects now hire program managers. Program managers then can be cast as extensions of staff or true independent consultants, and their duties can be defined contractually to meet the needs of the particular owner.

Discussion Questions

○ Are program managers in competition with architects in offering early services to owners?

○ How should architects respond?

○ Are program managers professionals? Should they be licensed? What are their true obligations to owners?

○ What are the salient differences between CM and PM?

Sources and Issues to Investigate to Maximize Learning From This Case

○ Research public school funding by use of bonds. What are the types of bonds and how are they generated; who are the investors, and how are returns paid to the investors?

○ Attend a public meeting where a presentation is being made regarding a new building project, and critique the presentation.

○ Obtain a milestone schedule for a multiphase project and evaluate it.

○ Review the AGC contract and guidelines for a PM agreement. Determine which parties have particular responsibilities in the format.

○ Draw an organizational chart for the overall program for Metropolitan City Schools.

○ Investigate forms of agreement for CM; understand reimbursables, fee structures, and payment processes.

MINI–CASE STUDY ON PM AS STAFF EXTENSION

Soon after the voters of Hamilton County, Ohio (Cincinnati), approved a half-cent increase in the sales tax to build two new sports stadiums, county officials realized that whatever PDS would be used, their staff personnel could not adequately manage the projects from an owner's standpoint. The county commissioners determined to hire a program manager as an extension of staff to represent them in a number of issues regarding procurement, liaison among designers and constructors, and actual construction.The program manager had less-than-umbrella responsibilities. The commissioners directly chose a design team consisting of two architectural firms and several consultants, and a construction team composed of three companies. The PDS became agency CM, with all contracts held by the county. Thus the PM had coordination responsibilities but no direct control over designers, constructors, or trade contractors. The PM operated much as a department head, managing information, approving submittals, and making reports to the commissioners. The PM staff grew to six persons at peak activity. The fee was on a per diem basis with no cap. The commissioners maintained that it was less expensive than actually directly hiring additional employees.

Case 4-5   Panhandle Christian College

Project:	Panhandle Christian College
Location:	Southwestern United States
Budget:	$30 million (for design and construction)
Project delivery system:	Program management

The Claremore twins were prompt as usual for their meeting with the president of Panhandle Christian College. He knew them to be devoted alumnae, members of the first class of 22 eager freshmen 70 years ago, and he thought that they might wish to discuss a bequest. He was optimistic enough to hope for a million dollars. The twins had no heirs and had led productive lives but lived frugally. The president deftly served tea and finger sandwiches while pondering how the meeting might unfold. Grace, the more vocal one, soon brought up the subject. They anticipated giving the college $42 million over the next five years. While the president tried to recover from the shock, Grace said that there were some strings attached. They wished two-thirds of the money to be used for two buildings, one named for their parents and one named for her late husband. The remainder could go into a permanent endowment for building maintenance and operation, plus grants to deserving students.

Grace had married a struggling builder soon after graduating from Panhandle in the depths of the Great Depression of the 1930s. She kept books and did what little secretarial work was available. Then the World War II buildup and the postwar building boom helped them develop a prosperous commercial construction company. Knowing the value of land, they steadily invested their earnings until they owned over 4000 acres, some of which became a major intersection of two interstate highways, and some of which contained abundant oil.

Faith Claremore did not marry but took a job in a nearby city with two men who had the audacity to begin an auto supply store in the early 1930s. They paid her scant wages but periodically awarded her blocks of stock, which were worth less than a dollar per share. Faith carefully put the stock away and became intrigued with the whole idea of equity investing. As the company expanded to dozens of sites, the stock grew—and grew. She became quite astute at investing, a substitute for family life. Soon after Faith retired and moved back to Panhandle to care for aging parents, Grace's husband died, and three company vice presidents bought her interest in the closely held corporation. The twins returned to the homestead, soon buried their parents, and resumed quiet, unpretentious lives. But the investments just kept growing! They fondly watched developments at Panhandle Christian, attending commencements and special events, and as the years passed, carefully planned their "surprise."

As the president of Panhandle Christian recovered from the surprise, his mind began to race. Certainly buildings would be built! Grace said further that they wanted a clear, financially sound plan of action before donating the money. She knew about construction and wanted evidence of how their money would be used. The president would be happy to comply. The meeting ended most amicably, with the twins leaving a check for $50,000 with the president for up-front expenses. The president called an emergency meeting of the board of directors and officers of the college. The college administration considered retaining an architectural firm for design and cost studies, but given the tenor of the women's request and Grace's husband's profession, they determined to first retain the Republic Construction Company as program manager. The overall management of the Claremore gift, and the resulting construction, was the responsibility of the college board of directors—who accepted the task joyfully (Figure 4-5).

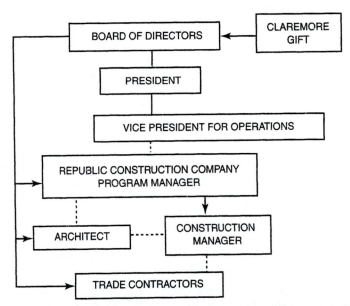

Figure 4-5 Pathway of decisions and responsibilities following the Claremore gift. The board of directors is the fiduciary body of the college; it is technically the receiver of all gifts and is signatory to all contracts. Republic Construction Company, first as program manager and then as construction manager, closely administers the other parties under contract to the board. The vice president for operations is the designated representative of the board and president for day-to-day design and construction activity.

Republic had performed well as construction manager on a tedious remodeling of their largest classroom building two years earlier. The company had made a very positive impression on the administration with its attention to detail and ability to keep much of the building in operation on a phased basis during construction. Also, at the conclusion of the project, Republic had made a contribution to Panhandle Christian's scholarship fund, aimed at attracting Native American students. Republic was a mid-size regional general contractor that performed work in several states under a variety of PDSs. The company had just recently engaged in PM for a hospital in a city 100 miles from Panhandle. Republic's marketing was low key, consisting of periodically writing letters to past clients to inform them of the company's continued interest in any projects that might develop and including a small brochure showing recent projects. Republic had included the college's classroom building in its most recent brochure.

Since Panhandle was a private institution, the selection process was straightforward. The college president called Republic's president and invited him to lunch. During the discussion, after learning the circumstances of the donation, Republic's president said that he had served on a construction association committee with the late contractor for whom one building would be named, and he thought that he could communicate effectively with his widow. The PM deal was made with a handshake following lunch, with the written details of an agreement to follow. The spirit of trust was immediately established and continued throughout the project.

> **Trust is an important ingredient of all relationships—in construction as well as in all other endeavors.**

At Republic's recommendation, the same architectural firm that designed the classroom remodeling was soon retained, along with a firm specializing in landscape architecture and site planning. This was seen as an opportunity to make a major impact on a small college. Republic quickly formed the participants into an effective team, which included the college vice president for operations and physical plant (who was an engineer and also taught mathematics). Three months were scheduled to produce schematic drawings, including overall site sketches and cost and schedule projections. When these documents were ready, the Claremore twins were invited to a special review. The proposal included:

○ A new formal entrance to the campus
○ A tree-lined main concourse

○ A quadrangle surrounded by three buildings, the larger of which, a student center, would be named for the contractor, and another, a new library, would be named for the Claremore parents

○ Projected cost figures, including life-cycle expenses

The president of Republic led the presentation but allowed all team members to participate. The sisters were thrilled, and they agreed to the suggestion by both presidents that the third building, a communications center, be named for them. The meeting was a triumph. The sisters wished construction to proceed immediately, left an additional $500,000, and promised that million dollar checks would continue each month. The money was in a trust fund with a local attorney and bank, ensuring its availability.

Republic then prepared a milestone schedule and a list of key issues to be decided during a two-day partnering session to be conducted the next week. Several faculty members and students were invited to participate in the session, which actually extended to three days. The excitement was profound. The campus became alive with stories about the improvements. The president of Panhandle Christian inquired about the possibility of accelerating the program, since he definitely wanted the benefactors to be present at the dedication of at least one building.

> **Partnering and project planning go hand-in-hand. Many issues are resolved that could become problems later.**

The outcome of a three-day partnering session included a number of decisions:

○ Campus utilities would need major upgrading.

○ Stormwater retention would be handled by a new decorative lagoon.

○ All infrastructure work would be done initially.

○ The construction would be phased over four years, based on anticipated cash inflow, impact on the campus, and availability of labor in a small market.

○ The student center would be completed first, 22 months from beginning of design development; the two other buildings would follow.

○ A ceremonial ground breaking would be held in one month, at which the Claremore twins would dig the first shovels of dirt.

Design development work had begun immediately after the partnering session so that some construction could continue following the ground breaking. A site preparation and underground utility bid package was prepared. Bids were slightly higher than anticipated, but contracts were let. Republic reviewed budgets and determined that they needed to broaden the base of bidders on future packages. They contacted trade contractors within a 100-mile radius and invited them to Panhandle for conferences. The overall project was reviewed, and the contractors were allowed to take design development drawings with them for further study in anticipation of bidding future packages.

The president of Panhandle opined that he would like the contractors to be as local as possible, considering the long-term position of the college in its community. Republic was faced with a dilemma. The local contractors were small, and most were not experienced in the type of construction being done—and had tended to overprice the work. Nonetheless, a meeting was called of all local parties who could supply construction labor or material. It was determined that Republic would directly manage (PM to CM) the work, and employ a number of local contractors. Training would be provided to all interested persons. The Claremore twins, who had taken a close interest in the project, heartily approved of this move. The work on the student center progressed with about half local trade contractors and half out-of-town participants. Republic's superior management merged their efforts efficiently. One result of the mix of contractors, however, was a 6 percent cost overrun on the student center. Republic had kept the college administration and the twins informed of cost growth through periodic reports, so there was no surprise when the building went over budget.

As the student center was being readied for the grand opening, the project team conducted a thorough postproject evaluation to determine successes and failures on the first building and how savings could be gained on the next two buildings. A series of 34 "watchouts" were listed on activities from concrete placement to landscaping. Four trade contractors were excluded from bidding on remaining work. Efforts ensued on the next two buildings, with Republic doing more direct management with an enlarged staff and a cadre of specially selected local subcontractors (plus mechanical and electrical contractors from the state capital). Republic's fees were adjusted accordingly. Republic held a second partnering session with all key subs. The watchouts were discussed in detail. The two buildings proceeded extremely well due to a high level of enthusiasm, learning curves, and continuous evaluation.

The buildings came to conclusion just beyond schedule and at budget. The entire "Claremore Quadrangle" was completed at a total cost, including all expenditures, of $32,140,500, somewhat over the original budget, but including considerable infrastructure and ancillary work—however, the Claremores had added $8 million to the gift due to Faith's extraordinary management of their investments. The twins were brought to the grand openings of "their building" and "their parents' building" in wheelchairs on their 92nd birthday to hear the assembled students, faculty, and workers sing "Happy Birthday." It was quite an emotional and rewarding experience for all.

Amplification of Issues to Allow Enhanced Understanding of This Case

Major gifts to institutions usually entail some strings attached. Not all donors are as enlightened as the Claremores. Institutions do have a moral (and sometimes legal) obligation to use funds as directed. It is important that all key participants understand the overall goals of any project. An integrative PDS, where all participants are engaged early, allows this. Also, partnering causes early exchanges during which salient issues become clearer. This was an ideal use of PM, given overall campus improvements and construction of three new buildings. Selection of trade contractors is crucial to any project. Generally, the more bidders on any segment of work, the more competitive the prices. Also, past experience relevant to that being bid is crucial. Work, procedures, or materials new to a particular contractor will lead to high bids.

Discussion Questions

○ If you were an architect, how would you react to being invited to a project by a contractor in a PM role? Is the entity still a contractor—or a new entity?

○ With whom would the architect contract for services, owner or program manager?

○ How does the architect's role change when providing traditional services to owners as compared to services rendered under a program manager?

○ Should architects become program managers?

Sources and Issues to Investigate to Maximize Learning From This Case

○ Invite a person from a university development office to explain endowments, equity investments, and procedures for naming buildings for benefactors.

○ Sketch a three-building quadrangle and plan a strategy for building the facilities over a four-year period with schedule milestones.

○ Investigate the process of a program manager becoming a construction manager. What change in responsibilities does the move entail? How should an agreement be developed?

MINI–CASE STUDY: THE LIMITS OF PROGRAM MANAGEMENT

The aging industrial city in New England faced tough times. A steady loss of tax base caused reduction of city services to a bare-bones level. The latest election brought a new, young mayor into office who promised to replace the malaise with a new robustness. He dreamed of a civic center to invigorate the city and was able to persuade the district's congresswoman to secure a rare urban renewal grant as seed money, for planning and feasibility studies. With no in-house personnel to even do adequate scope definition, the mayor persuaded the city council to retain the Essex Corporation as overall program manager to "do it all," beginning with the scope and moving to schematic design and possible funding sources—then to full project delivery as further funding would allow. Essex has an excellent track record in both design and construction, generally in engineering projects such as power plants and high-tech facilities. The mayor-driven "objective" selection process focused on Essex's superior management, information systems, and contacts with many consulting groups and financial institutions.

Essex quickly swung into action, retaining an urban planning firm and architectural group and calling its own feasibility people into the mix. A *charrette* (intense planning and sketching session) ensued for a week, during which political, business, and civic leaders, and citizens at large, were allowed to participate in exciting exchanges of ideas. Another two weeks of frenetic activity

Continued

produced dazzling computer-generated pictorial drawings and a preliminary model of a proposed complex, including a performing arts auditorium, historical museum, shops, and a hotel. It was to be a public-private venture estimated to cost $75 million. Essex pursued a hotel chain, retailers, and financiers, and developed an attractive package for the city. Then came crunch time. It would be necessary for the city to float a $45 million bond issue to pay its share, including the cost of infrastructure improvements. The mayor enthusiastically lobbied council to vote the authority for the bonds. Legal bond counsel provided an opinion that the city's financial status would give the bonds a low rating; thus high interest rates would need to be paid to investors to make the bonds attractive. The further advice was to increase city revenues to improve the bond rating. Council reluctantly agreed to place a two mill bond issue (two dollars of annual tax increase for each thousand dollars of property valuation) on the ballot for the next election. The issue was vigorously debated in the election season, with the mayor being opposed by three council members and a property owners' group. In the highest level of voter turnout in years, the citizens narrowly defeated the issue. The small amount of remaining seed money was used to put a few added touches on the drawings, making it easier to resurrect them in good order for further consideration when the mayor came up with another idea to bring the project to reality.

C H A P T E R 5

Case Studies Needing Solutions: Project Delivery Systems/Contractual Relationships; Public Sector Work

"Taxpayers are the true owners of public sector projects."

The case studies in this chapter are framed to allow several outcomes in design approaches, selection of PDSs, and establishment of contractual relationships. Since most real-life projects can be executed under more than one design approach and different delivery systems, each case can have multiple solutions. In fact, with hybrids and variations, several solutions may be nearly equally appropriate. The questions and assignments at the end of each case are composed to help guide the solutions. Participants may generate additional assumptions and questions in group sessions. It is important to develop sound rationales ("reasons why") prior to embarking on a particular direction. All cases

111

in this chapter are in the public sector, with its abundant regulations, as compared to private sector projects.

Case 5-1   New High School for Summit City

Owner:	Summit City (population 40,000) in the mid-western United States; board of education
Project:	New consolidated high school
Location:	Greenfield site on edge of city
Budget:	$29 million (exclusive of site costs and design fees)
Project delivery system:	To be determined

Summit City currently has two public high schools, both of which are aging and in need of repair. Declining enrollments recently caused the board of education to consider consolidation into one state-of-the-art high school. The board proceeded to compose referendum language requesting the electorate to fund a bond issue to build a $32 million comprehensive facility. Bonds will be sold with maturities of 5 years, 10 years, and 15 years, causing a total tax liability to Summit City property owners of $48 million over the 15-year period, or $3.2 million per year—if the voters approve the issue.

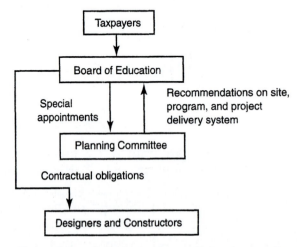

Figure 5-1   Organization for producing the new Summit City High School. Taxpayers elect and fund the board of education and schools. The board appoints an ad hoc planning committee for advice. The board is signatory to all contracts.

While the election campaign is being planned, the board of education is faced with deciding the best procedure to get the school designed and built. A planning committee, established to determine program requirements, has been given this challenge (Figure 5-1). The ad hoc committee is composed of representatives of the faculty, staff, board of education, parents, and community persons, all working with an architect who lives in the community and who has children in the school system. He is serving as a "user-friendly" consultant for a nominal fee. The architect is employed by a firm that primarily designs industrial facilities. His firm will not be a candidate to design the school project. In his industrial practice, the architect has become familiar with a range of PDSs, and while there is, of course, more latitude in the private sector, relatively new state laws allow both design-build and agency CM in public work, as long as the selection process is objective and most trade work is competitively bid. The architect consultant presents the following options to the planning committee:

1. Traditional qualifications-based architect selection process followed by full contract documents and then a competitively bid lump sum agreement with a general contractor—sometimes called *design-bid-build*.

2. Design-build under contract with a firm that provides in-house design services. At least three design-build firms in the state have experience in providing such services to boards of education.

3. Consultative or joint venture design-build, where a traditional general contractor retains a design firm to perform design duties—or the two firms jointly form a separate entity for the project. (*Note*: There are important legal differences between consultative design-build and true joint ventures, but for the purposes of this example, they are treated together.)

4. Bridging, a hybrid of design-build, where the board retains an architect in the traditional manner to prepare schematic designs and partial design development drawings and specifications, after which competitive design-build proposals are taken from contractors to complete the documents, meet all regulatory and permitting requirements, and execute construction.

5. Agency CM, where the board retains both a design firm and a construction company at the same time to provide dual agency for design and construction.

The planning committee carefully reviews each delivery system, the pros and cons of which are summarized below:

Option 1: Traditional Design-Bid-Build, Lump Sum Contract

Pros	Cons
Lump sum is a well-understood system that the board of education has used several times in the past, and for which there are ample guidelines in the way of state legislation, forms of agreement, bonding, and liquidated damages.	It takes a relatively long time to prepare full documents for competitive bidding. Although the school project is not on a fast track, there are obvious advantages to accelerated completion and early use of a new facility.
A number of regional architectural and engineering firms are experienced in school design and are eager for design contracts for the school. Competitive proposals, in regard to both quality of service and fees, would be anticipated by the board.	The board must be careful not to select the designers based primarily on fees, since this can lead to inferior documents and problems during construction. Comprehensive interviews and reviews of credentials are recommended.
Most of the board's constituents are comfortable with lump sum contracting and perceive that the best prices for construction are achieved in the competitive marketplace. Thus it is the politically safe way for the board to proceed.	Construction costs are not known until bids come in, and if the bids are too high ("bid-day surprise"), painful cutting occurs. Also, even after bidding, change orders can add additional cost—depending largely on the quality of documents.
The board and other interested parties will have a good understanding of all the physical aspects of the building (layout, appearance, and details), provided by presumably complete contract documents, before construction begins.	Adversarial relationships cropped up on previous jobs when designers and contractors disagreed on interpretations of several issues described in the documents. Claims and counterclaims that distracted from the project objectives were filed.

Option 2: In-House Design-Build

Pros	Cons
Single-point responsibility provides some efficiencies to the board of education. One selection is made for a contractor who is responsible for both design and construction.	The owner loses the agency relationship with an architect; thus the historical checks and balances between designer and contractor are lost.

Pros	Cons
Preliminary costs may be part of the selection process, based on owner's scope statement and programs. Approximate schedule projections may also be made.	Owners need to be cautious not to be deceived by early cost projections in the selection process—and certainly should not make a selection based only on cost or schedule.
A guaranteed maximum price can be established early. Bid-day surprises can be avoided. Integration of design and construction entails cost-control collaboration, including ongoing value engineering and constructability studies. Design fees are built into the construction costs, which may have advantages in financing the project. Design fees may be less, but this is not necessarily the case.	Thorough prequalification is recommended because most in-house design-build contractors work primarily in the private sector, where disclosure of information and bonding requirements are less prevalent. Objective selection is crucial, in regard to both capability of designers and reliability of constructors—and in the best interests of the taxpayers. Prequalification should include inspections of recent projects.
State law requires competitive bidding of trade work, and while this does not preclude self-performance by the design-build contractor, all costs must be demonstrated as being lowest and best in the marketplace.	Extensive use of subcontractors (similar to lump sum contracting) may reduce some of the efficiencies of design-build. Also, some monitoring of prices is required by any responsible owner.
Overall schedule can be compressed. Decision making is accelerated due to employment linkage of design and construction. Contract documents can be produced more quickly since some details and bidding aspects can be omitted.	To guarantee the price, a design-build contractor must have a good deal of control over design, which may be in conflict with uments may lead to owner-contractor disagreements.
Design-build contractors who have ample experience can reuse proven details and selected components from past projects. (Of course, independent architects also reuse proven components.)	Quality of design may be sacrificed. Designers in direct employment of contractors may be stifled in their creativity. (Technically, most in-house design groups are corporately separate, but they are still heavily influenced by the construction entity.)
Contractor selection can be quicker, based on proposals and interviews rather than on bids, which usually require a 30-day bid period followed by negotiations on details. (Obviously, careful investigation should be made of candidates' track records on safety and quality, as well as cost and time.)	It is difficult to have complete objectivity in selection of a design-build contractor. Competitive proposals are based on the owner's scope statement and program. These are not enough for firm price proposals, so the board must necessarily use some subjectivity in the process.

Pros	Cons
Major segments of buildings can also be design-built by specialty contractors, including plumbing, electrical, HVAC, and fire suppression systems, and special curtainwall and roofing systems.	To ensure efficacy of design-built systems, licensed professionals should bear responsibility for their design. Liability can become blurred in cases where systems do not function properly.

While it is important for owners to understand risks, liability, and insurance requirements in any PDS, there are some special peculiarities in design-build. The owner contracts with a construction entity for design, a service that requires licensed professionals in all states. Few contractors are licensed professionals, and thus they usually cannot be insured for design liability. (Like many construction issues, insurance continues to evolve.) Similarly, most designers are not qualified contractors, so they ordinarily cannot be insured for construction execution. Owners should seek assurances from the design-build contractor that all design is being done by insured, licensed professionals, so that, in a worst-case scenario, a major design flaw can be corrected, if need be, from the "deep pockets" of an insurance company. This same type of scenario is why most in-house design-build contractors set up their design component as a separate corporation—either entity may survive the litigious demise of the other. The same precautions hold for consultative design-build or joint ventures, with a few twists germane to those PDSs. Good advice for the board would be to seek its own counsel from an insurance agent, including guidance on the board's liability coverage and property and casualty insurance for the proposed project.

Option 3: Consultative Design-Build or Joint Venture Between Design Firm and Contractor

(*Note:* These ventures are rarely truly "joint" collaborations with equally shared responsibilities. Since contractors take prime financial responsibility for cost assurance, bonding, and liability, the construction entity usually becomes the prime contractor to the owner, and the design firm acts as a subcontractor. In any case, the legal relationship must be clear to the owner.)

Pros	Cons
There is single-point responsibility as with in-house design-build, with the owner usually having somewhat more traditional contact with the architect in an administrative relationship.	The design firm, if a subcontractor, has no true agency role, and while influence may be exerted on the owner's behalf, the architect is contractually linked to the contractor—and answerable to that entity.

Pros

Most contractors in this category have track records in public work and thus are bondable. They also understand issues such as the owner's desire for dialogue on design, public disclosure, and liquidated damages—and tend to be facile in collaborations with designers.

Pricing and schedule advantages are similar to in-house design build. The integration is not quite as complete, but as a trade-off, the designer has some additional autonomy and tends to research issues more thoroughly—to focus on design excellence.

Compared to in-house design-build, design quality tends to be better when consultative architects are involved. They depend heavily on design quality to maintain and expand clientele. Fees also tend to be higher—"you get what you pay for."

Cons

The contractor must have a high degree of authority on design to control price and schedule. The contractor will vigorously discourage agreements between designer and owner without the contractor's input, particularly as they may influence cost or schedule—and safety or constructability.

A small degree of efficiency is lost compared to in-house design-build by virtue of operating in separate offices. (Sometimes, on large projects, the design and construction team will move into the same office for document execution.)

The owner may feel encumbered by always needing the contractor to be involved in any salient discussions with the architect, and by being regularly reminded by the contractor of cost and time implications of design-related decisions.

Option 4: Bridging

Pros

The owner can proceed through much of the design process in the traditional manner, in close communications with the architect. Quality of design and special issues may be emphasized by both parties.

Some of the design costs are transferred to the construction process (but not all, as in complete design-build). Project costs are largely known prior to spending all of the design budget. Design-build proposals are typically lump sums or guaranteed maximum prices.

Clear marketplace objectivity can be maintained in contractor selection since competitive bids are taken on a well-described document package.

Cons

Some of the schedule efficiencies of design-build are lost. The design process takes about the same amount of time (or longer) as in traditional design-bid-build lump sum contracting.

Careful prequalification of design-build contractors is recommended, including bondability. They will be operating largely independent of the owner's architect, who will typically not have traditional agency responsibilities or any contract administration during construction.

Overall cost efficiency is not usually as good as in other design-build iterations. Design fees are higher, and there are fewer early value engineering/constructability studies.

Pros

The owner's architect can (but usually does not) provide some level of monitoring of final design and construction, thus maintaing some traditional checks and balances. This needs to be contractually determined, including extent of the achitect's authority—and fees. Careful prequalification of design–build contractors may include demonstrated understanding and compliance with the project goals.

Cons

Continuity of design may be lost with a change of design teams, particularly if the design-build contractor wishes to make changes to stay within a budget. The owner will need to monitor "bridging" of the gap. If the original architect is retained by the owner to monitor documents and construction, clarity of responsibility is needed to avoid possible resultant conflicts and possible claims and counterclaims.

Option 5: Agency Construction Management

Pros

Owner enjoys dual agency of both architect and constructor. They are contractually independent of each other but collaborate during planning and design to ensure that design decisions meet cost and time objectives of the owner.

Acceleration can be accomplished by an early start, and then efficient phasing is maintained through bid packages coordinated by the construction manager—all based on careful preliminary cost studies by the construction manager.

The construction manager as agent, on a fee basis, makes all decisions on the owner's behalf, rather than mixing in a profit consideration, as is done in lump sum general contracting. Such issues as minority involvement may be handled effectively under agency CM, if part of the prescribed duties is to seek such participation through contractor selection. This usually is handled better in an agency relationship than in general contracting.

Cons

The construction manager is not contractually responsible for means and methods. Prime liability for cost, time, safety, and quality is transferred to trade contractors, most of whom will need to be prequalified and bonded.

Any cost overruns in early bid packages must be offset in later packages, perhaps by reducing quality of equipment or finishes, if the project budget is firm. Guaranteed maximum prices are not typical in agency CM, but are used in hybrid forms.

Objectivity can be an issue in construction manager selection. Owners must be wary of selection based on low fees, since quality and experience of management personnel may be sacrificed. Additional paperwork is generated through bonds, payment applications, and so on. While the construction manager is expected to handle most of this, the owners, as stewards of the taxpayers' money, must stay "tuned in" and involved in proceedings.

Pros	Cons
It is possible to have lower overall costs under CM if the construction manager is skillful at assembling bid packages, seeking efficient trade contractors, and directly purchasing certain items for the owner, particularly long-lead-time components (boilers, chillers, elevators, and so on) with typically lower markups than a general contractor would charge.	Owners must be quick decision makers and actors, since construction managers will present abundant issues requiring owner decisions and many papers needing signatures. Not all public bodies are facile in this regard, because they must properly make "politically correct" decisions. One responsible owner representative is recommended.

Amplification of Issues to Enhance Understanding of This Case

Boards of education are part of the great American democratic tradition of citizen guidance of public institutions. Members are elected in most locales, and they serve with a mixture of altruism and desire to influence important happenings in their communities—frequently including the education of their own children. Most boards take their fiduciary responsibilities quite seriously, and indeed do try to spend their constituents' money wisely. Consensus on such spending is not always easily achieved, because genuine differences of opinion—and ample public (and private) lobbying—crop up on such issues as how to build important buildings. Thus a recommendation to depart from the time-honored design-bid-build lump sum delivery system will take well-documented persuasion. A suggestion is to set up graphic matrices with determinant variables on one axis and PDSs on another, and then rank the systems against variables with numerical ratings that are supportable based on research of market conditions. While it will be difficult to firmly tie down the ranking of each block, the process causes useful comparative analysis, which helps decision making (Figure 5-2).

Discussion Questions

○ The key, and first-priority, issue is why depart from traditional lump sum general contracting. Public bodies appropriately are loathe to take risks that are not fully understood—a condition of inertia. What are the most persuasive reasons for even considering other delivery systems?

○ How is objectivity of participant selection demonstrated in each delivery system?

	Lump Sum	In-House Design-Build	Consultative Design-Build	Bridging	Agency CM	Totals
Cost Assurance						
Schedule Efficiency						
Quality Design						
Quaility Construction						
Safety						
Other						
Other						

Figure 5-2   Matrix for evaluation of project delivery systems. Choose the remaining variables and prioritize them, 7 (high) and 1 (low). Then rate each PDS against the variables 10 (high) to 1 (low). Multiply the rating by the priority weight in each slashed box, and add the results. Then review and make crucial judgments.

Assignment: Which PDS to Recommend to the Summit City Board of Education?

Take the position of the board of education's planning committee and evaluate the options and provide a rationale for each. Use a matrix similar to Figure 5-2. Criteria should include:

○ Costs
○ Time
○ Safety
○ Quality
○ Aesthetics
○ Roles of designers

○ Roles of constructors
○ Owner's best interests
○ Stewardship of taxpayers' money
○ Fairness to all participants
○ Assurance of project delivery
○ Available forms of agreement

Draw diagrams of the parties involved and their relationships in various contractual arrangements.

Research the following related issues:

○ Bonding
○ Insurance
○ Project preplanning

○ Reporting systems
○ Safety assurance (While this was not discussed in the proceeding options, research how safety assurance is administered in various PDSs.)
○ Review laws in your state regarding use of design-build and CM in public work.

Recommendations: Organize participant teams to interview parties who have firsthand knowledge of design and construction and of various PDSs:

○ Architects
○ Engineers
○ General contractors
○ Trade contractors
○ Private building owners
○ Public building owners.

Participant teams may select different delivery systems and present their proposals. Then class members may debate the merits of the various proposals. Finally, consensus should be sought on the procedure to follow, and a recommendation should be made to the board of education that they could accept and, if need be, defend to their constituents.

Case 5-2   Bicentennial Library

Owner:	City of Newmont (population 245,000) in the mid-south United States
Project:	New public library to commemorate the city's bicentennial
Location:	Site of a former railyard
Target Budget:	$45 million (exclusive of site costs and movable equipment but including all fees)\
Project delivery system:	Design-build or construction management

The city government has authorized general revenue bonds to be sold as soon as a design and a guaranteed maximum price contract can be established. The resolution of authorization specified that the cost of the facility cannot exceed $45 million, and that said cost must be guaranteed before full contract documents will be funded. Thus it becomes necessary to employ a delivery system that allows an early guaranteed maximum price.

Programmatic direction: The library board desires a modern building with some of the glories of historic civic architecture. After touring several recently completed libraries, a committee's summary statements of criticism are:

○ Chicago: too heavy and somber
○ Denver: visually stimulating but will not stand the test of time aesthetically
○ San Francisco: too regimented in form
○ Cincinnati: a collection of elements with no clear theme

Additionally, the desire is to achieve a building that fits Newmont and its mixed ambience of:

○ Currently an important light manufacturing center
○ Cotton Belt history
○ "Laid-back" Southern style
○ Rail center, past and present

Site characteristics: The site was once a railyard and warehouse area near downtown Newmont. In the early 1980s, it was transformed to stage a year-long heritage festival. Since that time the site has not generated significant follow-up development. Nearby features are converted warehouses being used for mixed commercial activity, as well as a few lowrise office buildings, apartment houses, and a hotel, all on the fringe of the urban core. A short distance away are the local university and the Onieta River. The 3.5-acre site is adjacent to an artery leading to the city center, and 1000 yards from an existing rail line. Grade at the artery is 6 feet below the street and drops gradually toward the river. The site has flooded several times in the 20th century, to a maximum depth of 7 feet. Since the property is owned by the city, zoning restrictions will be waived if necessary. Principal programmatic spaces and elements:

○ Entrance "rotunda"—6000 square feet; not necessarily round, but a dramatic, lofty space
○ Reception area—500 square feet adjacent to the rotunda; up to ten persons checking books, parcels, and so on
○ Computerized "card catalogs"
○ Open stacks with groups of carrels and lounge furniture—30,000 square feet
○ Closed stacks—30,000 square feet
○ Meeting rooms—three, consisting of 200, 300, and 500 square feet, respectively

○ Auditorium—6000 square feet with full media capability
○ Administrative offices—8000 square feet
○ Display area for arts and crafts—4000 square feet
○ Retail bookstore—2500 square feet
○ Ancillary spaces for utilities, toilets, janitors, storage, and so on
○ Required circulation and egress
○ Parking garage for 750 cars, suggested to be placed under the habitable area to raise that space for flood-protection purposes. (Garage will be operated commercially to serve other activities in the area, with 100 spaces reserved to library users on "free ticket" basis.)

The library board wishes to take occupancy 26 months after retaining designers, in order to be part of a city bicentennial celebration.

Amplification of Issues to Enhance Understanding of This Case

Large civic projects frequently have substantial cost overruns that delight journalists, annoy taxpayers, and embarrass public officials. A reason for using design-build or CM is to have a contractor commit to a guaranteed maximum price (GMP) early in the process. Of course, this carries abundant risk—to guarantee costs with less than full information. Scope estimating, unit pricing, and projecting variables have become important skills. Necessarily, in order to give early GMPs, the contractor must have a good deal of control over final design—and should have one or more contingency funds to buffer against cost growth due to owner-driven design changes or unanticipated exigencies. Owners must understand the contractor's motives in a series of cost-driven recommendations.

Discussion Questions

○ Does it make any difference whether a contingency fund is within a GMP or added to the GMP?
○ How are contingency funds differentiated from change orders—when is a cost item to be absorbed within a contingency fund, and when should it increase the GMP as a change order?
○ What are fair fees for designers and constructors in a project such as Newmont's bicentennial library?
○ How are fees affected by invasions of contingency funds or by change orders?

Assignment

○ From the information provided, draw a diagram of the site and then sketch one or more layouts of the spaces to determine probable form of the library and total square feet required. Figure 5-3 may be helpful to start the process.

○ Verify that the budget is adequate by using a published pricing index.

○ Take the role of a consultant to the library board and prepare a recommendation regarding a PDS, offering more than one option. Conclude with a recommendation with a rationale, including the best system to:

1. Achieve programmatic elements, culminating in a distinguished building
2. Achieve quality design throughout
3. Meet schedule
4. Control cost
5. Meet public requirement of objective selection process
6. Meet other typical requirements of public work, such as prequalification, bonding, and possible liquidated damages

○ Develop a visual and oral presentation, with the audience simulating the library board. Different teams may present competing approaches and delivery systems.

Case 5-3   Satellite Campus

Owner:	University of Cincinnati
Project:	Satellite campus in a rural area
Location:	Southern Ohio
Budget:	$90 million over ten years
Project delivery system:	Program management

This case is for a hypothetical project similar to many actual projects done, past and present, by major state universities. An objective of branch campuses is to bring education to the clients, avoiding the high cost of student housing. Also, satellites provide less intimidating conditions to students who prefer more manageable environments. The core of this case is a proposed agreement between a university and a firm offering PM services. The assignment is to analyze and critique the agreement. The university's intention in using a PM agreement is to outsource significant responsibility for an extended project rather than taking on additional personnel to develop and manage the program.

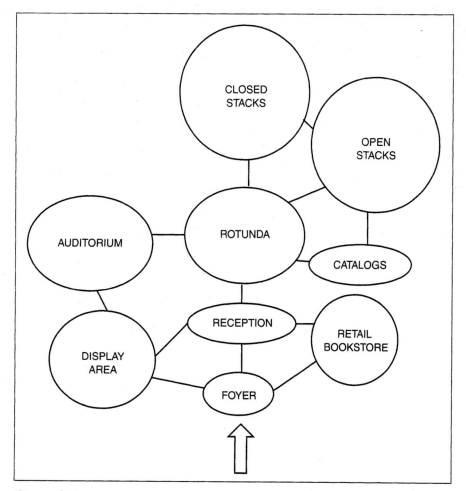

Figure 5-3   The idea of a rotunda being both an architectural element and a prime circulation space, as used in important public buildings for centuries. The diagram suggests possible spatial relationships for the proposed Newmont Library. There is no scale, and circles are representational rather than proportional to the assigned square footages.

AGREEMENT

Between the University of Cincinnati and Smith/Jones, Inc. For Program Management for the BROWN COUNTY CAMPUS

PARTIES

Owner: The University of Cincinnati as represented by its Board of Trustees and the Ohio Building Authority Cincinnati, OH 45221

Program Manager: Smith/Jones, Inc.
                        2350 Victory Parkway
                        Cincinnati, OH 45206

Date: March 1, 1999

Scope of the Project

A satellite campus in Brown County, Ohio, is to become an administrative and educational unit of the University of Cincinnati; said campus is to have four or five buildings (depending on final programming and enrollment trends) on approximately 50 acres (depending on actual site selected), including all ancillary services such as parking, public utilities, and educational and administrative support systems. Actual ownership is by the taxpayers of Ohio, through the governor and Ohio Building Authority (Figure 5-4).

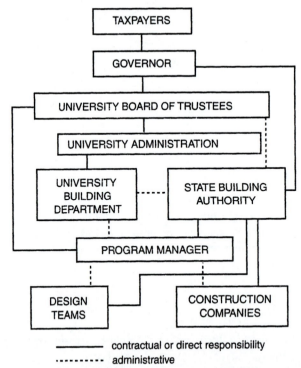

contractual or direct responsibility
administrative

Figure 5-4   Administrative chain of command for program management for a state university. The program manager would be responsible to both the university board of trustees and to a state building authority, the former for actual operations and the latter for legal purposes and funding approvals. While the program manager would administer designer and constructors, those entities would be under direct contract to the state building authority.

Target budget = $90 million for land, buildings, and fees
Target overall schedule = 10 years

Scope of Program Management Services

The program manager shall provide comprehensive services, as agent to the owner, to guide the overall project in the owner's best interests. Such services shall include but are not limited to the following:

○ Review owner's preliminary scope statement and program, and advise on amplifying those documents to clarify issues, objectives, and options, as required for professional relationships to ensue.

○ Review owner's budget and advise on adequacy and timing of expenditures.

○ Advise owner on site selection process.

○ Become familiar with all relevant state and local regulations that may impinge on the project.

○ Prepare milestone schedule of entire project, including phasing of buildings over time, under at least two options.

○ Prepare outline of infrastructure needs and relate such to the milestone schedule.

○ Investigate all public utility availability—and possible limitations—in Brown County.

○ Investigate traffic patterns and possible required improvements proximate to sites under consideration.

○ Order and monitor all necessary investigations of sites, such as subsurface conditions, drainage patterns, and soil peculiarities (actual costs of technical services to be paid directly by owner).

○ Evaluate site(s) for possible contaminants (with technical consultation as required).

○ Recommend site or sites to the university administration, prioritized as required, with decision criteria and rationale.

○ Provide liaison among university, property owner(s), and real estate agent in acquisition of site.

○ Develop and maintain liaison with public officials in Brown County for purposes of facilitating the program.

○ Establish criteria and guidelines for selecting design professionals and construction companies, and guide the owner in the selection processes (all contracts to be directly with owner).

○ Identify long-lead-time items or other materials and equipment that may be directly purchased by the owner.

○ Recommend actual project delivery systems (may be more than one with various buildings) and contractual relations to be used for both designers and constructors.

○ Prepare forms of agreement for owner to contract with both designers and constructors.

○ Monitor design processes for program compliance; keep owner informed of progress and salient issues.

○ Manage all legal requirements such as public advertisements, prevailing wages, and related matters.

○ Establish reporting systems, documentation, and information networks for design and construction activities.

○ Establish prequalification procedures for contractors, subcontractors, and suppliers.

○ Develop overall strategy for DBE participation.

○ Establish and monitor safety standards for all design and construction.

○ Establish and monitor quality standards for all construction procedures.

○ Monitor all construction and make periodic progress reports to owner.

○ Manage applications for progress payments and final payments for all work by designers and constructors, and advise owner accordingly.

○ Maintain a record of accounts on the entire program, providing the owner with periodic reports on expenditures and, particularly, alerting owner early regarding any irregularities or possible cost overruns.

○ Update schedules as required, and provide owner with periodic progress reports.

○ Coordinate building start-up, commissioning, item (punch) list completion, contract close-out, and procedures for warranty work for each building.

Comprehensive services shall include all other duties typically associated with a multiphase construction project, such activities usually being carried out directly by an owner or an owner's immediate agent. The program manager shall provide sufficient numbers of personnel to carry out the expected responsibilities.

Services Not Included in the Program Management Agreement

○ Actual design activity, which shall be performed by licensed design professionals under contract to the owner.

○ Actual construction activity, which shall be performed by construction companies under contract to the owner.

○ Related professional and investigative activity, such as real estate acquisition, soil investigation, traffic engineering, site planning, landscape design, and materials testing, all of which shall be contracted for and paid for by the owner (except for any testing required in construction contracts), but all of which shall be coordinated by the Program Manager.

○ Legal representation.

Performance by Program Manager

The Program Manager shall serve the owner in a comprehensive agency relationship under the following guidelines:

○ All performance, communications, and representations shall be provided with complete honesty, professional ethics, and reliability.

○ All information gained about the owner and the owner's activity shall be held in complete confidence. (It is recognized that the owner is a public institution, and thus all activity is technically public information; however, such publication should come from the university, not from the Program Manager.)

○ The Program Manager shall keep the owner fully informed of all relevant activity regarding the program and its execution.

○ All personnel employed on this project by the Program Manager shall be qualified by education, training, and experience to perform the duties assigned.

Responsibilities of Owner

The Owner shall provide the following:

○ A designated individual empowered to represent the owner in all decision making, and to administer duties related to holding the contracts for various activities.

○ Timely decisions on issues presented by the Program Manager.

○ Timely payments to all designers, constructors, consultants, and suppliers based on payment applications certified by the Program Manager.

○ Monitoring of the performance of the Program Manager.

○ Payment to the Program Manager for services rendered.

Remuneration for Services

The Owner shall pay the Program Manager in current funds for personnel assigned to this project, according to the following schedule of hourly rates:

Senior Manager	$150
Associate Manager	120
Scheduler	100
Estimator	80
Technical staffperson	70
Administrative staffperson	40

The following expenses shall be reimbursed at a multiple of 1.05 of net cost:

Reprographics and document printing

Photography, video, and special copying

Long-distance phone and fax

Travel from Cincinnati to Brown County, but not local travel

Lodgings in Brown County, subject to preapproval by Owner

Postage and other transmittal of documents

Special outside consultation expenses preapproved by Owner

Other expenses preapproved by Owner

Payments shall be made monthly based on applications by the Program Manager with supporting documentation. Payments shall be made within 14 days of receipt of application unless Owner has bona fide reason for delaying payment.

At the beginning of each month, the Program Manager shall provide the Owner with an estimate of the cost of services for the upcoming two months. If the Owner approves the amounts or does not respond within 7 days, those amounts are approved. However, each month's billing shall not exceed 110% of the forecast cost amount without written approval of the Owner.

The maximum charge to the Owner, including expenses, for complete services over the ten-year period shall be $1,200,000 (one million, two hundred thousand dollars). If the scope of services is changed, the fee will be renegotiated. The amount of change will be adjusted only by a mutually agreed-on amendment to this agreement, based on unusual or unforeseen circumstances.

Liability and Insurance Requirements

The Program Manager shall be liable for proper delivery of all PM services included in this agreement and shall hold the Owner harmless from any loss or damages experienced as a result of the delivery of said program management services. The Program Manager shall maintain throughout the project the following coverages:

General liability	$1,000,000 each occurrence; 3,000,000 total
Auto liability	1,000,000 each occurrence; 3,000,000 total
Workers' Compensation	State of Ohio requirements

Termination of Agreement

Either party may terminate this agreement for cause, with 30 days notice. Upon notice of termination, the Program Manager shall submit to the Owner an accounting of fees and reimbursables paid to date, those due, and anticipated costs until cessation of services. The Program Manager shall be paid for all work and reimbursable expenses duly provided to the project and so documented.

For: The University of Cincinnati   For: Smith/Jones, Inc.

_____   _____
            (Signature)   (Signature)

_____   _____
      (Printed Name and Title)   (Printed Name and Title)

_____ (Date)   _____ (Date)

Amplification of Issues to Enhance Understanding of This Case

PM is growing in use due to:

○ Increasing complexity of buildings, contractual relations, and regulations. Many owners simply do not have in-house expertise to properly administer projects.

○ The spirit of outsourcing, wherein companies or agencies use consultants rather than permanent employees, who frequently

carry cost burdens of 50 percent over actual salaries. Public institutions in particular find it difficult to release employees and are encouraged not to add regular staff for construction projects, but
rather to outsource much of the responsibility. Since PM is rather
new, contractual relations continue to evolve. The Associated General Contractors of America has developed a matrix-type multipage
form of agreement that assigns responsibilities to each party:
owner and program manager.

Discussion Questions

○ What types of individuals make capable program managers—contractors, architects, engineers, or others?

○ Is per diem remuneration (or hourly rates) valid in PM agreements—
or are lump sums more appropriate?

○ Should program managers be licensed?

Assignment

○ Analyze the agreement in regard to:
  1. Clarity of responsibilities
  2. Balance and fairness between the university and the program
     manager
  3. Risk distribution
  4. Things that should be added to make the agreement more complete
  5. Possible circumstances not anticipated by the agreement
  6. "Watchouts" for both parties

○ Diagram the relationships between program manager and various
  entities involved in the actual projects.

○ Take the position of a taxpayer in Ohio and critique the agreement as
  to whether it represents your best interests:
  1. Is it appropriate to outsource these responsibilities rather than
     handle them with direct employees?
  2. Does the PM approach appear to be cost-effective?
  3. Is the fee schedule appropriate? What do the hourly rates cover?

○ Offer alternative PDSs to accomplish the project either with or
  without a program manager.

Case 5-4   Community Recreation Center

Owner:	City of Westline (population 45,000) in the Rocky Mountains
Project:	Recreation complex
Location:	Open space near the edge of the city
Budget:	$21 million (exclusive of design)
Project delivery system:	Lump sum general contracting

Charles Amburgy was eager to have his own construction company. He was 14 years out of college and had risen through the management ranks of a national company, with various duties in a number of locations. When he was assigned to be project manager for a power plant near Westline, he felt that he had found the place to launch his dream. During the two years of the project, he made many friends in the community of 45,000 people, and evaluated the various contractors performing there.

As the power plant project was winding down, he negotiated an agreement to buy into an established general contracting company, Guaranteed Construction, Inc., which had an annual volume of approximately $45 million. The principal owner was nearing retirement and welcomed the new individual, who had a good knowledge of modern management and information systems. There was a cadre of estimators, superintendents, and hands-on team leaders who were quite capable in their jobs. None held college degrees, although several had taken course work at the local community college.

After giving his current employer six weeks' notice of resignation and agreeing to be available for follow-up work (warranty and otherwise) at the power plant, Amburgy left that company on good terms, with the understanding that if he changed his plans, he could come back to that employment. He accepted the position of vice president for operations with Guaranteed, and soon began a series of changes aimed at more efficiency, better marketing, and improved office processes. Two new office personnel were hired to operate the computer systems and to assist in marketing and government relations. The changes were met with mixed reviews by the long-time employees, but Amburgy was adept at personnel relations and kept everyone relatively satisfied.

The marketing efforts paid off with several new negotiated private sector projects, and the company was also low bidder on two public jobs. Then the new Westline recreation complex was announced by the city. It would consist of a multiuse stadium to seat 15,000 people for football and soccer, a baseball park seating 8000, a clubhouse with locker rooms and workout facilities, and a recreation building for a variety of indoor activities. The total estimated cost was $21 million, a really big project for the city of Westline. The city had determined to use a traditional lump sum contract. Two local companies capable of handling a project of this size (including Guaranteed) and three out-of-town contractors showed interest in bidding the job. Amburgy knew it would stretch Guaranteed's resources, but felt that it was a "must-win" project for the destiny of the company. The CEO had reservations for a number of reasons:

○ Guaranteed was already quite busy with the work Amburgy had negotiated.
○ The company's capitalization, although good for a company of its size, was still characteristic of a small business.
○ He was concerned about hiring new management personnel whom he did not know well.
○ The architect for the project, a Westline practitioner, while being quite capable, had never designed a project of this size or complexity.
○ Guaranteed's bonding agent cautioned against becoming overextended.

Westline used a standard AIA prequalification form A305 to determine the abilities of the five candidate companies to perform the project. The other in-town company was reluctantly disqualified by the town council because of two contracts underway that were experiencing problems with quality and completion. The council wished to have a local contractor, but would not risk taxpayers' money to satisfy that objective. The disqualification left Guaranteed as the only qualified local company.

Amburgy had become well known in the town during his two years there, and had become a friend of three council members. And, of course, the CEO, a lifelong resident of Westline, was highly regarded. The council members urged the two to bid the recreation complex and, after several detailed meetings with their bonding agent and insurance company, they decided to do so. They would seek subcontracts for almost all of the work so as not to stretch their current field forces. Also, they would hire an experienced superintendent from the local company recently disqualified for the recreation project.

Guaranteed's bid of $20,776,620 was $752,200 under the next-closest bid, which was just slightly lower than the other two. This gap obviously caused concern, but a close review of estimate sheets indicated that the amount was valid. Painful chagrin remained, however, about leaving three-quarters of a million dollars "on the table." There was also some unease caused by the 12 addenda issued during the bid period to provide corrections to the contract documents. It was obvious that the architect had been hard-pressed to turn out documents for the project.

The city council was delighted with the attractive bid by a local contractor, and a ground breaking was scheduled. On a bright April day, a dozen people equipped with gold-painted hard hats and equally luminous spades turned over shovelsful of dirt, and soon thereafter a bulldozer began clearing the site. That was the last day for two weeks that it did not rain. The sudden and extensive wet weather portended problems to come.

Amburgy had computer generated an aggressive critical-path-network schedule showing completion in 17 months, despite the fact that the completion date allowed 19 months. The earlier date would force overall efficiencies and reduce job overhead costs. Liquidated damages had been set at $1000 per day past 570 days. The two weeks of rain dictated the first change in that schedule. Another week of mud seriously slowed proceedings.

Amburgy had also designed a front-end-loaded schedule of values to ease the potential cash burden on Guaranteed. After some questions by the architect, the schedule of values was approved. Guaranteed's first application for payment, however, in the opinion of the architect, exceeded the value of the work completed. The application, which showed somewhat less than the total scheduled work for the first month, nonetheless had figures for mobilization, general conditions, and excavation that the architect felt were inflated. The application was returned, and relations between the architect and Guaranteed suffered appreciably. In a heated session, Amburgy severely criticized the contract documents and the architect's capabilities in managing contract administration, which the firm's sole principal was handling directly. An adjusted payment application was approved by the architect, and Guaranteed was paid—three weeks late.

The second payment application was equally debated, and Amburgy complained to city council members about the treatment by the architect. All contracts—primarily owner-architect and owner-contractor—were reviewed, and the council concluded that, as their agent, the architect was acting appropriately. The poor relations continued, and the architect became critical of some of the quality of masonry work. The masonry subcontractor had been on the job for ten weeks, and after a few off-handedly critical remarks regarding quality, the architect became quite negative about the brickwork on a prominent wall. He maintained that it did not match the approved sample panel. The masonry subcontractor and foreman argued vehemently that there was appropriate compliance. The masonry crew left the job, both as a result of the criticism and because of nonpayment by Guaranteed, which refused to pay for work not accepted by the architect.

The masonry subcontractor filed a claim against Guaranteed and a lien against the property owned by the City of Westline. A number of other problems ensued:

○ After six months, the project was five weeks behind schedule.
○ The superintendent, hired specifically for this project, left Guaranteed to return to his original employer.
○ The cash flow on the job was slow, and the pay-when-paid practice of Guaranteed caused complaints by subcontractors.
○ Several subcontractors reduced their crews and sent tradespersons to other projects.

Amburgy took over field management of the project directly, but some old-line subcontractors resented his aggressive tactics. Lack of attention to other Guaranteed projects caused them to progress less efficiently, and the capital condition of the company eroded. Nonetheless, Amburgy persevered, and by working 70-hour weeks, he was able to keep the recreation project and other jobs moving satisfactorily.

The CEO, however, was quite concerned and, on his 67th birthday, announced his plans to retire. While this was not totally unexpected, the timing was not beneficial to the company. The veteran contractor, however, was concerned about the immediate future and wished to get out reasonably intact financially. He thus was prepared to draw significant assets out of Guaranteed for his retirement. This concerned everyone in the company. Amburgy threatened suit to guard the company's assets.

This whole set of activities detracted from management of all the company's work, particularly the recreation complex. As the dispute over company assets heated up, subcontractors went unpaid, job progress deteriorated, and the architect advised the city council to prepare for default by Guaranteed. This company had never failed to complete a contract in 45 years of existence, and this was indeed a serious matter for all concerned. A special city council committee was appointed to review the status of the project. The committee retained a consultant, a retired architect, to help them appraise the situation. After one month of review, the findings were as follows:

○ After 13 months of activity, the project was 4 months behind schedule.
○ Four subcontractors had left the project not having completed their work, and all had filed liens.
○ Leaking was occurring in the clubhouse and in the recreation building.
○ Stadium seating was poorly attached to the concrete structure. Several units of plastic benches had cracked since installation.

○ The underground irrigation system had frozen and was inoperable.

○ The architect and contractor were in serious disputes regarding:
1. Responsibility for quality problems
2. Nonpayment for work done
3. Means of rectifying many problems

The city's consultant advised that, despite the architect's control of payments and retainage, there was probably not enough money in the construction account to correct and complete the necessary work. The bonding agent was called in to confer on possible actions to be taken. He immediately called the surety company to request legal counsel. The architect and members of city council conferred with the agent and counsel, seeking the best way out of the dilemma.

The surety, of course, had a duty to complete the project to the owner's satisfaction. In surety terms, the owner is the obligee, one who is owed an obligation (Figure 5-5). There are a few options on how to carry out this obligation.

To become bonded, a contractor must indemnify the surety. Thus Guaranteed's assets may be seized by the surety to help pay for the cost of project completion—and in most legal domains, the surety has priority rights over those assets. Amburgy's threatened suit may be moot. A default seems inevitable, in which case a number of "shirts will be lost."

Amplification of Issues to Enhance Understanding of This Case

Default of contracts, while not really frequent, haunts the construction industry. This is why public owners, in particular, insist on third-party assurances through bonds provided by surety companies, which are frequently components of large insurance companies. In case of default, the surety becomes the contractor of record, but having no resources to directly provide construction means and methods, it typically retains replacement contractors to complete the work. In some cases the surety will "prop up" the defaulting company long enough to complete the project at hand. All the obligations of the contractor pass to the surety, including project completion, close-out, and warranty work. In a default, usually everyone is damaged—owner, designer, contractor, subcontractors, and surety company—both directly, financially, and due to extensive effort that goes unrewarded.

Discussion Questions

○ What is indemnification? How does it influence the outcome of this case?
○ What is the relationship of sample panels (mock-ups) to finish installation?
○ How is poor construction quality rectified when default occurs?

Assignment: Problems to be Addressed Regarding the Case

○ Analyze events to date, and cite decisions and actions that led to the current problems. Suggest how the problems might have been avoided or mitigated.
○ Research defaults, indemnification, liens, and bonds. Seek advice from a bonding agent.
○ Review issues of contractual compliance, liability, and default, including language in AIA A201, and summarize the legal aspects at hand. Consult with a lawyer or veteran architect.
○ Place yourself in the role of consultant (retired architect) to the council committee. Summarize the job status. Review options and provide a recommendation.
○ Devise a plan for completion of the project.

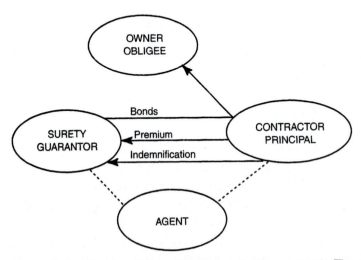

Figure 5-5   Bonding relationships in construction contracts. The surety sells bonds to the contractor to protect the owner against loss. The contractor pays the premium and indemnifies (to varying degrees) the surety with the contractor's assets. The agent represents the surety, prequalifies the contractor for bonding, and brokers the sale.

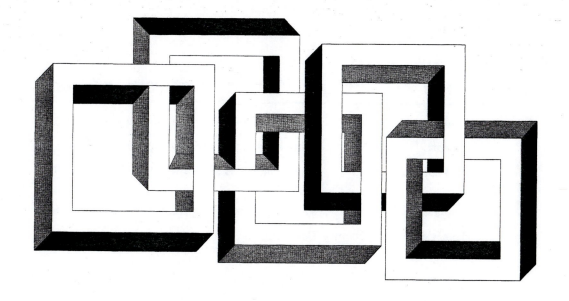

CHAPTER 6

Case Studies Needing Solutions: Project Delivery Systems/Contractual Relationships; Private Sector Work

"The private sector continues to be the crucible of innovation in design and construction."

The case studies in this chapter cover privately financed projects, which allow a wide array of approaches to design and construction. Largely unfettered by regulatory requirements, private owners, assisted by their consultants, can be quite inventive in creating strategies to bring their visions to reality. Of course, all buildings must meet zoning and building codes, and all construction must adhere to safety requirements.

Case 6-1   Early Morning Retirement Center

Owner:	The Foothills Consortium of Churches
Project:	Early Morning Retirement Center
Location:	Near a mid-size city in the northwestern United States
Budget:	$25 million (including design and construction)
Project delivery system:	Design-build

A consortium of churches plans a retirement facility offering a range of services from independent living through full nursing care. The budget is $25 million initially, with the intent of doubling the size of the facility in the future. Twenty-five acres of land have been purchased near a mid-size northwestern city. Zoning allows the proposed use. All public services are available; no public financing is involved. Fees will be charged to residents on an affordability basis. The operation will be subsidized by the religious consortium. The preliminary program is to provide the following facilities:

- Independent living for 100 adults, half of whom are married couples
- Assisted living for 100 adults, 25 percent of whom are married couples
- Full nursing care for 100 adults, 10 percent of whom are married couples
- Central kitchen and dining facilities
- Hospital-level services in the nursing facility
- Small shopping area with barbershop and beauty parlor
- Four bowling lanes
- Lounges and recreation areas
- Typical ancillary services
- Parking for 400 cars
- A water feature (pond), which serves as a stormwater-retention device, on the campus
- External recreation consisting of three tennis courts, three shuffleboard courts, and a putting green
- Attractive landscaping, walking paths, and gathering places with seating and amenities for groups of various sizes

A consultant to the owner advises soliciting design-build proposals for the project. It is important for the selection process to be as objective as possible, given the broad constituency of the consortium. A two-stage selection process is devised, with requests for qualifications (RFQs) to be sent to a long list of possible design-build providers. Respondents are to be evaluated, and then reduced to a short list of candidates who receive requests for proposals (RFPs) involving more detailed submissions. The consultant recommends a five-person selection committee, four church leaders plus himself.

Amplification of Issues to Enhance Understanding of This Case

Obviously this project could be built under several types of PDS. Design-build is applicable because it allows early integration of designers and constructors, early cost commitment, and overall project acceleration. A key question is whether in-house or consultative design-build is preferable. This is a large project for most in-house design-build companies. If consultative design-build is employed, candidate teams of designers and contractors should join forces to seek selection for the project. The more complete the scope statement and preliminary program, the more objective the selection process.

Discussion Questions

○ What special issues would a religious consortium bring to a senior housing project?

○ As a designer or constructor, how would you tailor your approach to this client group to win the project?

○ What type of consultant should the consortium hire to guide the process?

Assignment

The first task is to critically review the choice of design-build as a PDS: What are the pros and cons of design-build versus competing systems? Then prepare the following:

○ A broad scope statement and RFQ to be mailed to contractor candidates. Review diagram in Figure 6-1 to enhance understanding of the overall process. Considerations for the RFQ should include:

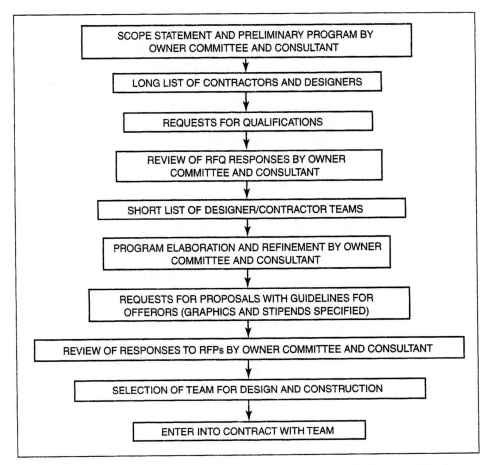

Figure 6-1   Process for selecting design and construction team for the early Morning Retirement Center. While the owner consortium intends to select a design-build team, the selection process could also be used for other project delivery systems.

1. Summary of key programmatic elements
2. Adequate description of project to allow companies to determine their levels of interest and capability
3. Statement regarding design guidelines, such as preference for traditional versus modern design, contextual influences, and local guidelines
4. Indication of whether there is a preference for in-house or consultative design-build or a joint venture between a design firm and construction company, possibly in a hybrid CM relationship with the owner
5. Good level of assurance of attracting teams that can work well with the consortium

○ Statement of what will be expected in responses to both the RFQ and the RFP. In the latter case, whether design submittals are anticipated and, if so, the judging criteria and whether stipends are offered.

○ A response to the RFQ, taking the role of a contractor or of a team of designer and contractor. Assume a company brochure(s) is to be included. Prepare a submittal including the following:
1. Level of interest in the project
2. Experience in this type of development
3. Source of design and capabilities of designers
4. Possibility of assistance in financing
5. Key personnel from among whom the project management team will be selected
6. Other factors that will persuade the client to place your team on the short list

○ An RFP, to be sent to three or four short-listed design-build teams, including:
1. Overall guidelines for submittals and interviews:
   a. Length of interviews
   b. Audiovisual media
   c. Limits on graphic submittals, including drawings or CAD/video presentations
2. Clear statement on expectations of the jury, so that all teams prepare comparable material
3. Identification of jury members
4. Restatement and expansion of criteria for final selection, with priority of relevance of items among:
   a. Site planning
   b. Design quality
   c. Budget and its fixity
   d. Constructability
   e. Life-cycle issues
   f. Milestone schedule
   g. Ease of future expansion
   h. Organizational structure for the project
5. Restatement of stipend rules, if part of the process
6. Sequence of submittals and interviews—that is, whether submittals are required prior to interview
7. Composition of scoring sheets, if used

○ (Optional) A full program for the facility

○ (Optional) A response to the RFP, including:
1. Site plan and sketch preschematics
2. Cost estimate

3. Milestone schedule
4. Statements on constructability and life-cycle issues
5. Organizational chart

(Optional) Hold a jury to judge the proposals, preferably including both professionals and students.

Case 6-2   Ms. Merritt Builds Her Dream House

Owner:	Adelaide Merritt
Project:	Private residence
Location:	Lake Anna, Virginia
Budget:	$300,000 to $400,000 (including design and construction)
Project delivery system:	To be determined

Adelaide Merritt pondered both the past and the future on her 50th birthday. Life had had its ups and downs, and the future looked perplexing. Growing up in Richmond in a family with antebellum roots, she had enjoyed a carefree and privileged youth. Educated at the best places, she was in her last year at Duke Law School when events turned. Her father died, leaving the family with far fewer resources than expected. Maintaining their lifestyle had been expensive, and his debts equaled their assets.

After Merritt graduated from law school, her first client was her mother, who had gone into depression and had no idea what to do. An older brother had moved to California several years earlier and had his own family to attend to. Merritt sold their fine old house and moved her mother and herself into a smaller home in a historic district. As her mother's condition ebbed and flowed, Merritt gradually built her legal practice. Long hours and demands at home precluded social life, and Ms. Merritt seemed destined for bachelorhood.

Her practice grew in the fields of domestic relations and property. She took an interest in historic preservation and became active in two groups promoting restoration of historic architecture. She retained an architect to add an office suite to their small historic home, and worked closely with her in the design and construction. By moving the law practice there, she could spend more time with her mother, still in poor health but stabilized.

In her late forties, Merritt was enticed to fulfill a dream, a vacation house to enjoy deferred relaxation. She purchased a 1.5-acre lakefront lot on Lake Anna in central Virginia for $70,000. She had a few casual meetings with the architect who had designed the office addition. Discussions involved whether to use historic architecture or to open the house up to the lake with large-view windows. Also, she wished to accommodate her mother in the new house, and needed an office where she could do professional tasks during moderately extended stays.

As she was thinking through the program, another turn took place. While attending a legal conference in Washington, she chanced on an old beau, Edward Byrider, from Richmond, who had also pursued a legal career, most of which was spent at the U.S. Department of Justice. Now ready to retire from that service and enter private practice, he discussed opportunities in the Richmond area. Of equal significance was the fact that Byrider had been widowed two years earlier. His two married sons each had a child, and he loved being with his grandchildren. After several meetings and phone discussions, he brought up the prospects for marriage. Merritt was attracted to him and to the idea, but was committed to her mother and her law practice, which was now quite prosperous.

So, on her 50th birthday, she sat on a lawn chair on her lakefront property gazing at the water, wondering what to do. She had already decided to build the house in any event, but the program, layout, and amenities would vary widely based on important and timely decisions. Would the house be for just her and her mother, or for an extended family? The latter would obviously mean more bedrooms, baths, and other facilities for the visiting kin—and about $100,000 additional cost, to be shared by her prospective husband.

Amplification of Issues to Enhance Understanding of This Case

Many architects start their practices in residential design, and it remains a fertile field for inventive ideas. Most well-established architects cannot afford the economics of home design (limited fees for the work involved) but still enjoy that process on occasion. Residential design has been the most wide open in regard to delivery systems. In fact, most houses arrive through some form of design-build where a builder gets a design somewhere—perhaps (though rarely) from an architect—

and proceeds to build for a client or the marketplace. Second homes or vacation places usually allow more inventiveness than most primary residences because of the expected casual lifestyle.

Discussion Questions

○ Romantic readers may first wish to decide Merritt's marital future— what should she do?

○ Figure 6-2 (in Case 6-4), titled "Anatomy of a Project: 'Capturing the Vision'," includes a build versus no-build decision juncture. Does this apply to Ms. Merritt's dream house?

Assignment

Outline two programs for the house:

○ One for Merritt and her mother.

○ The other for Merritt, her mother, and her husband, with facilities for the visiting offspring.

○ In either case, the mother's bedroom should be on the main living floor to reduce the need to climb stairs.

○ Relevant contextual issues:
1. The lot is on the north side of the lake, with 200 feet of frontage running due east-west.
2. Setback requirements are 100 feet from the lake (except for boathouses or gazebos) and 30 feet from side property lines.
3. The lake is a cooling reservoir for a nuclear power plant, which is 2 miles to the west and plainly visible on most winter days.
4. The only deed restrictions are a prohibition of fences and limits on boat docks not to project more than 50 feet into the lake.
5. A county building code is in effect, derived from the state code, which is based on a widely used model code. Permits are issued by the county building department.
6. The only public services are electric and phone. Water comes from domestic wells, and sewage is handled by mechanical aerators with sand filters, the systems being carefully regulated to avoid lake pollution.
7. Heating systems are fueled by oil or propane gas.

8. Most of the site is former pasture. A scrub growth line begins 200 feet back from the lake. Three handsome, mature sweet gum trees are spaced at approximate one-third points in the open space, 125 feet from the lake.
9. An access road runs along the north property line. A cut may be made into the property at any point.
10. There is even topography, with an approximate 3 percent slope up from the lake.
11. The lot immediately to the east contains a 3000-square-foot two-story house of modern design with a wall of glass facing the lake. It also has a two-unit boathouse and a gazebo of similar design on the lake. The lot immediately to the east is vacant, but the next lot has a brick home of quasi-Georgian design.

○ Sketch a location plan from the information given plus relevant assumptions.

○ Select one of two program directions and write a program for the house.

○ Evaluate siting and directional influences on design—that is, sun, views, water, vehicular access, and so on.

○ From the program, sketch a site plan, floor plans, and massing studies.

○ Determine a strategy for design and construction. Possibilities include:
1. Complete drawings and specifications, and then lump sum competitive bids for the entire project
2. Lump sum contract for the house, with separate contracts for the well, septic system, driveway, boatdock, and landscaping
3. Early selection of a builder, who can then work with the architect on material selection, pricing, schedule, and so on, with the intent of establishing a fixed price prior to construction
4. A process similar to the above, with construction to proceed on a cost–plus a fee basis with a guaranteed maximum price
5. Merritt to act as general contractor and issue trade contracts for various segments of the work
6. Architect to act as general contractor
7. Architect to act as agency construction manager

○ Provide a rationale for the selected PDS.

After the several assignments are completed, a jury should review the various recommendations. An ideal jury would include an architect, a builder, and an attorney.

Case 6-3   Evans Investments, Inc.

Owner:	Evans Investments, Inc.
Home office:	Portland, Maine
Project:	New regional center
Location:	Near Mobile, Alabama, 26 acres facing Mobile Bay
Budget:	$33 million (initially, to be expanded later to $50 million)
Project delivery system:	To be determined

Evans Investments, Inc., has $24 billion under management in 18 mutual funds. Clients reside in 22 countries. Mobile was chosen for the new regional center, partly to provide both a functional and symbolic address for the increasing clientele in the Southeastern United States, and also to target a perceived large market in Latin America. Multilingual employees will be sought from throughout the Gulf Coast region. Salient proposed building functions include:

O Communications center
O Intelligent office building
O Training center
O Regional sales center
O Community center

Site restrictions: The site is essentially flat and rectilinear, rising away from the bay road at a 2 percent slope. The only recent history of flooding occurred during Hurricane Camille in 1968. The road along the bay forms a levee to manage periodic water-level fluctuations. The site has been filled over the years with dredging and excavated material to an average depth of 6 feet. The current land use is a strip shopping plaza, a few houses, and several old foundations. Zoning height restrictions progress from 30 feet at 30 feet setback to 100 feet at 150 feet setback. Nearby uses are midrise apartment buildings, lowrise commercial, and single-family houses.

Programmatic issues: The company wishes to become a recognized entity—and a good neighbor—in the local community. This will be manifested as follows:

O An architectural landmark will be displayed on media pieces, stationery, business cards, and journals.

○ The community services center, to be available for use by organizations and individuals, will include:
  1. Two meeting rooms, for 80 and 25 people
  2. Recreation room
  3. Combination soccer and softball field
  4. Five tennis courts

○ A training center will provide skills to employees recruited in the region.

○ Well-landscaped grounds will have seasonal flowering trees and plants.

The company is open to design recommendations regarding grouping of salient elements in one overall structure versus a series of smaller structures. Guidelines include:

○ One landmark element carried to 90 feet in height, with antennae and dishes atop

○ Visual distinction of the community center, and easy access to it

○ Massing aimed at visual identification of salient elements

○ Unity of design, with ease of future expansion of all elements

Guidelines for particular elements (all areas are best estimates based on information from current users and facility managers in Portland):

○ Communications center—50,000 gross square feet:
  1. "Nerve center"—8000 square feet, with 50 fully computerized workstations
  2. "Boardroom"—4000 square feet, with several large boards (screens) containing constantly updated information on funds, international currencies, and markets; workstations for ten people
  3. Administrative office area—3000 square feet with open landscaping
  4. Conference rooms—two at 900 square feet, each with complete built-in media
  5. Equipment space—12,000 square feet for transmitting and receiving information; no human occupancy; ample circulation space for ease of service of equipment
  6. Main lobby—1600 square feet; to create a distinctive arrival area with display of information electronically on a prominent lighted panel; two reception stations
  7. Storage for disks, tapes, and hardcopy—9000 square feet
  8. "Black hole"—3000 square feet; highly secure area for handling sensitive information and transmissions; ten workstations
  9. Employee lounge/rest area—1200 square feet
  10. Typical ancillary areas: toilet rooms, general storage, and so on

○ Intelligent office building—60,000 square feet; completely equipped with smart systems:
  1. Internal and external voice communications systems
  2. Motion sensors to detect appropriate or inappropriate presence, to control illumination and air management systems, and to alert security if required
  3. Natural-light sensors to control artificial illumination
  4. Security systems
  5. Energy control systems
  6. Ergonomic workstations with individual control of all systems, including lighting, HVAC, and white noise

○ Most of the intelligent office building will be open-office landscaping, with huddle spaces located periodically. Activities in the work areas include:
  1. Marketing strategies and macro marketing
  2. Research into investment opportunities
  3. Corporate regional planning
  4. Tracking and storing abundant data
  5. Communications connections with offices in 22 countries

○ Training center—14,000 square feet, used for both group and individualized training for new employees, as well as existing employees who typically receive 100 hours of continuing special training each year:
  1. Three classrooms at 1100 square feet each, with workstations that can be equipped with various devices
  2. Twelve individualized training areas at 125 square feet each equipped for two persons, trainer and trainee
  3. Administrative area—3800 square feet
  4. Library—6000 square feet
  5. Lounges—two at 1000 square feet
  6. Typical ancillary areas

○ Regional sales center—15,000 square feet, used by salespersons operating primarily in the southeastern United States, who typically spend 50 percent of their time out of the office in face-to-face sales. Workstations are less sophisticated than those in the intelligent building:
  1. Several large open offices—10,000 square feet total
  2. Secretarial pool—1500 square feet
  3. Conference rooms—two at 1000 square feet each, with full audio-visual media
  4. Lounge—1100 square feet
  5. Typical ancillary areas

- Community center—8000 square feet:
  1. Meeting room—1400 square feet with full audiovisual media
  2. Meeting room—600 square feet
  3. Lobby—120 square feet
  4. Kitchen capable of serving both meeting rooms—250 square feet
  5. Recreation room—3500 square feet
  6. Shower and lockers—800 square feet
  7. Typical ancillary areas
  8. Adjacent outdoor recreation areas
- Dining facility, with commercial kitchen, for entire workforce
- Day care center
- Adequate parking
- Fully landscaped grounds

Amplification of Issues to Enhance Understanding of This Case

This is a true high-tech project requiring expansive thinking by all parties. Experienced facility management people will huddle with designers, constructors, and specialists to fully program and design this complex (the appropriate label), which will be a functional symbol of the information revolution. A sort of virtual organization may be formed (see page 31). An open PDS will be necessary to allow maximal cross-fertilization. Perhaps a hybrid of two or more delivery systems is appropriate. It is time to use one's imagination, both in regard to how to get the building designed and built, and also in regard to how the architecture will express the activities and company statement, including the "good neighbor" objective.

Discussion Questions

- What are the principal distinguishing characteristics of intelligent buildings? How are they incorporated into building design?
- Should an intelligent building look intelligent? Should an architectural statement grow out of the high-tech function?
- How can a building be designed to be a "good neighbor"? Is this a valid programmatic issue?

Assignment

○ Expand the design program for the facilities. Do not necessarily repeat the spatial and resource requirements listed previously, but focus on design approach, owner expectations, architectural statement, circulation, and so on. (See Pena, 1987.)

○ Determine the most appropriate PDS among several options. Identify pros and cons of each option, and move to a selection, with a clear rationale.

○ Prepare a milestone schedule for design and construction.

○ Prepare a request for qualifications to be sent to teams of designers and constructors for integrated services.

○ Prepare a financing proposal, with sources of funding.

○ Compose a circulation diagram for the project, showing how salient elements should relate to each other.

○ Design a site plan illustrating an arrangement of buildings to carry out the circulation scheme. The site is 2000 feet along the bay road, which runs almost due north-south, on the east side of Mobile Bay.

Case 6-4   The Tomorrow Company, Inc.

Owner:	The Tomorrow Company, Inc.
Home office:	Lexington, Kentucky
Years in business:	Twelve
Product and service line:	Health and exercise equipment, apparel, and accessories for active senior citizens
Projects:	Several in the southern United States
Budgets:	To be determined
Project delivery system:	To be determined

Owner Background

The Tomorrow Company was founded by three former executives of Nike, Liz Claiborne, and IBM, respectively, who realized the tremendous developing market among people aged 60 to 85. Many in this demographic group resist the notion of growing old and are looking for exercise equipment suited to their particular needs, plus apparel and accessories to match their desired image of the active, healthy mature citizen. Tomorrow's intent is to continuously develop a connection with seniors, the way Nike has captured a more youthful market. After a few developmental years, Tomorrow's sales are now growing at 27 percent per year, and the company is on the verge of major expansion, initially in the southeastern and south-central United States.

Operations

The Tomorrow Company contracts out manufacturing around the world, with strict quality control standards. The company's central focus is on marketing, distribution, sales, and service after sales. All processes are computer controlled and tracked. A huge database of potential customers is being developed for direct sales via catalogs and the Internet. Retail sales are through Tomorrow's own stores, and through general and specialty retailers, typically in shopping malls.

The Tomorrow Company's Vision Statement

"The Tomorrow Company believes that everyone has many happy tomorrows. The golden years will be the best years for those who stay active mentally, physically, and socially, and who take pride in themselves, their independence, their appearances, and their sense of well-being."

The Mission Statement

"The Tomorrow Company is dedicated to providing the finest-quality equipment, apparel, and accessories to the world's mature citizens, and to providing a level of service that will ensure their becoming our long-term customers."

Organizational Philosophy

Since two of the Tomorrow's founders were "riffed" (reduction in force) from their former companies, the goals are to carefully build long-term regular employment, retain a flat organizational structure, outsource as many activities as possible, provide excellent working conditions for a core of permanent employees, and hire seasonal temporary employees as required.

Current Growth Strategy

Tomorrow's leading competitor operates from Los Angeles and has gained relative dominance on the West Coast, plus a foothold in the Northeast. Tomorrow's current strength is in the South, where it wishes to become more overarching; it plans to then gradually extend sales worldwide. Two distribution centers have been built to date, in Lexington and Tampa. A third is scheduled for New Orleans, with five more to follow at the rate of one per year.

Project Delivery Systems

The Lexington distribution center was built using a traditional competitively bid lump sum contract. Design and construction took 25 months. There was an 11 percent cost overrun and two serious disputes. The Tampa center was executed using at-risk CM with a guaranteed maximum price. The project was fast-tracked, which reduced total design and construction to 18 months, but a number of coordination and quality problems occurred, plus a cost overrun of 5 percent, half of which was paid by Tomorrow, with the other half currently in litigation.

The Tomorrow Company wishes the New Orleans center to be state-of-the-art in sales, communications, distribution, computer operations, and architecture—and project delivery system. It will be an "image building" that is clearly visible along Interstate 10, and will be used in Tomorrow's upcoming advertising campaign. The center will be a prototype for the next five centers. Tomorrow wishes to design and build the New Orleans center in 16 months, and then continue to compress the schedules on the succeeding centers to support the overall marketing and growth strategy.

Tomorrow is searching for an optimal design/construct/maintain system and ideal financing, including the possibility of facility ownership by others. The company vice president for facilities, Harry Bossman, a former construction company executive, has sent a request-for-information letter to 25 developers, design firms, and construction companies with the following information:

○ Tomorrow has budgeted $28 million for a state-of-the-art sales and distribution center on a prominent site near New Orleans.

○ Major components of the center are:
   1. Entrance lobby to receive busloads of visitors for direct shopping
   2. Lunch facilities with kitchen
   3. Retail area displaying full lines of equipment, apparel, and accessories
   4. Warehouse to stock all items in the many lines, with fully automated storage-and-retrieval system
   5. Shipping and receiving area with loading dock
   6. Phone service facilities,with superior ergonomic design, for 200 catalog and Internet salespersons
   7. Offices for manager, supervisors, and customer service personnel

8. Ancillary spaces to support the operations and personnel, including full computer facilities, intelligent systems, typical utilities, toilet rooms, janitor closets, and so on
9. Ample parking for personnel and visitors
10. Capability for expansion

O Tomorrow requests the following from interested parties:
1. Statement of interest in participating in the selection process
2. Experience in this type of facility, or similar operations
3. Safety experience
4. Experience in various PDSs
5. Experience in providing or seeking funding for projects
6. Willingness to team with developers, design firms, and contractors
7. Openness to innovative thinking
8. General overall approach to this project
9. Preliminary recommendations for PDS, including:
   a. Contractual arrangements
   b. Document preparation
   c. Preconstruction services
   d. Execution of construction
   e. Postconstruction services
10. Understanding of intelligent workplaces and ergonomics
11. Recommended design approach, including 3-D modeling and simulation techniques
12. Recommended innovations in the design/construct/maintain continuum, including whether the party will be interested in undertaking facilities management
13. Recommendations for:
   a. Partnering
   b. TQM
   c. Dispute prevention and resolution, and risk management and risk sharing
14. Projected time frame:
   a. Preconstruction
   b. Execution
   c. Commissioning, start-up, transfer
15. Probable division between self-performance and subcontracting
16. Preliminary response to budget
17. Willingness to respond to a more detailed RFP
18. Willingness to enter into a long-term alliance with the Tomorrow Company for design and construction of several centers
19. Availability for an interview in Lexington within a month

Amplification of Issues to Enhance Understanding of This Case

This is characterized as an entrepreneurial-driven project—or true speed-to-market. In the fast-moving global economy, the company that beats the competition to customers with products realizes handsome returns. And enlightened companies are willing to pay for quick, good-quality service. Computer generation of information and images will aid the pace of decision making. Collaboration is crucial. Very likely a hybrid PDS will evolve to optimize a yeasty process. The team will probably include a developer to obtain the site, arrange financing, and coordinate overall economic activity; a design team to complete the program and graphically articulate the vision; and a construction team to expedite construction, commissioning, and delivery of a functioning facility to the owner.

Discussion Questions

○ What is (are) the true driver(s) of this project—time, market share, return on investment, ego, or other criteria?

○ Are the vision and mission statements valid? Do they drive the program?

○ What would you change about the case to better fit your personal vision, mission, or fundamental values?

Assignment

Task 1

Form teams of three persons, one taking the role of developer, one designer, and the third, constructor. Prepare a response to Tomorrow's request for information with answers to each point and other relevant information, including a strategy for *capturing the owner's vision* and thus capturing the New Orleans project and the five to follow (Figure 6-2). Give particular emphasis to your abilities to work as a team, the PDS recommendation, preconstruction services, and postconstruction services. The worksheets in Figure 6-3 may be used to guide each team.

Task 2

Prepare a basic program for the New Orleans center, estimating areas needed, height requirements, and special needs. Consider architectural statement (near an interstate), spatial relationships, and other key issues.

Task 3

Draw a spatial relationship diagram for the life of the project.

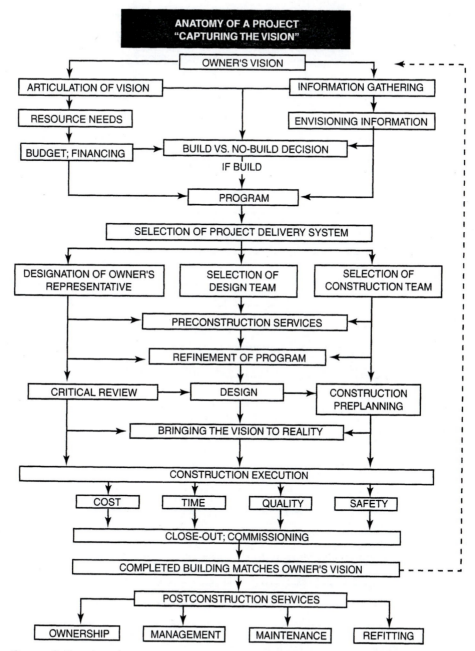

**ANATOMY OF A PROJECT
"CAPTURING THE VISION"**

OWNER'S VISION

ARTICULATION OF VISION   INFORMATION GATHERING

RESOURCE NEEDS   ENVISIONING INFORMATION

BUDGET; FINANCING   BUILD VS. NO-BUILD DECISION

IF BUILD

PROGRAM

SELECTION OF PROJECT DELIVERY SYSTEM

DESIGNATION OF OWNER'S REPRESENTATIVE   SELECTION OF DESIGN TEAM   SELECTION OF CONSTRUCTION TEAM

PRECONSTRUCTION SERVICES

REFINEMENT OF PROGRAM

CRITICAL REVIEW   DESIGN   CONSTRUCTION PREPLANNING

BRINGING THE VISION TO REALITY

CONSTRUCTION EXECUTION

COST   TIME   QUALITY   SAFETY

CLOSE-OUT; COMMISSIONING

COMPLETED BUILDING MATCHES OWNER'S VISION

POSTCONSTRUCTION SERVICES

OWNERSHIP   MANAGEMENT   MAINTENANCE   REFITTING

Figure 6-2   Capturing the Vision, a flowchart of initiatives and activities by designers and constructors to effectively serve owners, as in Case 6-4.

RESPONSE TO REQUEST FOR INFORMATION
THE TOMORROW COMPANY, INC.
(WORKSHEETS)

Statement of interest: _____
_____
_____
_____

Relevant experience: _____
_____
_____
_____

Safety experience: _____
_____
_____
_____

Experience in various project delivery systems: _____
_____
_____
_____

Experience in funding: _____
_____
_____
_____

Willingness to team with developers, designers, or constructors: _____
_____
_____
_____

Overall approach to project: _____
_____
_____
_____

Figure 6-3   Worksheet for responding to Request for Information.

Preliminary recommended project delivery system: _____

_____

_____

_____

Contractual arrangements: _____

_____

Design document preparation: _____

_____

Preconstruction services: _____

_____

_____

_____

Execution of construction: _____

_____

_____

_____

Postconstruction services: _____

_____

_____

_____

Understanding of intelligent workplaces and ergonomics: _____

_____

_____

_____

Recommended design, modeling, and simulation techniques: _____

_____

_____

_____

Figure 6-3   Continued.

Recommended innovations in the design/construct/maintain continuum:

_____

_____

_____

Recommendations for:

    Partnering: _____

    _____

    _____

    TQM: _____

    _____

    _____

    Dispute prevention and resolution: _____

    _____

    _____

    Risk management and sharing: _____

    _____

    _____

Projected time frame:

    Preconstruction: _____

    _____

    _____

    _____

    Construction execution: _____

    _____

    _____

    Commissioning, start-up, transfer: _____

    _____

    _____

    _____

Figure 6-3   Continued.

Probable division between self-performance and subcontracting: _____

_____

_____

_____

Preliminary response to budget: _____

_____

_____

_____

Willingness to respond to a more detailed RFP: _____

_____

_____

_____

Willingness to enter a long-term alliance: _____

_____

_____

_____

Availability for interview in Lexington: _____

_____

_____

_____

Team strategy for capturing the owner's vision to win this project and the five to follow: _____

_____

_____

_____

_____

C H A P T E R   7

Case Studies Needing Solutions: Risk Distribution and Dispute Resolutions

"Risk is inherent in construction. Adroit practitioners know how to manage risk."

The management of risks and disputes is crucial to success in design and construction. Exposure to liability should be part of early planning by all parties. Risk distribution should be based on which parties have the most direct responsibility for segments of a project and on their abilities to mitigate risk through proper preparation—and their abilities to acquire proper insurance coverage.

Dispute resolution begins with prevention through good planning and communications. Nonetheless, there should be in place, either contractually or through partnering, a series of steps to resolve disputes. It is crucial to reach agreements prior to entering malevolent cycles that degrade relationships and sap energies from the project execution. Dispute resolution steps include:

○ Negotiations

○ Third-party mediation

○ Medarb (a combination of mediation and arbitration)

○ Dispute panels

○ Minitrials

And if all else fails, either:

○ Arbitration

or:

○ Litigation

Each step tends to be more extreme than the previous ones, is more expensive and time-consuming, and pushes responsibility and control further away from the parties to the dispute. However, all alternative dispute resolution methods are preferable to either arbitration or litigation, which are lengthy, costly, and rarely fully satisfactory. Good legal advice aims at avoidance of arbitration—and most particularly litigation (except in special cases where grievous wrongs need correcting in a public forum).

Case Study 7-1   Riverside Condos

Project:	Midrise condominiums
Location:	Louisville, Kentucky
Budget:	$30 million (for construction; masonry repair, pending)
Issue:	Leakage through masonry

The condominium tower in Louisville was designed to attract empty nesters back to the central city. Good views were afforded of the Ohio River, Indiana across the river, and the downtown business and cultural districts. Financing, including land acquisition, was completely private.

The building design combined a formal architectural statement with residential features. The structure was in-situ concrete frame and flat plate slabs. Brick veneer on metal studs provided the envelope system. Soon after completion, moderately serious leakage became apparent at each floor level during and after storms. Investigation indicated that water was penetrating the single wythe of brick veneer and traveling down the inner side of the brick. When it accumulated at the bottom of the cavity between brick and sheathing, it was gradually seeping into the living space through the sheathing, insulation, and interior plasterboard. This is considered a *building failure*, which, by definition, is any significant lack of performance of a completed building. The envelope ledge detail showed the metal studs running from slab to slab, with channel plates above and below anchored to the slabs. The wythe of brick sat on steel ledge angles bolted to slab edges at midpoints of the 10 inch slab thicknesses.

Amplification of Issues to Enhance Understanding of This Case

A single wythe of brick, $3\frac{3}{4}$ inches thick, will not reject all wind-driven precipitation. Hairline cracks develop at joints due to mortar shrinkage, and if flexure occurs due to lateral (wind) loads, joints open further. Then direct flow and capillary action allow water penetration. It is crucial that water entering a wall be allowed to flow back out. Flashing and weepholes provide safe passage out—but they are not foolproof. Inadequate installation of flashing or clogged weepholes can cause moisture to migrate internally rather than to the outside. This is not an unusual condition in highrise curtainwall design.

Forensic investigation involves after-the-fact research into why something happens. This can be done on a cursory level or by retained professionals such as architects, engineers, contractors, or researchers who cultivate investigative skills and extend their services into this arena. Forensic investigators are frequently hired by lawyers for disputing parties after a building failure. They research issues and then testify as expert witnesses. Frequently, opposing sides present expert testimony that is diametrically opposite in findings, causing critics to call them "hired guns."

Nonetheless, good information that may be helpful in avoiding future problems is frequently compiled. If the dispute gets to court, however, "gag orders" are usually imposed to protect parties from further claims. Thus, much good forensic work stays in court files and is not available to educate practitioners against repeated mistakes.

Discussion Questions

○ Are there better types of wall construction for excluding water? What are they, and what are their pros and cons?

○ If a contractor refuses to rectify such problems, what are the owner's options?

○ What is the purpose of ledge angles? How frequently should they be placed?

Assignment

(*Note:* Some assumptions will need to be made in order to work through a series of issues. These assumptions should be knowledge based and reasonable, dependent on the information provided, but researched further through building materials texts, product catalogs, standard details, and design and construction practitioners.)

○ Draw details of how the envelope engages the structure. Consult Architectural Graphic Standards, Sweets Catalogs, and architects' drawings of similar conditions.

○ Speculate on what might be causing the leakage. Possibilities include:
   1. Inadequate or improperly placed flashing
   2. Inadequate or improperly placed weepholes
   3. Partial filling of the cavity with mortar droppings, thus clogging weepholes
   4. Improper tying of brick to studs, allowing inordinate flexure of the brick and leading to joint failure
   5. Combinations of the above

○ After reaching one or more points of consensus on the cause(s) of the leakage, plan an approach to rectify the problem. Consult with an experienced designer or constructor, ideally one who has performed forensic studies of building problems. Possible approaches include:
   1. Provide a thorough coating of a silicon sealant to retard moisture penetration (this will need to be restored at about two-year intervals).
   2. Completely replace brick envelope and replace damaged sheathing.
   3. Remove lower courses of brick at each level (while properly bracing upper courses), clean the cavity, replace sheathing and flashing, and then replace brick with proper weeping.

○ Estimate the cost of each proposed remedy by consulting a pricing index or a contractor's cost database.

○ Determine how the cost of the remedy will be afforded. Considerations include:
   1. Design liability: If deficiency can be shown in the design as manifested by the construction documents, the architect may have liability, which is typically covered by professional liability insurance, sometimes called *errors and omissions* coverage. Such insurance always has a deductible amount, which places some of the architect's fiscal resources at risk.

2. Contractor's general liability: If it can be demonstrated that the design was adequate, the fault probably lies with execution. If subcontractors were involved with any part of the envelope (which is probably the case), the general contractor will attempt to gain restitution from one or more subcontractors. However, from the owner's point of view, the prime contract is with the general contractor, and that is the party to whom the owner will look for claims of damages—that is, costs of repair and loss of rental income. All contractors, generals and subs, carry liability insurance to cover issues such as this. However, since there is usually a deductible and since insurance claims can affect premiums, no contractor prefers to accept the burden.

3. Owner's casualty loss: Owners should always have property and casualty insurance for a project in effect prior to its commencement. The basic rule of ownership is that once materials are built into a structure, they belong to the owner, regardless of payments to date. A builder's risk insurance policy is another way to handle this exposure during construction. However, following completion, the builder's risk lapses, and the ongoing property and casualty insurance covers damage to the completed building. The question in this case is whether remedies to construction problems are appropriately covered by either builder's risk or property and casualty insurance.

○ Consult with an insurance agent to help in determining how the loss may be covered by the various parties and policies.

○ Obviously a dispute is at hand. No party will willingly accept the responsibility for full coverage of the cost of the problem. While basic professionalism should cause architects and constructors to seek a solution, and while the owner will be pressing for full use of the building, differences of opinion will surely occur in regard to payment for remedies. Insurance companies do not pay claims with alacrity. Take the position of an independent mediator and attempt to bring the dispute to conclusion. Research the Construction Industry Rules of the American Arbitration Association, findings of the College of Construction Attorneys, and recommendations of the Dispute Avoidance Round Table (DART).

○ Lay out a dispute avoidance or resolution procedure with a series of possible steps.

○ Diagram a "decision tree" showing dispute resolution options and "if-then" procedures based on success or failure of each proposed step.

○ Investigate the concept of consequential damages to determine if the owner could rightfully pursue such.

Case Study 7-2   The Racetrack Default

Project:	Vista View Auto Racing Pavilion
Location:	Southeastern United States
Budget:	$50 million (for design and construction)
Issue:	Default by owner

Vista View Racing Corporation planned a major new facility at its auto racing track in the southeastern United States. An old grandstand would remain on one side of the track, while bleachers on another side would be razed to allow for a new, modern, fully enclosed air-conditioned grandstand with video and sound systems, a motor racing history display, and related activity. The budget was set at $50 million, and design-build was selected as the PDS. An Associated General Contractors' 410 form of agreement (following an AGC 400 preliminary agreement) was signed between Vista View and Arnold Construction Company of Atlanta, which had recently built two similar structures in the Southeast. By prearrangement with Vista View, Arnold retained Prescott & Thornton—a comprehensive AE firm—as subcontractor for design, using an AGC 420 form of agreement. The project was totally privately financed, but the local county government agreed to upgrade infrastructure to support the facility.

The project was fast-tracked, with a contractually firm completion date of 18 months after signing of the design-build contract—to be ready for a major event that should draw 75,000 people. A guaranteed maximum price contract for $50,227,550 was signed, including design and construction fees, and a contingency fund of $950,000, under joint control of Vista View and Arnold, was agreed on. Arnold would receive 20 percent of any savings within the GMP. As soon as the contract was signed and design was underway, Arnold sent RFQs to many trade contractors in the region and began prequalifying potential participants. Arnold planned to self-perform demolition, all site work, and foundations, and then to subcontract out all the other work in ten packages. Thus there would be ten subcontractors, many sub-subcontractors, and over 100 suppliers, many of whom would be responsible to sub-subcontractors. Some of the subcontractors would be mid-size general contractors who would take on packages such as envelope or interior finishes, using sub-subcontractors for specialty aspects of the packages. Other subcontractors would provide both design and construction (see later discussion).

Arnold began demolition one week after signing a contract, and then proceeded to narrow down the long list of potential subcontractors through review of prequalification forms, phone discussions, and interviews. While having the objective of subcontracting most of the work, Arnold retained the option of self-performing any activity for which a competent subcontractor could not be placed under contract for a reasonable price. Arnold's project preplanning efforts consisted of:

○ Careful overall scheduling
○ Scheduling AE document deliverables to match the construction schedule
○ Determining contents of bid packages
○ Projecting costs of all components of the project
○ Establishment of daily cost-reporting systems to continuously monitor actual expenses compared to projections
○ Setting a rigorous safety program, with training and drug compliance
○ Establishing quality control through a team of Arnold veterans in quality assurance.

As the first bid package was finalized, competing subcontractors were invited, along with their salient sub-subcontractors, to the AE office to review documents currently in preparation and to be thoroughly briefed by Arnold's project executive and AE personnel. Construction document deliverables were timed to provide adequate information to bidders. Design-build subcontract proposals (six of the ten packages) were solicited for:

○ Envelope system
○ HVAC
○ Plumbing
○ Electrical services and illumination
○ Fire suppression
○ Elevators

Professionals in the AE firm were retained to review and coordinate the design-build subcontract proposals, but not to take design responsibility, which would reside with licensed professionals employed or retained by the respective trade contractors.

The project proceeded well. Arnold expedited demolition, site preparation, and foundations while the bid packages for superstructure and envelope were being finalized. Subsequent packages were organized on schedule, and bids were within the parameters set in advance by Arnold. After one year, all bid packages were set, and the project was on schedule in regard to both time and costs. Payments were made in a timely manner, and there were a minimal number of disputes, all manageable.

Then the chairman of Vista View Corporation was sued by the U.S. Internal Revenue Service for tax evasion over the past six years. Since he was a majority stockholder of Vista View, and since the claims of the IRS ran to millions of dollars including penalties, serious consequences boded for the project. The chairman steadfastly proclaimed his innocence. Nonetheless, the IRS proceeded deliberately in developing its case, and other members of the Vista View board of directors became apprehensive about the future of the corporation, and thus of the racetrack project.

Though seriously concerned about payment, Arnold realized that contractual obligations dictated that work continue. A work stoppage would place Arnold in a position to be declared in default, and thus be weakened in the dispute that was becoming evident. (*Note:* All contracts have termination clauses, but contractors are advised to persevere until termination is unavoidable.) The news of the chairman's problems quickly spread throughout the construction community. Arnold was bombarded with inquiries from subcontractors and suppliers about the status of the project, particularly prospects for payment. The concern was exacerbated by the owner's lapse in payment of Arnold's next monthly application. Subcontractors and sub-subcontractors began reducing staff on the project, and several then stopped work altogether.

Arnold's project executive had had a number of discussions with Vista View's project representative about the financial aspects of the project, and now the dialogue became daily and intense. All pertinent matters were documented, and file drawers filled with paper. As a construction company, Arnold already had excellent documentation procedures; now the documents became more voluminous. Arnold's president took personal interest and involvement in Vista View, and he assigned another assistant project executive just for documentation and preparation of data for claims and answers to counterclaims.

Vista View's project representative urged patience and requested continued progress on the job—and tried to persuade all parties that the problems were temporary and would be resolved without loss to anyone. Several parties had already alerted their attorneys to be prepared to take action. The first actions were the filing of liens by several subcontractors, sub-subs, and suppliers. The laws of the state prescribed that liens must be filed within 75 days of the last date of work on the project by the respective parties. All contractors who had ceased performing work filed liens soon after such stoppage. Some contractors who continued working nonetheless filed liens to seek priority consideration in case the owner defaulted.

When the owner missed the second successive monthly payment, the president of Arnold authorized the company's legal counsel to cite Vista View for default of the contract, to file a claim for back payment (in the state court system), and to file a lien on the property in amount of such payment. Copies of the documents were sent to the subcontractors with the advice that they should cease work and remove all personnel, tools, and materials from the site. Arnold's personnel then proceeded to close the site with barriers and warning signs to reduce liability regarding trespassers. The project came to a halt.

Vista View's attorneys filed a counterclaim charging Arnold with improper design, unsatisfactory management, poor-quality work, not complying with contractual requirements, and leaving the project without the owner's authorization to do so. Several subcontractors filed claims for payment on both Arnold and Vista View, the latter as follow-ups to previously filed liens. The project transitioned from the execution phase to the legal phase. Now everyone read the forms of agreement and related documents with extreme care. The AGC 410 standard form of agreement, used for the contract between owner and contractor, called for binding arbitration to resolve disputes, but the agreement allowed for alternative means of dispute resolution—including litigation—if both parties agreed. Vista View's attorney requested that Arnold agree to medarb, a process beginning with mediation and then, if such fails, moving into binding arbitration. The attractions of the medarb process were a possible earlier resolution than standard arbitration, and less legal expense. As the case stands now, Arnold is considering whether to accept the proposal for medarb (Figure 7-1).

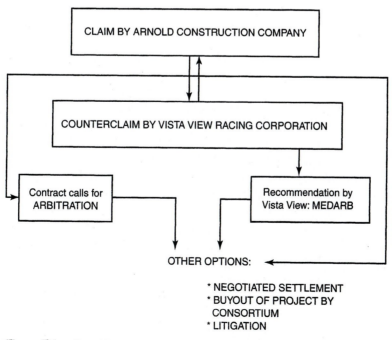

Figure 7-1   Possible tactics to resolve the default by the owner, Vista View Racing Corporation.

Amplification of Issues to Enhance Understanding of This Case

Three salient issues in the case, besides the actual default, are design-build by subcontractors, liens, and pay when paid. The first is becoming more frequent, the second has been around a long time, and the third is controlled by law, contracts, and tradition.

An important concept of design-build, single-point responsibility, makes the integration of design and construction attractive for building systems made up of many components, such as HVAC and building envelopes. Consequently, one party can be responsible for design, procurement, sub-contracting (or sub-subcontracting), handling, storage, installation, and warranty of the entire system. There are usually requirements for licensed professionals—architects or engineers—to be involved in the design and thus to take professional responsibility for the integrity and performance of the systems. These design professionals may be in the employ of the specialty contractors, or may be retained in consultant roles. In either case, they are contractually responsible to the specialty contractor, whose responsibility passes up the chain to the prime design-build contractor, who carries overall responsibility to the owner (Figure 7-2).

The project design team usually reviews—and to a degree may coordinate—documents regarding the systems, but they eschew design responsibility. They remain contractually linked to the design-build prime contractor. Insurance coverages are required accordingly for all the players.

Liens are more than a century old in the United States, and are the historic way for parties who contribute to built projects to be remunerated when timely payment is not forthcoming from the owner. Since the original intent of the laws was to protect workers, they have become known as *mechanics' lien laws*. In fact, most liens are now filed by subcontractors and suppliers. (Governments sometimes file liens for unpaid taxes—but those follow different regulations.) Rules for filing and "perfecting" liens vary from state to state, but actions are always time sensitive—that is, filings must be made within a prescribed period following the contribution of labor or material. Essentially a lien is an attachment to a tangible asset, which claims value from that asset to satisfy a debt or damages. Thus a contractor, supplier, or tradesperson who has not been paid can claim part of the built asset for compensation. Of course, this usually involves legal action to perfect the lien—to actually gain payment. Many liens are negotiated to settlement; others are parts of bankruptcies wherein reduced payments to claimants can be time based or priority based (amounts and criticality to the project). In most states, designers have low-priority

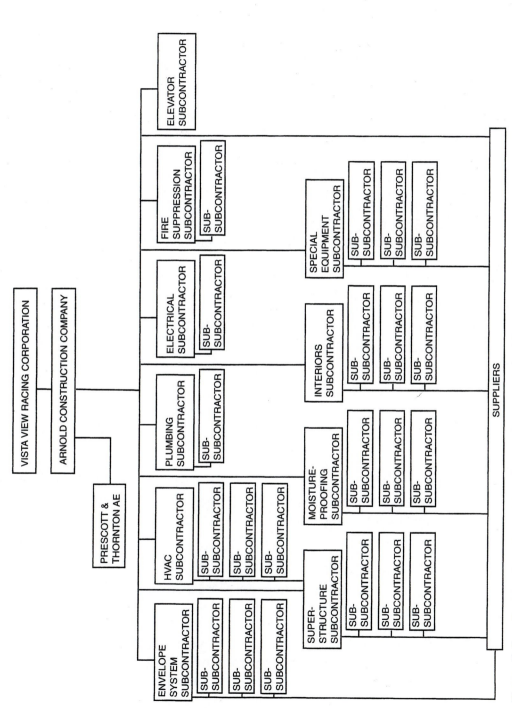

Figure 7-2   Organization of Vista View Racetrack project. Arnold Construction Company is the prime design-build contractor. Prescott & Thornton are overall design subcontractors. Ten bid packages are let. Those shown on the upper tier have design-build responsibilities; those on the lower tier do not. All subcontractors and sub-subcontractors are linked to their respective suppliers.

standing. Even on relatively harmonious projects, suppliers may file protective liens if payment has not been received and the clock is ticking down.

Obviously owners hate liens—particularly if they are the result of non-payment to subcontractors and suppliers by contractors to whom owners have made payment. Thus there are complex networks of affidavits, certificates of materialmen, and lien waivers built into the payment process to try to avoid liens.

The concept of pay when paid remains controversial. Is the contractor required to pay subcontractors and material suppliers if that contractor has not been paid by the owner? Tradition and most subcontracts support the pay-when-paid idea—that, if the owner witholds payment, nobody gets paid (except the contractor's direct employees, usually). However, some contractors, whether based on ethics, business reasons, or legal tactics, pay "down the chain" prior to being paid. Several states address the issue with legislation, which obviously prevails over tradition.

Discussion Questions

○ What particular skills must Arnold have to manage this project?

○ Is design-build the best PDS here?

○ Did Arnold act correctly when it became clear that the owner had financial difficulties?

○ Should Arnold pay the subcontractors prior to receiving payment from the owner?

Assignment

Place yourself in the position of project executive for Arnold and prepare a recommendation to the company president in regard to proceeding on the dispute resolution. Options include:

○ Accept Vista View's recommendations for medarb

○ Hold to the contractual requirements for binding arbitration

○ Counter the Vista View offer with your own recommendation; possibilities include:
   1. Resort to litigation (if you think that Arnold has a strong legal position)
   2. Retain an independent factfinder to investigate the case and present a third-party analysis and recommendation
   3. Retain a three-person dispute panel to expedite a binding resolution outside the rules of the American Arbitration Association

○ Make the subcontractors parties to the dispute to resolve many issues

○ Form a group to purchase Vista View from the current owners and thus generate capital to complete construction and pay all debts—and perhaps have a profitable enterprise

To develop background for your recommendation, investigate the following:

○ The Construction Industry Rules of the American Arbitration Association (AAA)

○ Legal standing of arbitration in your state, whether using AAA procedures or other rules; and whether courts accept the binding resolution or allow appeals to arbitrate decisions

○ The lien laws in your state: perhaps called mechanics' lien laws since their genesis was to protect workers from nonpayment by employers

○ Bankruptcy laws in your state: how assets are distributed to creditors when an owner declares bankruptcy

○ The design-build contractor's obligations to the AE firm: review AGC 420 and state laws to determine whether lien laws cover design services

○ AGC contracts 400, 410, 450, and 460 to determine responsibilities among the parties, including what obligations Arnold has to the subcontractors while awaiting payment from the owner

○ The efficacy of the "pay-when-paid" thesis, from standpoints of:
   1. The prevailing law
   2. Sound business practices
   3. Ethics
   4. Future relations with subcontractors

○ Obligations of subcontractors to sub-subcontractors. Since subsubs have no contractual relationships with either the owner or the design-build contractor, they are "at the mercy" of subcontractors—depending on their forms of agreement, which range from standard documents to their own specially prepared forms, to relatively simple purchase orders. All three were used on the Vista View project. Obtain samples of such and determine which provide equitable relief for sub-subcontractors. Also, what are the obligations to suppliers?

Prepare the recommendation with a series of options and then a prioritization of them with brief rationales for each.

Case Study 7-3   The Unfinished House

Project:	Custom residence
Location:	St. Louis, Missouri, suburbs
Budget:	$500,000 (for design and construction)
Issue:	Death of contractor

Henry Herron was the classic "Old German carpenter," a 62-year-old second-generation American who displayed the skill and work ethic so admired in construction. Those attributes had made him a successful builder of fine homes in and around St. Louis. Herron typically built just two to four homes per year and became heavily involved personally in each. Most projects were for individual customers. He was much in demand by knowledgeable clients. Herron operated as a sole proprietor. A nephew and four other long-time employees did much of the work, and he subcontracted out the specialty tasks such as tile setting, electrical, HVAC, plumbing, and paving.

Herron's daughter was an architect with a small local firm. She produced his residential drawings sufficient for building permits and basic construction. The drawings and contracts with clients were somewhat "bare bones" because Herron worked out many details on site, and many issues were simply "understood." The contracts were a three-page listing of items to be included in the house, the contract amount, and the completion date. Changes were handled in a matter-of-fact manner in simple negotiations. Herron was known for his honesty and ethical behavior, and he tended to select clients in whom he saw the same characteristics. He always had more potential customers than he could serve.

After 30 years of successful projects, he contracted with a prominent attorney for a house, to cost in excess of $500,000, on the attorney's property. The drawings and contract were completed, and the job got underway in good order. As the construction progressed, the attorney made a series of changes, most of which added costs to the contract. Casual notes were kept of the discussions, along with Herron's estimates of the added cost of each change. The actual costs would be finalized on a time and materials basis, with Herron's overhead and profit being 10 percent added to the actual costs.

After three months' progress on the house, catastrophe struck—Herron died of a heart attack on the jobsite. By the time emergency vehicles arrived, he was gone. Obviously, production was nil the rest of the day and for the week thereafter. Although his nephew and the other workers were competent, they relied heavily on Herron for leadership and supervision. Also, Herron handled all the payroll and accounting in his own simplistic manner. While his daughter was generally aware of her father's operation, she was not attuned to the details. His wife, a lifelong homemaker, was not involved in the business at all. Two sons worked abroad and could not return long enough to be of much help. Work slowed to a halt, and the crew sought other employment.

Herron's wife and daughter met with the attorney-owner in an attempt to settle the financial side of the agreement. The attorney had entered negotiations with another builder to complete the house, which was closed in, with mechanical and electrical rough-in completed. He told the Herrons that prices being quoted to complete the house, plus what he had already paid, exceeded their original agreement. He maintained that no additional money was owed to the Herrons.

The Herrons contacted their own lawyer, who, after discussions with them and the attorney-owner and a review of the records available, determined that indeed the Herrons had a legitimate claim—the question was for how much. A meeting among the Herrons, their attorney, and the attorney-owner was aimed at an agreement on compensation, but the owner held firmly against any additional payment. He stated that the substitute builder estimated that the value of work satisfactorily completed equaled the amount already paid to Henry Herron.

The Herrons' attorney then advised them that the only way to recover any money was to file suit and develop a case for the money owed. The Herron women, by this time generating growing hostility toward the owner's intransigence, agreed to the suit. Developing a case entailed having an expert examine all aspects of the project, and then produce a credible report to become the main evidentiary matter in the trial. Court testimony of that expert would, of course, be required.

A homebuilder friend of Henry's was recruited by the Herrons for this expertise. He examined all the records (which were sparse) and the job, which had not yet resumed. He then created a basic schedule and cost breakdown, which showed $185,000 of value built into the project, but just $140,000 paid, for an owed amount of $45,000. He added interest for the anticipated ten-month delay in payment and the estimated legal fees and court costs, and subsequently the Herrons' attorney filed suit with a claim for $80,000. The attorney-owner, representing himself, filed a counterclaim against the Herrons, requesting $20,000, stating some unsatisfactory work, overcharges, and the value of his own legal time.

Six months later, a trial was set before a county common pleas judge, with no jury. Discovery consisted of depositions taken of the Herron's expert and of the substitute contractor retained by the owner. Work had not continued on the house pending settlement of the suit. Since it was closed in but did not yet have water service, there was no danger of deterioration or freezing.

Amplification of Issues to Enhance Understanding of This Case

Continuity or succession is a critical issue in any enterprise. Life is full of unanticipated events. "Passing the torch" is easier in a corporation than in a proprietorship. The latter form of organization, while having good profit potential for the proprietor, is full of risk, and sole operators are notorious for maintaining poor records. As the case suggests, if litigation occurs, the lack of records increases exposure. Good standard contracts, by AIA or AGC, identify in advance procedures to be used in dispute resolution—usually arbitration under the rules of the American Arbitration Association.

Discussion Questions

○ Are "old school" contractors like Henry Herron becoming obsolete? If so, is this good or bad?

○ It is not unusual that the sons and daughters of skilled mechanics are becoming architects, engineers, lawyers, and computer whizzes—what does this bode for the construction industry?

○ When you build your "dream house," how will you contract for the design and construction?

Assignment

Now it is the day before the trial, and the owner calls the Herrons' attorney and asks for a conference that may lead to a settlement. Take the position of the Herron daughter, on whom the mother has grown to rely and who has done some of her own investigation to become quite familiar with all the exigencies of the project. How will you advise Mrs. Herron on procedure? Mrs. Herron is uncomfortable about testifying in court and does not really need the money for continued modest living, but she is driven by a strong sense of fairness to her beloved husband. Here are some options:

○ Continue with the trial, since the owner is showing doubts about his case by requesting a settlement conference.

○ Instruct their attorney to seek a beneficial settlement with no less than a net amount of $40,000 to the Herrons.

○ Instruct their attorney to settle for any reasonable amount, based on the fact that, given the weak contract and poor records maintained by Herron, they would be vulnerable in a court where the judge would decide the case on the evidence presented.

Issues to consider:

○ Why was arbitration or other alternative means of dispute resolution not employed?

○ Do courts usually allow charges of legal fees to be included in suits?

○ Will an out-of-court settlement be upheld by the court?

○ Will Mrs. Herron ultimately be paid any settlement amount agreed on? What is the mechanism to ensure payment?

○ If the case is decided in the court of common pleas, what are the prospects of it being appealed to a higher court by either party?

Sources of information:

○ Seek sample contracts and advice from the local chapter of the Home Builders Association of America.

○ Invite a homebuilder and an attorney to discuss the issue.

Your recommendation by Ms. Herron to her mother and her attorney should by backed by a clear rationale, readily understood by Mrs. Herron and easily transferred to the attorney-owner. It is advisable to have a "fall-back position" or option in case your recommendation is not accepted by the owner.

Ms. Herron is giving thought to taking over her father's business, and although she would not consider finishing the subject house given the adversity, she sees an opportunity to combine her design talents with her cousin's construction skills. She is tempted to regenerate the old crew into a renewed Herron Homes enterprise, continuing the reputation established by her father. If she is to do so, what advice would you give about conducting that business?

○ Should she incorporate?

○ Should the cousin be an officer in the corporation?

○ What chain of command should be established?

○ Should she have site responsibilities as well as design responsibilities?

○ Should the design activity be part of a design-build venture, or should she have a separate design practice—with separate corporate status?

Summarize your recommendations with rationales.

Case Study 7-4   The Apartment Building Fiasco

Project:	Rehabilitation of a historic residence
Location:	Dayton, Ohio
Budget:	$95,000 (for construction and CM fee)
Issue:	Dispute between owner and architect

A young architect in Dayton, with a sole proprietorship practice specializing in residential and small commercial designs, was approached about "saving" an old, large condemned residence by converting it into four apartments. Current zoning allowed this action. The owner pleaded that if the city did not see evidence of some progress to salvage the building within a month, demolition orders, already issued, would be executed, and the old house would be gone in the name of the health, safety, and welfare of the community, well within the police power of the city, granted by the laws of Ohio.

The architect, intrigued by the character of the house and having sympathy for historic preservation, accepted the idea and prepared an AIA B141 agreement for design services, with a fee that he felt appropriate. The owner and her attorney, who had now appeared on the scene, both stated that the fee was beyond the owner's means. The owner had recently returned to Dayton to take a position with a real estate company while working toward her real estate license. No income was yet forthcoming; she had invested her resources in buying the property and was limited in her ability to pay for design or construction. She offered the prospect that her brother, with construction experience, would be the contractor and that thus the documents could be simplified—adequate for permit purposes and general description of the work, but not necessarily detailed for competitive bidding. There would be no separate specifications, all information being directly on the drawings.

A bit apprehensive, but seeing an opportunity to display his historic preservation talent, the architect agreed to a reduced fee; deleted his contract administration and produced a modified agreement that was signed by both him and the owner. He thoroughly measured and photographed the building, which, while on the verge of becoming a derelict, was still fundamentally structurally sound. He quickly produced schematics of the four-apartment layout. The units ranged from 800 to 1200 square feet, appropriate for that neighborhood. With a few changes, the schematics were approved by the client. Then the agreed-on working drawings were completed and were submitted for a building permit. A particularly demanding plan examiner requested several more details than the architect thought necessary. These included:

○ Details of full support and anchorage of balconies (there had recently been a collapse of a balcony on an old converted residence, injuring several people)
○ Wall sections of all walls, including existing ones
○ Complete sections through all stairs, even those already in place
○ Several interior elevations

Initially, the plan examiner stated that the building would require sprinklers for fire suppression, but when he and the architect went over the code carefully, it was determined that this was not the case if all units were separated by walls rated at one and a half hours. The differences over the drawings were resolved, and approval for a permit was granted. The architect did not actually secure the permit, which was priced at $428; this would be the obligation of the owner.

The architect sent the permit approval notice and a statement for final payment to the owner. There had been no agreement on services during construction. After waiting two weeks, he called the owner to ask about the status of the project—was her brother proceeding on the work, and could they wrap up their agreement with her payment? She requested that he meet with her and her attorney. The meeting was set, and the attorney did most of the talking. The client still was having financial difficulty, and the attorney was thinking of buying into the project. Together they were investigating financing of the rehabilitation. The brother was having health problems and could not undertake managing the construction. While several options were explored, the team asked the architect to manage the construction. They said that they could not get a loan until a reliable cost estimate was given, and the implication was that he would not receive final payment (nearly 40 percent of the fee) until a loan was secured. The architect said that he would consider it and get back to them. He was torn between rejecting the proposal or accepting the challenge and moving ahead. The options he saw were:

○ Reject the proposal outright and probably not be paid the remainder of his fee—$3200, which was a substantial sum at that stage in his practice. He recognized that to sue the client would cost more than that in legal fees.

○ Accept the proposal with an agreement that would shield him from excessive risk. He carried minimal insurance.

○ Seek another party to undertake the construction, perhaps with the architect as collaborator in some role.

The option of taking on construction responsibilities was not a "wild idea." The architect had already performed contract administration on a number of projects, and had contracted the expansion and remodeling of his own house. He knew a number of small contractors who might become engaged in the project. In the meantime a local elected officeholder, whom the architect had supported in a recent election, called to state confidence in the owner's attorney, "who would probably be appointed to a judgeship in the relatively near future."

The culmination of several issues—most particularly the challenges of saving the old house (about which he had now developed a bit of romance) and engaging construction more fully than he had before—caused the architect to propose a construction management contract using AIA Form A101/CM. He would line up several trade contractors to do the actual work and, acting as the owner's agent, manage them through to a completed building. The client insisted on a guaranteed maximum price and that the architect hold all the contracts and take responsibility for them. Having already developed his own estimates as part of the design effort, and having received some preliminary prices from contractors, he compiled a GMP 12 percent higher than the earlier estimate (including his own overhead and profit), citing the risk involved and the fact that the earlier estimate was based on the brother doing the work. Some haggling took place. A number 7.5 percent higher than the earlier estimate was agreed on, and the contract was signed in June.

The architect immediately directly hired some students from the construction program at the local college to begin wrecking the necessary parts of the building. They also placed concrete foundations for new supporting members and performed several other miscellaneous chores to get the project ready for the carpenters and mechanical trade contractors, who began in July. The architect filed monthly payment requests for the direct hires (whom he had paid) and the trade contractors. June, July, and August payments were made by the owner, and most of the framing and rough-in plumbing, wiring, and ductwork were completed. Drywall work was to begin in September, but the team that originally agreed to do the plasterboard work declined to perform, citing other higher priority work. The electrical inspector rejected some wiring, necessitating rework, which the electrical contractor sought payment for. The owner and her lawyer, now partners in the project, visited the site regularly and, after initial excitement, showed more and more apprehension. She requested that one unit be completed by Thanksgiving for her to move into. This would be difficult, but the architect stated that he would try to do so. After resolving the electrical issue, he recruited three young men to hang drywall in the evening and on weekends. They worked hard with moderate skill. Several new problems developed:

○ The owners objected to the quality of drywall and other work.

○ Neighbors complained about the noise of night work and the accumulating debris on the site.

○ A building inspector demanded evidence that the old partitions were properly firestopped. Several had to be opened, inspected, and then refinished.

○ The owner paid only half of the September payment application, citing unacceptable work.

○ The architect was spending an inordinate amount of time on the project, to the detriment of other important work.

○ The building inspector, feeling triumphant in his firestop investigation, pressed aggressively on other issues.

The architect, realizing that he had a "true loser" on his hands, knew that the only solution was to press forward to completion. All exterior work, except painting, was completed by the carpenters; drywall was finished (though with less than stellar work); and the mechanical trades finished their work, with the exception of setting of actual fixtures. The October payment was also only half of the submittal (the architect was tempted to submit inflated statements but did not do so). He paid for work from his own resources, and kept careful accounting of all activity. He persuaded the owners to directly purchase plumbing and lighting fixtures, cabinetry, carpeting, and other amenities to expedite the project.

The Thanksgiving move-in date was missed, and the owner, expressing outrage, refused to make the November payment. Relations among all parties deteriorated. The architect and owners became increasingly hostile toward each other, and carpenters, sensing the situation, were reluctant to return for finish work. The architect had to pay the plumbers in advance to come back and set fixtures, and the architect self-performed much of the cleanup and final painting, hiring students to help. The architect examined the ethics of the situation many times, and was quite anxious over whether he was performing correctly:

○ Despite his disdain for the owners, one of whom had indeed been appointed to a judgeship as predicted, he kept them informed of activity through regular memoranda.

○ He paid workers on time, although one complained of underpayment and threatened physical damage to the building if not more fully compensated.

○ He strove for the best possible quality, while realizing that several compromises had been made.

○ He remained fully truthful in all his dealings.

○ Yet he obviously could not be proud of the potential outcome.

The architect, never having needed legal service, contacted a lawyer acquaintance who advised:

○ Pushing the project through to completion—as a necessity, if litigation were to transpire

○ Documenting a calendar of events with as much detail as possible

○ Filing regular (every two weeks) statements with the owners

○ On final completion, filing a complete review of the project with the owners, including a request for full payment

○ If payment in full was not made within 30 days, filing a lien on the property for the outstanding amount plus accrued interest

○ Beginning to line up witness who might testify favorably in case of arbitration or litigation

Completion of the project came early the next year; a certificate of occupancy was approved by the building inspector after a few miscellaneous alterations, and the owner immediately took occupancy of her unit. The architect considered trying to preclude this, but his attorney advised against it. The architect did, however, retain the keys to the other three units. This led to a call from an attorney who said that he was representing the owners, who were prepared to file suit if the architect did not immediately release all obstacles to their gainful use of the entire building. The owners' advertisement in a local newspaper described excellent apartments, close to business and cultural facilities.

The architect clipped and filed that with his other documents arranged for the suit. A month of haggling over various issues culminated with the architect filing a lien on the property for $33,000. This included labor, material, CM fee, and interest charges. The architect had paid all participants for whom he had responsibility. The owners had paid for several finish items and to redo some interior finishes at their volition. They had changed locks and proceeded to rent out the other units at marketplace prices.

The AIA A101/CM contract had a clause requiring arbitration, unless other action was mutually agreed to. Both parties desired litigation: the architect, on advice from his attorney that he had a good case because indeed the building was producing gainful return on the owners' investment; the owners, because they thought that his judgeship would be valuable in local legal circles. They had already retained a well-regarded, flamboyant lawyer, a friend of the judge.

The architect's attorney, a mature, dignified individual, filed suit to enforce the lien, and the owner's attorney filed a counterclaim to dismiss all claims due to improper execution of the contract. The heavy local court docket caused visiting judges to be called to Dayton to try cases, and a judge from Steubenville was appointed to this case, thus removing one of the advantages the owners sought (while removing possible uncomfortable circumstances for local judges). Ten months after completion of the project, the case went to trial. Both sides produced expert witnesses, who were first deposed in attorneys' offices during discovery, and later testified in the trial (Figure 7-3). The architect and his witnesses maintained that the quality of the project was "at a market level" for projects such as this, with the argument reinforced by the renting of all units soon after completion. The owners and their witnesses argued that the interior finishes, particularly drywall, were inferior, and that the late completion had deprived her of a place to live and of rental income.

The most persuasive evidence was photo slides shown by the architect of the original state of the building (slides made from the black-and-white prints shot to record predesign information) and then slides in color of the finished building. The comparisons were dramatic, and the owners protested the use of this evidence. The judge opined that it was a legitimate substitute for a site visit, and the owners had to admit under examination that the photos were "generally accurate." The agreement for CM services contained no liquidated damages, and there was no specific language on quality, except standard language in A201, included by reference, which essentially made the architect the determiner of quality standards.

The case concluded after two days of testimony. The flamboyant lawyer did not particularly impress the out-of-town judge (in fact, the lawyer was relatively poorly prepared, this not being his highest-priority case). The architect's lawyer, about the same age as the judge, handled himself with aplomb, collegiality, and confidence; with the extensive help of the architect, he was quite well prepared. Following the trial, briefs were filed within 30 days, with considerable input from the architect, and 30 days after that, the judge announced the verdict of the finding for the plaintiff (the architect) in full, and awarded the $33,000. Of course, the defendants appealed, primarily as a stalling action—which could take another year. The parties sought a settlement, which concluded with the owners paying $27,000 (the interest and certain other claimed items were deleted).

The legal fees for the architect amounted to $9750, which were somewhat "friendly" based on his past relationship with the lawyer plus his own hard work helping to prepare the case and his persuasive evidence. The net result was indeed a "true loser." The architect computed his net loss on this project to be $28,000 when he included actual cash losses, unpaid time, and lost work on other projects. Nonetheless, with family support and forebearance, he was able to get back on track and resume his practice. The case had no ongoing fallout. Anyone familiar with the situation knew that he had won in court, and experienced architects know the vagaries of the profession and the pitfalls one can encounter. In fact, he gained the admiration of several fellow designers by persevering both in completing the project and then in winning in court, without compromising his professional ethics—and in particular by beating a local judge at his own game. He still had misgivings about some of the issues, but accepted the learning value and moved on. Ten years later he was elected president of the Dayton Chapter of the American Institute of Architects.

Amplification of Issues to Enhance Understanding of This Case

Architectural practice has inherent risks, many self-imposed. As a service profession, it is easy to extend valuable services to clients less ethical than the architect. Also, architects tend to overcommit—that is, to take on more work than they can effectively complete—with the rationale that this situation is better than having too little work. Sole proprietors in particular suffer from the "romance of architecture" and the engagement of marginal projects. And life is full of lessons to learn from. A salient skill is continually learning to learn.

Discussion Questions

○ How can architects gain better commitments from clients?
○ What are the pros and cons of architects acting as construction managers?

Assignment

Thoroughly review the case and cite the key decision points and whether the architect made the right decision each time. Draw a graph (like a decision tree) showing actual outcomes and possible outcomes if different decisions had been made. Place yourself in the architect's position and state what you would have done at each crucial point along the way. Sources to consider:

○ AIA A201
○ AIA A101/CM
○ Codes of ethics of professional behavior
○ Rules of evidence in civil cases in your state
○ Interview with an architect to seek advice on how to avoid such problems or to work through them
○ Interview with an attorney about legal procedures pertaining to filing suits

A debate may be set up with one team taking the role of the architect and the other team that of the owner. Each team should list the strengths and weaknesses of its side of the case and then argue for an appropriate outcome of the dispute.

Extra Issue

Investigate the advisability of hiring students or others "off the street" for construction labor. What are the liability issues? Are they independent contractors? What do your state laws say about independent contractors?

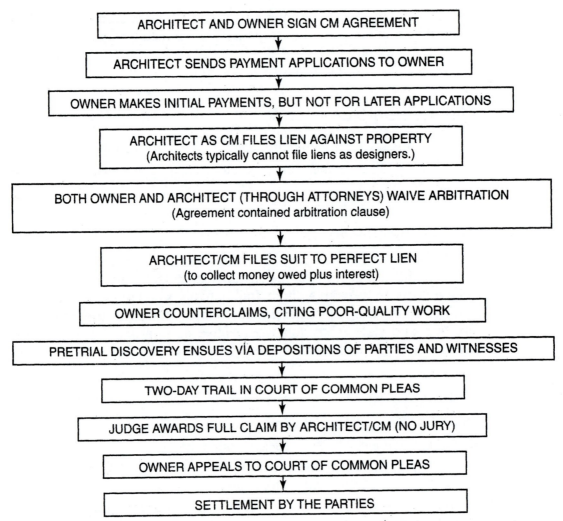

Figure 7-3   Steps leading to dispute between architect and owner, and to the resolution of that dispute.

Case Study 7-5   The Family Comfort Nursing Home

Project:	The Family Comfort Nursing Home, senior care center
Location:	Upper midwestern United States
Budget:	$2.85 million
Issue:	Claims, counterclaims, and arbitration

The growing need for good-quality care for senior citizens in the upper Midwest caused a successful homebuilder and a co-investor to consider developing a nursing home in their hometown community. They researched the economics and programmatic needs to their satisfaction, obtained necessary financing for 75 percent of the costs from a bank, and then retained an architect who had designed several large residences for the builder's clients. Both the architect and builder liked stucco exteriors. They had used both portland cement stucco and the newer polymerized synthetic stuccos (exterior insulation finish systems, [EIFS]) on a number of homes and found that the former, while more expensive, held up better over time. The builder had employed a father-and-son specialty contractor to place the portland cement stucco on his houses, with generally good results. Close inspection would show some hairline cracks and other imperfections, but by controlling panel size and breaking up the surface with masonry and wood members, the stucco was quite acceptable. Portland cement stucco would be the main exterior material on the Family Comfort Nursing Home.

The architect produced a pleasing design for the two-story, 80-bed facility. It combined residential characteristics with an institutional function. This was by far the largest project ever attempted by either the architect or the homebuilder, and they went about the project much as they would a large house, except for the more demanding code issues. The builder had requested, and paid for, only minimal drawings from the architect, enough for necessary permits, pricing, and obtaining subcontracts. He retained only a very small directly hired crew, so 95 percent of the project was subcontracted out, primarily to small specialty contractors who ordinarily performed in residential work. The structure was wood frame with fire-rated plasterboard-protected interiors, primarily stucco exteriors, and several fire separations as required by code.

Construction got underway in good order, with grading, excavation, and foundations placed on schedule. The framing subcontractor began the work with enthusiasm and made good progress during the first five weeks. Then he assigned three workers to frame two houses for another builder, and the nursing home fell behind schedule. The nursing home builder came to the job and challenged the framing contractor's decision. A major shouting match developed that nearly led to a fistfight. Not much productivity occurred that day. The situation deteriorated further, and the framing contractor finally sent his workers off the project, demanding immediate payment for work to date.

The builder, of course, did not make any payment to the framer, claiming breach of contract by that subcontractor, who called his attorney for advice. The advice was to document the framing activity as fully as possible and then to send a claim and to place a lien on the property. Such was carried out by the framer and his lawyer.

The builder directly hired three young carpenters as independent contractors and supervised their completion of the framing, which culminated two months behind schedule. The stucco work had begun over the partially completed structure while the remainder of the framing was being completed. The process included:

○ An asphaltic felt membrane over the particleboard sheathing, properly lapped and fastened to retard moisture penetration
○ Ribbed expanded metal lath over the felt
○ Three-layer application of stucco
   1. Scratch coat
   2. Brown coat
   3. Finish coat with beige tinting

○ Metal corner beads and divider strips to separate the stucco into panels with a maximum size of 100 square feet

The father-and-son stucco subcontractors took on two helpers to try to stay on schedule. However, the helpers were neither skilled nor highly motivated, and the whole operation also fell behind schedule.

The builder became particularly fretful since he had promised the co-investor and families of potential patients that the facility would be ready by December 1. Since both framing and stucco were obviously on the critical path, several other trades were delayed. To allow interior work to continue, the asphaltic felt wall membrane was placed all around the building as soon as framing and sheathing were completed.

By mid-November the stucco was only 60 percent completed; progress was slowed because of the loss of the two helpers, and suddenly cold nights were inhibiting the amount of material that could be safely placed. If stucco freezes, it must be completely replaced. By December 1, the project was not nearly completed, and the stucco work stopped. The senior member of the team refused to risk poor workmanship. The builder hired a semiretired plasterer and one of the erstwhile stucco helpers to continue the work, using tarpaulins to cover fresh stucco every evening.

Because they had not been fully paid, the original stucco team filed a claim and a lien. Several other subcontractors did likewise as the job administration continued to deteriorate. By January all exterior work stopped, and interior finishes moved ahead slowly. Stucco work resumed in April, with yet another subcontractor. Much of the work placed in December was replaced due to unacceptable surface textures and cracking. In fact, there was abundant cracking in the stucco overall, with the seriousness increasing toward the later applications. The worst failures were replaced, and the entire project was completed on May 15. By this time there were seven claims against the builder, and liens against the property for a total of $312,562. The co-investor and bank were holding back money because of the delay and quality questions, and the bad publicity impinged on the marketing of the facilities.

The builder filed counterclaims against all claimants, while he desperately sought loans to equip the facility and get it into operation. He had already invested over half a million dollars of his own money in the project. He retained a claims specialist to aid in developing a case and to assist his lawyer. His lawyer, and lawyers for the various claimants, negotiated settlements in all the cases except for the stucco. The father and son took pride in their work and wished to prove to all interested parties that their product was not at fault. They cited several issues:

○ The framing work was inferior, and its excessive movement caused much of the cracking. This was particularly the case with the later work framed by the independent contractors under the guidance of the builder.

○ The persistent driving of the builder for higher productivity and longer hours caused a decline in quality—and safety—and thus causing concern for well-being as well as performance.

○ The work performed by replacement stucco subcontractors was the worst of all, and the builder was using it as one of the reasons for refusal to pay for their work.

The builder's claim agent hired a stucco expert to produce a report stating that the stucco work was faulty. The stucco subcontractor and his lawyer retained a local architect to state that the work done by the father-and-son team was adequate, "at marketplace standards, but that the work done by others, particularly framers, was below standards." The architect who designed the project carefully remained neutral. He had only a two-page agreement with the builder, which included no contract administration. The specifications were minimal, and there were no details of the actual stucco application.

The lawyers for the opposing parties persuaded them to use arbitration rather than litigation, which would cause at least a year's delay. They further decided to use their own form of arbitration rather than the construction industry rules of the American Arbitration Association, in order to speed up proceedings. The stucco claim was for $79,252, including unpaid work, extra effort required to file the claim, and so on, plus interest on the original amount of money. The builder had filed an updated counterclaim for $85,000 to repair and coat the stucco. The three-member panel for arbitration included a retired architect, an attorney, and a professor of construction management from a nearby university. The panel took a thorough tour of the project and then were prepared for testimony, all to be done in one day. The opposing lawyers were well prepared and presented testimony from the parties and witnesses. By mid-afternoon it was clear that the case would go to the second day. The presentations of evidence were concluded at noon on day 2, and the panel went into executive session. Within three hours they reached consensus on the following points:

- ○ The homebuilder had overextended himself by taking on a project much beyond his usual scope of work without broadening his management team.
- ○ The framing of the building was barely adequate. Some misalignments and poor detailing were identified during the site visit and through testimony.
- ○ The builder had misled some subcontractors in regard to expectations and payment.
- ○ Subcontracts were minimal, with little language regarding quality and no language about dispute resolution.
- ○ The quality of stucco was adequate at the beginning of the project and then gradually deteriorated. None of it was considered to be superior work.
- ○ Cracking in the stucco occurred throughout the project, with increasing intensity toward the last work done. Some sort of repair work would be necessary for intermediate-term durability.

Amplification of Issues to Enhance Understanding of This Case

Frequent problems result when parties who are competent in one area of construction take on projects with which they are less familiar. Several business failures could result in such a case.

Arbitration is provided by practitioners with minimal compensation. It is considered to be an extraordinary service to the professions—as a valid alternative to litigation. Once having distinct cost and time advantages over litigation, arbitration now takes nearly as long and costs nearly as much as going to court. All parties are searching for ways to resolve disputes more quickly under *alternative dispute resolution,* or *ADR.* The best method, of course, is adequate preparation to avoid disputes. Next, negotiation is preferred. Then, third-party mediation or a neutral review panel may be attempted. Review other sources for more extensive discussions of ADR.

Discussion Questions

○ What is the balance between entrepreneurial zeal and blind risk-taking?
○ Is arbitration the best way to resolve this case? What are valid alternatives?
○ Would a phased construction/move-in schedule have produced a better project?

Assignment

Place yourselves in the positions of the arbitration panel and move to a consensus. Consider the evidence presented and the points just made. Together agree on additional assumptions, and then render a decision including a dollar amount, time frame for payment, any additional responsibilities of any parties, and a rationale for the decision. Possible resources include:

○ Books, manuals, and producers' literature on stucco
○ Discussions with a builder who engages buildings such as nursing homes
○ Arbitration procedures other than those of the American Arbitration Association

C H A P T E R   8

Government Regulations

"Design and construction function as regulated capitalism."

The cases in this chapter exhibit the role of government in the design and construction arena, and show how adroit practitioners must deal with the rules and officials who can aid the process or set up serious roadblocks. The construction marketplace is essentially *regulated capitalism*. The concept of government having police power to protect the health and safety of citizens is well established in jurisprudence. While debate ensues about the appropriate level of regulation, the fact is that abundant rules are already in place, and they must either be obeyed or be challenged in the courts. In this regard, wise business practices may conflict with ideology. In the case studies that follow, readers may decide which has priority in each case—seeking the most practical business solution or standing by one's principles—if the two conflict.

Case 8-1   Township Zoning

Project:	Community unit plan for condominiums
Location:	Suburb to a midwestern city
Budget:	$14.8 million (for land, design, and construction)
Issue:	Zone change

Townships adjacent to large cities are the most rapidly developing areas in the Midwest. Established as government units in the early history of the United States, and modeled on the medieval notion of rural land administration used in England, townships were impressed on the Northwest Territory in 1789 in 36-square-mile grids across what would become five states of the Union. Cities and towns were chartered, and township borders changed over time. Townships remain unincorporated (not chartered), and thus many of the local powers are sparser than those adopted by incorporated municipalities. Following World War II, a massive housing market pushed beyond city limits, and development came to surrounding townships before adequate preparation for such expansion could occur. Roadways, schools, utilities, and storm-water management were all inadequate, and an ongoing race to try to install government services to catch up with development played out over the next 50 years.

Although zoning, as a mechanism of land use planning and control, was established and judicially supported early in the 20th century—as within the police power of government, in the interests of health and safety—most suburban and rural areas had no zoning by 1950. People who moved to the green-belt "Nirvanas" to enjoy their single-family homes on large lots were shocked when a strip shopping center or apartment building was built across the street. Demands for better planning and controls led to actions by county or township governments to create zoning resolutions and then to submit those resolutions to the citizens for referenda votes, an ideal example of grassroots democracy. Most areas close to cities adopted zoning; some did not. Once zoning was adopted in an area, development patterns did not immediately change. The attractiveness of inexpensive open land still brought development, and many zoning codes adopted land use patterns similar to ones already unfolding in an area. Nonetheless, there were frequent cases of where a property owner, developer, contractor, or architect thought that the new zoning regulations restricted logical development, and a zone change would be sought—technically a legal process to amend the zoning resolution and accompanying map. Zone change cases are classic illustrations of conflicts in local democracy—the individual rights to develop one's property versus community-adopted land use regulations. The proceedings are usually cast as individual constitutional rights versus the demands of the citizenry, who are typically opposed to proposals for commercial development, apartments, or smaller lots than allowed, based on the perceived protection of their property values and rights to enjoy the community that they had moved into—"our rights versus their rights."

Zoning regulations are indeed elastic, but carefully drawn procedures must be followed for changes to take place. Submittals, public notices, hearings, recommendations, and public decisions are all part of the process. Whereas most applications for change come from private parties, sometimes government itself proposes changes (following the same rules that private applicants must follow). With experience in land use and administration and learning from new ideas that succeed in other parts of the country, local officials tinker with their own resolutions. Thus unit developments (PUDs) and community unit plans (CUPs) came into being planned as ways to allow integration of different usages on plots of ground, rather than only one use, such as single-family houses, apartments, or retail—various uses could be mixed together into a "planned community." The actual zoning process is shown in Figure 8–1.

The case at hand involves a proposal for a CUP for condominiums consisting of attached units, detached single-family units, and a central clubhouse and recreation area, all on smaller land parcels than allowed by the zoning resolution, but the overall intensity of which is equal to that allowed in this zoning district. As a result of the clustering, ten acres of green space is planned, with deed restrictions precluding its ever being developed. The application was technically filed by the absentee property owner but, in fact, the process was initiated and managed by a developer/building contractor who had purchased an option on the property. A planning and architectural firm with a strong track record of functional and aesthetic design of such developments was commissioned to produce the necessary visual documents for the development, and a land use attorney prepared legally required instruments. A series of requisite filings, mailings to adjacent property owners, and project descriptions led to a formal meeting with the county planning commission, which was the first step in the process. Though it was

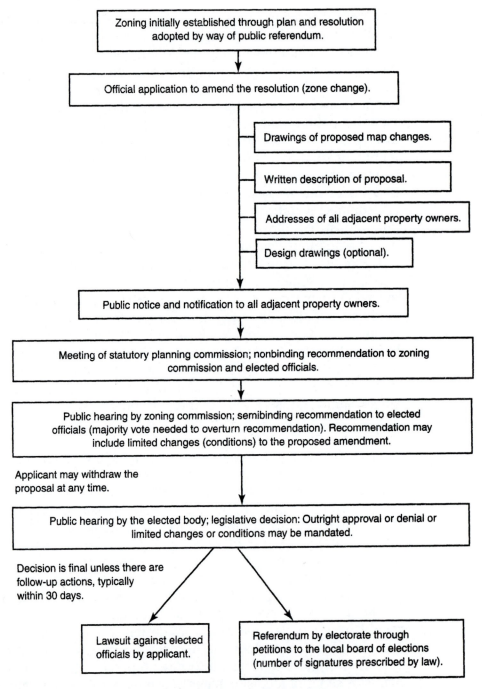

Figure 8-1   The zone change process as described in Case 8-1.

not a hearing per se, several interested citizens attended to become informed. They questioned size and pricing of units, traffic generation, effects on services, encroachment on their privacy, and a change in the character of the community. The proponents were experienced professionals and portrayed their project in the best possible light. They also agreed to meet interested citizens in their neighborhood—not a required meeting, but a tactical ploy. The meeting was arranged, and over a hundred people attended a spirited gathering. Commentary ranged from general support to invective about bringing low-income people to the neighborhood and schools. Results of the meeting were "definitely mixed."

The county planning commission approved the proposal at a subsequent meeting, but the decision was not binding on the township zoning commission or on the elected officials, a three-person board of trustees. The hearing before the township zoning commission, a five-person body appointed by the trustees, was so crowded that fire laws were violated; the meeting was postponed for a week and then held in a school auditorium. Neighbors in the subdivisions bordering the proposed development had met subsequent to the developers' neighborhood meeting and, after ample discussion, determined that it was in their overall best interest to oppose the project. They retained an attorney and came well prepared for the zoning commission hearing. The formal proposal by the developer's attorney and designers emphasized the following points:

○ Because the site had not yet been developed as a standard subdivision, as had most of the surroundings, it obviously was best suited to alternative uses.

○ The owner, a long-time resident in the township (but not now living on the property), has the traditional American right to realize gain from his property, as had so many nearby owners previously.

○ The plan will provide an appropriate mix of dwellings, allowing a range of citizens to live happily in the community, including many senior citizens who will pay taxes but have no children in school.

○ Senior citizens currently living in the township in single-family homes will have an added option for remaining in the area.

○ The attached housing will be placed away from existing single-family subdivisions, and the new single-family houses will be proximate to existing single-family houses in adjacent subdivisions.

○ Ten acres of green space will help buffer the old and new developments, and will be a community asset in a rapidly expanding area.

○ The design is superior to most existing development in the township, with amenities such as walkways, bikeways, a clubhouse, and abundant landscaping—plus buildings designed by award-winning architects.

The opposition, carefully prepared by their attorney, countered:

○ This township has traditionally been a single-family area with houses on large lots, and this style is healthy for family living and should not be violated.

○ The project is a potential precedent setter. Several other similar tracts of land in the township could easily follow in this development pattern.

○ If developed as a single-family subdivision, there would be fewer units than proposed because of topographical constraints—thus the proposal is actually for an increase in density.

○ Traffic problems will be exacerbated more than they would be by single-family houses.

○ There is inadequate planning for storm-water management. While a drainage detention basin is shown, it is deemed to be in the wrong place and not large enough.

○ The ten acres of green space is sited on irregular land that is not likely to be developed anyway.

○ There is a potential for increased enrollment in schools without con-comitant tax generation.

Some citizens spoke in favor of the development, stating that:

○ There are too few units available in the township for senior citizens who no longer can afford their homes or who do not wish to keep them, and who face the prospect of being forced to move from the community.

○ The township should be progressive and allow alternatives to "mun-dane subdivisions."

There were some responses like "not in my backyard" (NIMBY) and "put it your neighborhood if you like it so much." The skilled and experi-enced zoning commission chair, an architect herself, managed the meeting well and limited the hostilities. The meeting closed with the two attorneys giving summary statements and the zoning commission taking the issue under advisement for a decision within 20 days, as required by state law. The decision would be a recommendation to the elected board of trustees, who would then have their own hearing.

Amplification of Issues to Enhance Understanding of This Case

On paper, the zone change procedures are logical, deliberate, and well defined (the process typically takes six months). Ample opportunity exists for all interested parties to be heard. The legislative decision—to amend the existing resolution and map—rests with elected officials directly responsible to the citizenry. All deliberations and decisions must be made in public, as required by "sunshine laws" in most states. It seems a well-crafted, almost ideal democratic process. But any political process brings the nonprocedural into the picture. Lobbying of public officials, behind-the-scenes maneuvers, threats, intimidation—and sometimes even illegal payoffs—have occurred. Obviously, all citizens should insist that laws be strictly followed, but most people are preoccupied with their day-to-day activities and do not pay much attention to government, sometimes to their regret.

Applicants focus their resources on the case at hand, and, in response, usually only those citizens directly affected provide resistance—and those folks are as capable of distorting positions and motivations as readily as are developers. Elected officials depend heavily on recommendations from their appointed boards and commissions for sound advice, and as a defense for decisions that may prove unpopular. In truth, the elected officials are frequently caught in the difficult position of satisfying a segment of their constituents versus satisfying a major campaign contributor who happens to be seeking a zone change. "Money is the mother's milk of politics," said Jesse Unruh, long-time California legislator.

Further, both sides have recourse following the elected officials' decision. Applicants can sue the officials based on procedural errors or for denial of basic property rights. Citizens can overturn decisions through legal action or via petitions for referendum—that is, by placing the issue on a ballot in a local election—where usually the electorate, whether informed or not, selects the status quo.

Discussion Questions

○ What should the designers do during this entire process—besides preparing the best possible documents?

○ Should designers expect to be paid whether or not the zone change is successful?

○ Is the referendum process valid, or should elected officials not be second guessed by the electorate?

Assignment

Place yourself in the role of a zoning commissioner or five-person teams representing the entire commission. Draft a recommendation to the trustees. Options include:

O Approval with no recommended changes in the plan
O Approval with recommended changes, such as
   1. Improved landscaping and buffers
   2. Fewer units
   3. Enlarged green space
   4. Improved storm-water management
   5. Reconfiguration of elements (but the commission is limited by law in the degree of redesign)
O Denial

The elected trustees anticipate a written rationale to help guide them in their decision, which will be binding unless either party follows with legal action, or the citizens pursue a referendum to overturn a decision not to their liking. The trustees will have their own hearing and wish to be well prepared for arguments to be made. Issues to consider:

O Overall benefits or detriments to the community, including:
   1. Impact on health and safety
   2. Compatibility with the established land use patterns
   3. Compatibility with the official land use plan, a strategic document that shows the subject site as being single-family residential but has text allowing clustering of units
   4. Impact on services, including schools
   5. Precedent
   6. Economic impact on the total community
O Status of the township: 35,000 people on 30 square miles, of which 23 square miles are developed in a mixture of residential, light commercial, and institutional:
   1. Single-family zoning = 85 percent of total area
   2. Existing attached units = 1600 condominiums and apartments
   3. Several assisted care facilities and nursing homes
   4. No industry or industrial zoning
   5. The remaining undeveloped land is mostly wooded, ranging from moderately to extremely irregular in topography
   6. A few farms, primarily in a floodplain

○ Politically/economically the citizenry (which, of course, elects the board of trustees) is generally conservative, with priorities of:
1. Home ownership
2. Education; half of the households have at least one college graduate
3. "Family values" (subject to various interpretations)
4. Minimal government intrusion
5. Expectancy of good service delivery

○ The township provides basic services of:
1. Government unit of three elected trustees, elected clerk, and appointed administrative support staff
2. Police
3. Fire and rescue
4. Road maintenance
5. Zoning control
6. Parks and recreation
7. (Education is under a separate board of education)

All members of the zoning commission live in this community and were selected on the theory that they represent the interests of their fellow citizens (while also belonging to the majority political party).

Case 8-2   The Urban Design Review Board

Project:	Proposed insurance company tower
Location:	West Coast United States
Budget:	$70 million (for construction)
Issue:	Urban Design Review Board

For the past 20 years, the mid-size West Coast city has had a special board, appointed by the mayor, to review, comment on, and guide urban development in the central business district (CBD) and adjacent transitional areas. In totally private work, the Urban Design Review Board (UDRB) has limited powers, including:

○ Planning and design advice relative to the overall CBD plan
○ Recommendations to the owner and designers regarding the contextual "fit" of a proposed project relative to surrounding conditions

○ Guidance on integration of the proposed project with any adjacent city-funded projects such as street or sidewalk improvements, land-scaping, and so on

○ Suggestions regarding aesthetics

Private owners may or may not accept this input. They have no legal mandate to do so, as long as they follow all codes and engineering requirements for street access and utilities. Most owners, however, do cooperate with the UDRB unless there are obvious disadvantages in doing so, such as added costs, delays, or radical changes.

However, in public projects or in public-private projects—that is, those that have some level of public assistance—the board has substantial authority. Besides having the preceding functions, which can become mandatory, the board may:

○ Require certain exterior building materials

○ Require setbacks greater than those stipulated by zoning

○ Preclude casting shadows on adjacent buildings or property

○ "Highly recommend" such items as entrance treatment, detailing, cornice alignment, and colors

The board is composed of three architects (two of whom are also academicians), a real estate broker, and a member of the city council. While they have wide-ranging authority and sometimes exercise it in arcane ways (particularly in the eyes of project designers), they are not ordinarily "second guessed" by other public officials. The board's decisions are, however, legally subject to review and possible alteration or overturning by the city council, upon petition by a building owner (Figure 8–2).

The case at hand involves an insurance company based in the city, which plans to build a new headquarters building with a $70 million budget on a prominent half-block in the city. The insurance company owns most of the subject property. An edge parcel makes up 20 percent of the total proposed site, and it is owned by the city. There are advocates in city government and in the general citizenry for making that parcel a small feature park on an important corner. Campaign promises were made regarding such a park in the most recent election. The insurance company proposes incorporating a parklike segment within the total property, more inboard to the total site—essentially designing the building around a park. The company has directed its design firm to study various concepts in preschematic form. While early negotiations about possible transfer of the city's property are proceeding, company executives and their architects meet with the UDRB. Three possible approaches are presented:

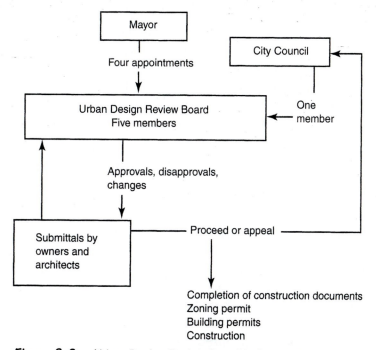

Figure 8-2 Urban Design Review Board in Case 8-2. The mayor makes all appointments except one council member elected by council to the board. All proposed projects in a defined urban core are submitted for review. Public projects or publicly assisted projects must accept recommendations of the board or seek appeal to council. Approved projects then proceed through the remaining normal process of zoning review and permit, code review and permits, and construction. Both zoning and building regulations are considered by the review board, but authority still rests with statutory bodies controlling each.

1. A rather traditional eclectic building (with elements of postmodernism and art deco) in a "U" shape, covering the entire site (including city property) with a formal parklike forecourt open to the street—and thus to the public.

2. Also covering the entire site, a mostly glass-enclosed building, with various hues of glass and stone, and a large garden that is partially indoors in a winter garden and partially outdoors as a public space. The winter garden would be open to the public during certain hours.

3. An extraordinarily tall building (with strong vertical lines), the configuration of which allows half the site to be open space, to be landscaped through both private and public funds, the latter to justify the development of prime open space in the CBD—and to address political exigencies.

The UDRB is nearly overwhelmed by the presentation, which is made by the insurance company's chief operating officer, a cultured, prominent local figure; the design firm's chief architect, a polished spokesman; and a landscape architect, a particularly articulate woman. Rarely has the board had such an opportunity—with three possibilities— and a private project owner willing to positively engage their involvement at such an early point in development of a key project. Typically, presentations to the board are by developers who have very specific ideas expressed in one well-developed scheme, and who are resistant to significant changes.

However, the surfeit of riches did not lead to the most admirable response on the part of the UDRB. Each architect on the board liked a different proposal and openly debated its respective merits in terminology not readily understood by the other two board members. The real estate broker talked about land values, highest and best use, and impact on surrounding property. He had a preference for the tall scheme with the largest park because he thought that it would enhance surrounding values. The member of council was noncommittal: The insurance company COO had contributed generously to his last two campaigns, and the councilman was searching for that executive's preference. The meeting ended with no decision and no clear direction on which to proceed. The advice to the presenters was to further develop all schemes, providing enough additional information to allow the board to more readily render a decision. The dilemma of the proponents was as follows:

❍ The use of the entire half-block was quite appealing, and they wished to reach accord with city council on acquiring the edge piece.

❍ It had become clear that dealing with the UDRB was problematic:
   1. Longer time would be spent in schematics.
   2. A divided board could further delay a decision.
   3. A potential dispute could develop if the owner preferred one scheme and the board another.

❍ The insurance company executives were sufficiently politically adroit to know that the city council favored having this hometown company develop this prominent "foreground" site, rather than possibly having its development go to an unknown party—a prospect if the insurance company became frustrated and sold the property. But they also knew that neither the council nor the mayor would openly pursue actions until a recommendation was forthcoming from the UDRB (despite some behind-the-scenes maneuvering).

○ The insurance company could greatly simplify its approach by dropping the city-owned parcel from its planning and proceeding to design for their already-owned, reduced site. A review would still be required by the UDRB, but outcomes would be nonbinding.

The owner retained an experienced construction company on an agency CM contract to begin making cost studies (the designers had done preliminary projections), schedules, and value engineering/constructability reviews of the various alternatives. A meeting has been called for next week by the COO, to include one other company executive, two design team members, the landscape architect, and two construction team members. The one agenda item is to determine whether to proceed with or without the city's property.

Amplification of Issues to Enhance Understanding of This Case

Historically, governments have had difficulty regulating aesthetics; art is too resistant to legal definition. However, in attempts to bring some order and harmony to urban development, many cities have established design review boards—with mixed success. The whole process remains controversial. Free-market advocates rail against such processes as being stifling; leading architects do not like to have their designs second guessed (and they frequently endeavor to "outpersuade" the review boards); owners complain that it usually adds costs; and some urban critics cite the dullness of controlled development as contrasted to the vitality of mixed design. The opposite arguments should be clear—one role of government is to bring order to society.

Discussion Questions

○ Debate the efficacy of design review boards—do they aid or inhibit good design?
○ What is the ideal makeup of such boards? Should they be dominated by architects? Should engineers, contractors, or others be included?
○ Would you like to serve on such a board? Why or why not?

Assignment

To solve the case study, seven roles should be assumed:

○ Insurance company chief operating officer
○ Insurance company chief of facilities

○ Principal architect of the design firm
○ Lead designer of the firm
○ Landscape architect
○ President of the construction company
○ Project executive of the construction company assigned to this proposal

Simulate the meeting, chaired by the COO, and review the various aspects of the three proposals already presented to the UDRB, plus adapting one or more of them to the reduced site. Include all the issues identified to date plus other assumptions that are plausible. The meeting ends when a firm recommendation is made to the insurance company board of directors, with a rationale for the recommendation.

Information that may be developed to aid the decision:

○ A drawing of a site plan showing private and public spaces, including streets (assume a 225 foot by 450 foot half-block, with 20 percent of it being the city-owned parcel)
○ Sketches of the three schemes presented to the UDRB
○ Sketches of one or more schemes on the reduced site
○ Approximate costs of each scheme, on a comparative basis, keeping in mind that the budget is $70 million
○ A list of issues that should be considered:
  1. The four prime success criteria of any project: time, cost, quality, and safety
  2. The prospect of something other than a park going on the city property, if it does not, in fact, become part of the building site (It is not "locked-in" yet as a park, and governments have been known to do the unanticipated, such as sell the property for revenue.)
  3. Architectural impact
  4. Political issues
  5. Other points that you may regard as germane

Possible additional learning resources include:

○ Attendance at a hearing of a design review board if one exists in your area
○ Guest discussion by a person knowledgeable in such proceedings:
  1. A member of a review board
  2. An elected official
  3. An architect or owner who has dealt with the process
○ Review of an ordinance authorizing a design review process

As an optional exercise, other people may represent the UDRB and review the selected proposal.

Case 8-3   The Building Code Appeal

Project:	Hoffman Middle School remodeling
Location:	Western Pennsylvania
Budget:	$52,500
Issue:	Building code appeal

The school district was upgrading a number of old schools for general-improvement purposes and to modernize them in regard to advancing technologies. One problem encountered among many was compliance with current building codes. The stance of the city building department was to allow moderate degrees of noncompliance until major rehabilitation was planned. As with all legislation, there is an appeal process for extremely difficult cases, or "hardships," which typically occur in remodeling projects. The appeal processes are aimed at providing conditions that protect the health and safety of building users, while not necessarily complying with the full "letter of the law."

One school building for which an appeal was filed was the Hoffman Middle School, a 1925 building built into a hillside. The lower-level rooms received daylight on the downhill front side, but rear rooms were buried in the uphill side. Those rooms had historically been used for utilities and storage. The modernization plan called for them to be converted to computer suites. The rooms were quite dry, a huge old boiler had been removed, and accumulated junk was discarded. The high ceiling spaces allowed air-conditioning ducts, and the rooms were to be equipped with up-to-date artificial illumination. The code in current effect calls for all classrooms to be naturally illuminated, but officials previously accepted appeals for alternative lighting, so this was of little concern. The major issue was means of egress. The two rooms have only one means of escape, through a level corridor to the main entrance podium, which is two feet above sidewalk level, with steps down to grade plus a wheelchair access ramp added five years earlier. The egress path is across a wood floor built above a crawl space. Also, that egress goes past clear (no wire) glass windows into administrative offices just inside the main entrance. The code requires:

○ Two paths of egress from all classrooms

○ Fully fire-protected passageways to exits (fire ratings of one and a half hours on all dividing elements: floors, wall, ceiling, doors, and openings)

○ A flame spread rating of less than 30 for all materials in the passageway

○ No glass larger than 100 square inches in any doors or walls

The project architect conferred with the city's building department plan examiner to discuss various options. It appeared that all the issues could be resolved by upgrading materials, except for the required second egress. The front rooms were sufficiently close to ground level that the large windows could be considered an additional means of egress. The rear rooms had no windows. The plan examiner was sympathetic with the problem and had had good professional relations with the architect. Nonetheless, policies and procedures must be followed. The plan examiner explained the appeal process as follows:

○ Owner or architect applies for a building permit.

○ Plan examiner officially rejects the application with citations of non-compliance with particular sections of applicable codes.

○ Owner or architect files appeal with the Building Code Board of Appeals, a group of knowledgeable citizens (including architects and engineers) appointed by the legislative body responsible for the code.

○ Hearing is held before the board at which various interested parties may testify.

○ Finding is announced by the board within 30 days (in actuality usually sooner; sometimes immediately following the hearing).

The entire process typically took two months. Time was an issue, since the improvements needed to be completed prior to the next school year. The architect was faced with several options:

○ Pursue the appeal process and try to expedite the cycle, by
   1. Accelerating the completion of contract documents and applying for the permit, knowing that such "hurry-up" may lead to omissions having other code implications.
   2. Request priority treatment by the plan examiner. This was not un-usual, but such requests are granted typically only under truly crit-ical circumstances.
   3. Prepare such a persuasive case that the Board of Building Code Appeals grants a quick positive finding at the hearing.

○ Change the design to allow adequate egress.
   1. The addition of sprinklers would enhance the safety of the situa-tion but would not specifically meet code requirements. Sprinklers relieve egress distance requirements and surface restrictions, but

not the need for two means of egress. However, sprinklers would certainly help in the appeals process.

2. Add a corridor to a side of the building by reducing the size of one of the front rooms: one an administrative space and the other a classroom. Both spaces are barely large enough now.

Amplification of Issues to Enhance Understanding of This Case

All professionals in private practice and in public service (most building officials are architects or engineers) desire safe buildings—both as a moral issue and for liability purposes (injury due to a building code violation is a very serious issue). Bringing older buildings "up to code" is frequently a problem, and an ever-increasing segment of design practice is rehabilitation and additions to existing buildings. Appeals boards are usually made up of persons experienced in code writing and implementation, such as architects, engineers, and contractors. Appeals are not unusual, and all parties try to find solutions that will allow improvements to be made to buildings while ensuring the highest probability of health and safety of the occupants (Figure 8-3).

Codes have become sufficiently complex that another specialty niche has been created—code consultants, who are frequently retained by architects on very difficult projects just to work out the compliance issues. Consultants may also prepare the submission and presentation to the appeals board.

Discussion Questions

○ How restrictive should codes be to protect health and safety? Should some remodeling, otherwise beneficial to the occupants, not be allowed because of code issues?

○ Compare the roles of plan examiners and field inspectors—what are their duties and how are they carried out?

Assignment

Develop a decision sequence. Weigh all the issues and make an initial determination of whether it is advisable to pursue an appeal. Develop a rationale, pro or con, for each option. Then make the assumption that an appeal will be sought and prepare a strategy for it. Points of the strategy could include:

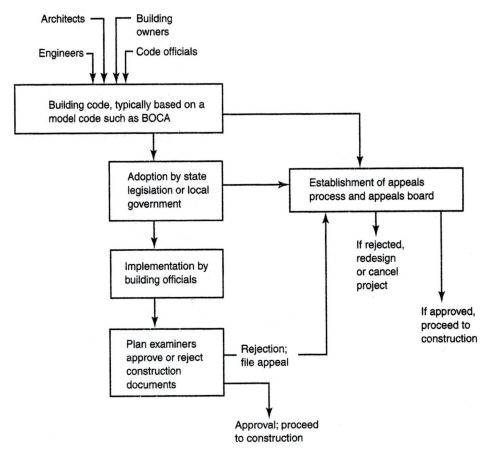

Figure 8-3   Building code establishment and appeals process. Most codes are currently based on model codes, such as those promulgated by the Building Officials and Code Administrators (BOCA). They are adapted to local issues by interested parties (committees of architects, engineers, building owners, and code officials) and then legislated, into official adoption by state or local elected bodies. The appeals process is also legislated, and provides for possible relief from "hardship cases."

○ Use of sprinklers (cited before):
   1. Any fire in the building would be quickly suppressed, thus reducing the hazard and allowing a calm egress. Or, with sprinklers operating, children could be led through the spray—getting an unwelcome bath, but a safe and exciting exit.

○ Upgrading all egress enclosures and materials
○ Providing smoke detectors (probably required by the code anyway)
○ Adapting one of the lower-level classrooms as a flow-through egress (without corridor); determine what changes this would entail

○ Asserting that children in the computer suites will be under regular supervision, and that teachers could quickly lead them to safety

○ Citing regular fire drills

Create a scenario where one team presents the case before the appeals board and another team acts as that board, which questions a number of issues presented and then comes to a decision.

Resources

○ The building code in effect in your area
○ A guest code official
○ A member of the local board of appeals
○ Architects who have dealt with such cases
○ First floor plan—draw it from the information available

Case 8-4   Historic District

Project:	Remodeling of a vacated convent
Location:	Small town near an eastern city
Budget:	$185,000
Issue:	Historic preservation

Ferndale is a self-anointed exclusive town near a large city. It grew up around a commuter rail stop in the late 19th century, when wealthy executives chose the area for their mansions and English-gentry lifestyle. The town incorporated at the turn of the century and included a green belt within its boundaries, which is now a delightful oasis amid urban sprawl. Over time, a variety of housing types intermingled with the mansions, and currently Ferndale is a pleasant middle- to upper-middle-class community of 3000 people. In the 1970s, following national and state enabling legislation, the town council adopted a historic district covering 65 percent of the town's area and including most of the significant buildings. Regulations were written for the area, and strict guidelines were put in place for new construction and remodeling in the district. The inhabitants of the town support the restrictions as important factors in maintaining its character and their property values.

A small Catholic community began a century ago in one section of the town. It was first composed of Irish railroad workers and domestic servants, but three generations later, the congregation completely blends with the rest of the town and has a fine stone church and a grade school. The earlier brick church became a school, and then a convent for teaching nuns. As the nuns retired and moved elsewhere, the building was vacated. The parish council wishes to utilize the building for parish offices and meeting spaces, and the pastor wishes to use the second floor for apartments for retired priests.

An architect has been retained to evaluate the building, perform code research, and draft studies for adapting the building to the desired uses. One scheme works quite well on the interior, and includes a new front entrance vestibule plus secondary egress to the rear. Since both are building additions, they must be reviewed by the town's Planning and Historical Review Commission and receive a certificate of appropriateness prior to proceeding on to zoning or building code review.

At the hearing of the commission, the architect presents schematic drawings, at $\frac{1}{8}$ inch = 1 foot, which he thought to be sensitive to the historic context. The commission immediately criticizes both the added vestibule entrance as being "too contemporary" and the secondary egress as being "too utilitarian." Further comments are that the drawings are too small and not sufficiently detailed for review. The architect, having read the Historic District Regulations, responds that the guidelines set different criteria for backs of buildings or those elements out of view, and there is no mention of scale of presentation drawings. He senses that the commission, all middle-aged or elderly men, does not receive his comments kindly, and he further senses that any argument on his part would be counterproductive.

Having encountered many boards and commissions in his practice, and having served on a planning commission in his own community, the architect believes that this commission is being quite arbitrary. This is further heightened by the chairman's recommendation that he seek assistance from one or both architects on the Planning and Historical Review Commission. He finds this mildly offensive, but saves his comments until after the conclusion of the meeting, at which no action is taken on the convent proposal.

On the sidewalk following the meeting, he discusses the issue with one of the architects, who seems quite hostile regarding the whole submission. Perplexed by this, a few days later he calls on the town manager, who earlier had been helpful in explaining the review process. The manager tactfully explains the "personalities" on the commission, while generally defending their good intentions, and makes suggestions on proceeding. The town manager offers several options:

○ Redesign both additions based on the comments given during the hearing.
○ Send the redesign for review to both architects prior to the hearing and consider their advice.
○ Send the redesign to the less critical architect only.
○ Redesign without review, and take your chances at the next hearing.

The remaining option, of course, would be to try to push the current design through the commission, since the members had not, in fact, rejected it. Discretion seemed the better part of valor, however, and the client (the parish priest) also recommended redesign—not wishing to needlessly alienate the commission.

Amplification of Issues to Enhance Understanding of This Case

As historical preservations become more popular, the scenario described here becomes frequent. Communities do indeed strive to protect their character, and recent legislation and legal cases uphold their right to do so. Citizens are willing—even eager—to serve on the commissions, out of civic duty and interest in participating in government to a limited degree. Architects are almost always in the membership: Some become quite zealous, particularly if they engage historical preservation as part of their practice. Historical preservation is subject to many interpretations, and architects carry differing viewpoints on what is appropriate. So, differences of opinions—even heated discussions—are not unusual.

Discussion Questions

○ Are historic districts a good idea overall? Are they beneficial, or elitist and antidemocratic?
○ Is historic preservation an appealing way to practice design or construction?
○ How would one get into historic preservation as a business?
○ Would you like to serve on a historic preservation commission?

Assignment

Help the architect decide how to proceed. Should he seek review by either or both of the architects on the commission, or should he redesign strictly under the client's and his guidelines? Is there an intermediate position? Issues:

○ Professionalism—What is the appropriate path to seeking a certificate of appropriateness?
○ Being of service to his client
○ Schedule

The assignment may be fulfilled by individual opinions in oral or written descriptions, or by discussions with different people taking different positions.

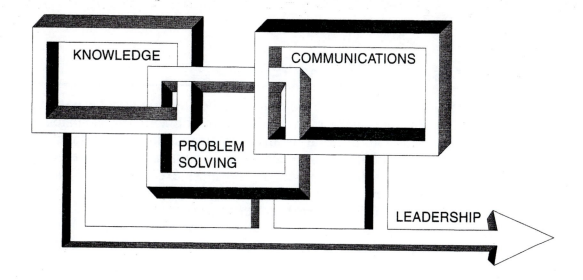

CHAPTER 9

Cases in Leadership

"In a changing society, one attribute continues to be extremely important in design and construction—leadership."

Both design and construction companies—like all enterprises—depend on leadership skills among key personnel. This chapter presents cases that highlight these skills, or the lack of them. Much study has been made of leadership in various settings, and a working definition is described below.

> **Leadership is a combination of traits and skills forming a personality with distinctive characteristics that cause others to trust and follow or collaborate with that leader. Leadership is the ability to cause others to perform at high levels for the good of the overall organization.**

Leadership Characteristics

Discussions of leadership always include the question: What is more important, skills or traits? Or, are leaders born or made? This is analogous to the discussion of what is most influential in our personalities, heredity or environment. The debate will continue for the foreseeable future, with behaviorable scientists, business executives, and military strategists regularly reviewing new findings and looking for information to support their opinions. There have been treatises on what type of political systems produce the best leaders, the main comparisons being between democracies and dictatorships. And the small town versus big city argument has been visited frequently, with the citation that a remarkable number of U.S. presidents, military leaders, and astronauts have come from small places. On the flip side, composers, artists, editors, and other "opinion leaders" tend to grow up in cities.

> **Whether leaders are made or born is an ongoing debate. We have all heard the phrase "a born leader"—but what does it really mean?**

Traits (hereditary aspects of personality) that seem to contribute to leadership are:

○ Basic intelligence
○ Ability to quickly grasp concepts
○ Well-developed senses of vision, hearing, and perception
○ Basic mobility and bodily coordination

Traits that do not seem to be important to leadership are:

○ Physical size
○ Facial features
○ General physical appearance

(Historically, all of these have been of greater importance than they are today.)

The positive traits can all be improved by certain environments and training. The most crucial of these influences seems to be parental guidance and modeling. Studies have shown that early interaction with parents and stimulating exercises (reading, talking, music, physical activity, and introduction of various objects) guided by those parents can enhance intelligence and ability to grasp concepts. Perceptive abilities and coordination can also be improved. So that raises the question of whether learned skills are more important than traits, and the answer is "probably." The model of leadership shown in Figure 9-1 suggests that skills are primary and traits are secondary. Important skills relevant to leadership are:

○ Fundamental honesty; trustworthiness
○ Dependability; punctuality; keeping promises
○ Awareness of duties and responsibilities
○ Vision: the ability to anticipate and direct events
○ Knowing the goals and objectives of an organization and having the ability to articulate them to others
○ Excellent communication skills: written, spoken, and graphic
○ Problem-solving capability, both technical and interpersonal
○ Good decision-making skills, and the ability to employ those decisions as quickly as required

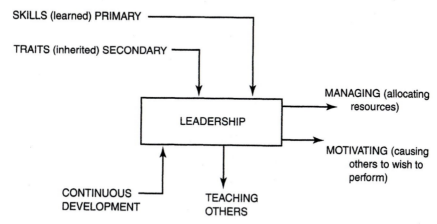

Figure 9-1   A simple model of leadership. It is composed of skills and traits. Almost everyone can learn leadership skills—but to varying degrees. Traits, such as basic intelligence and quick grasping of concepts, influence the ability to learn, and thus are important secondary factors. Leadership demands continuous development, because the world keeps changing. Leading others always involves some degree of teaching. Management is closely related to leadership. Motivation is the most important skill of a leader—causing people to want to perform so that they require little direct supervision.

Attitudes and Behaviors

Leaders are identified by other persons primarily by the behaviors of those leaders. Behaviors are the external manifestations of attitudes, which are defined as beliefs and positions developed within people over time and through education and training. Important attitudes and resultant behaviors expressed by leaders:

○ Accepts responsibilities; does not blame others
○ Accepts directions from superiors, but is willing to question directions that do not seem valid or ethical
○ Offers suggestions to superiors; follows up with supporting information
○ Receives suggestions from subordinates; considers and uses those that help the organization
○ Leads by example; models appropriate performance
○ Handles several issues at one time; can prioritize and pursue them by levels of importance to the organization
○ Understands social psychology and is skilled at applying it to the workplace
○ Urges independence in others; seeks to empower subordinates to make decisions
○ Helps others develop leadership skills
○ Is sensitive to the needs of others, while urging them to seek solutions to problems
○ Delegates responsibilities to others when appropriate
○ Seeks continued improvement through training, learning by experience, and cross-fertilization with others
○ Helps develop self-esteem in others
○ Knows how to build effective teams
○ Is a good teacher
○ Is willing to share credit for accomplishments with subordinates and colleagues
○ Plans ahead to anticipate problems, and has various solutions ready depending on the circumstances at the time
○ Can be authoritative when conditions require; can be democratic when other conditions require
○ Is consistent in temperament, behavior, and treatment of others
○ Possesses a drive to achieve, but also has this drive under control
○ Motivates others to perform for their own good and for the good of the organization

> **With all the expectations, can anyone really be a truly good leader? Yes, but it requires constant development.**

Motivation and Training

The most important aspect of leadership is motivation. A leader must cause others to perform, and ideally to perform through their own desires to do so. True motivation reduces the need for authoritarianism in leadership, reduces the need for supervision, improves productivity, and enhances cohesiveness in the organization. Motivation is built on many of the characteristics listed previously, but most important are trustworthiness, communications, and teaching. Most leaders need training in motivational skills. These skills are not easily achieved, but are extremely valuable once gained.

It can be readily seen that leadership has many facets, but it should also be clear that most of the characteristics are the results of learning rather than inborn traits. While indeed there are hereditary aspects in all human behavior, a basic premise in a democratic, performance-oriented society is that the majority of people can become leaders—at some level. Certainly this is true in the design and construction professions. Executives, chief designers, project managers, superintendents, and team leaders all must possess the necessary ingredients of leadership skills to be effective in their positions. Most leadership skills are assumed to be acquired over time with exposure, experience, and observations. However, this acquisition can be accelerated with special training and coaching, and many companies as well as some colleges now offer instruction in leadership—attempting to cause everyone in an organization to perform better—to "move the bell curve" (Figure 9-2).

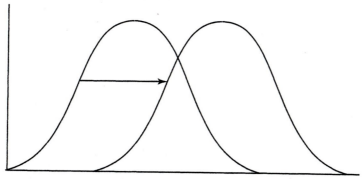

Figure 9-2   Moving the bell curve—making the entire organization more effective through leadership. The ultimate goal of motivation is an organization full of productive, self-reliant people who proceed toward effective outcomes with little supervision.

> An outcome of leadership training in an organization should be to cause everyone to perform better—to "move the bell curve."

Cases in Leadership

Cases in this chapter are designed to motivate students to think through leadership issues and to generate solutions to the problems posed. As with other case studies, there are no right answers—but many possible solutions. Students are urged to develop sound rationales for their positions, including cause-effect relationships, expected behavior versus emergent behavior, and possible outcomes of various solutions.

Case 9-1   The Carpentry Crew

Project:	Elementary school
Location:	Suburbs of a midwestern city
Status:	Basement columns being formed
Issue:	Irregular performance by a crew member

You are the project superintendent and have been on this site for two months. You have established a four-person crew to assemble forms for concrete columns:

Max: experienced carpenter, lead man
Harley: moderately experienced carpenter
Burt: laborer/helper/trainee
Hank: new employee, first assignment with company

Max and Harley work well together: Max figures things out quickly, and then they move ahead with good productivity. Burt is in his second year with the company and is progressing satisfactorily. Hank, having been with the company for two months, has much enthusiasm for his new job but is irregular in performance. Once assigned a task, he will carry it out rather well. However, he is slow at catching on to new ideas and at thinking for himself. After a month of regular attendance and punctuality, Hank has been late two or three times per week and has missed two work days during the past month. Once, Burt was absent the same day as Hank. That really hurt productivity. Both men claimed good excuses for missing work: Burt took his wife to the doctor but did not mention it to Max ahead of time; Hank said that he had to appear in court one day and stated "family problems" for the other absence.

Max comes to you for advice. He likes both men personally, and states that when they are all "in sync" they are a really good crew. Max himself is rather easygoing, not a taskmaster. He leads by example, but admits to being a reluctant teacher and really hates "chewing people out." He senses that because he has not disciplined Hank, Burt may be getting a little lax. The crew's output is good, and they are slightly ahead of schedule. Forming columns is definitely on the critical path, so it cannot be allowed to fall behind schedule.

Amplification of Issues to Enhance Understanding of This Case

Max may be characterized as a dedicated career carpenter, a vanishing breed that populated U.S. construction for a century. These mechanics were skilled, motivated, self-reliant, quality conscious—and sometimes irascible. They had varying levels of leadership skills, most acquired over time, with little actual training in "people skills." Their sons, daughters, and grandchildren are now doctors, lawyers, architects, and computer experts. Many less-well-qualified personnel are being drawn to construction, and most do not make it a career. So there is regular need for training and motivation.

Discussion Questions

○ Would you consider a career in construction trades—why and why not?
○ What must be done to attract capable, career-oriented people to the trades?

Assignment

As the superintendent and Max's immediate superior, evaluate the situation, determine other assumptions as required, and then identify various approaches you can take to improve the crew's overall performance. Review the leadership characteristics identified at the beginning of the chapter and determine which apply. Think through the various actions and their probable outcomes. Options include:

○ Motivate Max to be somewhat more authoritative. Possible outcomes:
   1. Everyone may respond positively, and the problem may be solved.

2. Max may be uncomfortable with this suggestion and allow it to affect his performance.
3. The crew, accustomed to Max's traditional relaxed behavior, may be "turned off" by a new manner, and productivity may suffer.

○ Move Harley into the lead-man position and make Max a regular crew member. Possible outcomes:
1. Again, the results may be very positive.
2. Harley may not function well in a leadership role.
3. Max may be demotivated, particularly if a pay cut ensues.
4. The entire crew may not function well under changed circumstances.

○ Fire Hank. Possible outcomes:
1. A reliable, productive replacement may be hired, and the crew will be revitalized.
2. The actions may motivate the remaining three crew members to work more diligently and actually equal the productivity of the prior full crew (this sometimes happens in industry).
3. A replacement may be unavailable and productivity may suffer.
4. The crew may be disturbed emotionally by the action and respond negatively.
5. There is always a learning curve for a new employee, and initial productivity will suffer even with the replacement worker.

Identify other options and possible outcomes, and then plan a path of action. Be specific about the superintendent's procedures. Remember that the superintendent has many other responsibilities besides this crew. He cannot spend an extraordinary amount of time on the problem.

Case 9-2   The Recalcitrant Designer

Situation:	Architectural engineering firm with 95 employees
Projects:	A number of institutional and commercial design commissions
Location:	Dallas, Texas
Issue:	A demotivated architect

The Center Group prides itself on high-quality design and has won several awards for schools, hospitals, and office buildings. There are many return clients, and there is a regular backlog of work. Melissa Alberta MacMurty is one of the most talented designers in the firm, both in regard to overall building concepts and in producing stimulating interiors. MacMurty has a history of hard work and positive collaborations with many team members over the eight years that she has been with the firm. She is a licensed architect in three states and has been directly responsible for four design awards. MacMurty has a total of 15 years of experience following a master's in architecture degree.

All was going "swimmingly" until three coworkers, all men, were elevated to principals and stockholders in the professional corporation, bringing the total to nine principals, one of whom is a 60-year-old woman, a cofounder of the firm. The three new principals are all competent, experienced persons, one architect and two engineers. Two are senior to MacMurty in employment; one has been there two fewer years but is two years older than she is. She had known that new principals would be appointed, and fully anticipated to be one of them. She bears no resentment to those elevated, but genuinely believes herself to be equally valuable to the firm.

MacMurty's disappointment soon influences her behavior. She considered a gender discrimination suit, but her husband, an attorney, dissuaded her. In the month since the promotions, her attendance has become erratic, and she is overtly less collaborative. Nonetheless, she has effectively pursued the design of a new church assigned to her just prior to her disappointment. The design has excited the church building committee, with whom she continues to work very professionally.

You are her immediate supervisor, an architect and principal in the firm. Your relations with her have been quite professional—efficient, businesslike, and friendly—but without a close personal relationship. She needs little supervision, but has regularly asked for your advice—until recently. You are impressed with her concept for the new church, but are concerned that she is not collaborating with structural and mechanical engineers, drafters, and specifications writers in the firm. She is too valuable an employee to lose, but her current behavior is unacceptable:

○ The firm is based on strong team relationships.
○ MacMurty's behavior is evident to everyone in the firm, and people are beginning to discuss it.
○ If not corrected, her behavior will affect other employees.

Amplification of Issues to Enhance Understanding of This Case

Architecture was long a "gentlemen's profession." While there were a few important women architects in the United States early in the century, such as Julia Morgan, who designed many buildings in California, including the

Hearst Castle in San Simeon, it was not until the 1960s that a significant number of women began entering the profession. Their impact has been quite positive, bringing new sensitivity to design and client relations. Many have moved into leadership positions in firms, in the American Institute of Architects, and in academe. Still, men hold most of the power positions in architecture, and the profession does not yet provide truly equal opportunity for women—but things are changing.

Women also bring different leadership styles to any occupation, being more supportive of subordinates and placing equal importance on how people feel about their work and on how they perform that work. Certainly feelings are an issue in this case.

Discussion Questions

❍ Is MacMurty correct to feel slighted—or might she be oversensitive to the issue?

❍ Would this case be handled differently if the individual were a man?

❍ Is architecture truly performance oriented—or are there other factors that determine success in a firm?

Assignment

As MacMurty's supervisor, devise a plan to redevelop her enthusiasm for the firm. Your options range from seeking a promotion for her to terminating her. There are obviously several middle-ground options. Identify three or four paths and possible outcomes, and then move to a recommended solution—with a strong rationale—to your fellow principals.

Case 9-3   Contract Administration

Project:	Addition to Children's Hospital
Location:	Northern Plains City
Budget:	$27,500,000 (for construction)
Project delivery system:	Traditional lump sum contract
Project status:	50 percent complete
Issue:	Conflict between an architect and a project superintendent

The Children's Hospital project is not going well. At midpoint it is six weeks behind schedule, and there are several disputes—with claims—already documented, and others brewing. You are the architect's contract administrator on the project. You were involved in the design and looked forward to seeing "your" project grow out of the ground. You have administered five other jobs, but this is the largest in your experience. The firm has a full-time field person, a senior engineer, but he is busy with other projects. You spend about 20 hours per week on the hospital, performing typical administrative duties:

○ Interpreting contract documents as required
○ Representing the owner's interests
○ Reviewing shop drawings and submittals
○ Observing the work and citing quality problems when necessary
○ Processing applications for payment
○ Helping to settle disagreements when appropriate
○ Processing change orders
○ Other acts aimed at advancing the progress of the job

The relationship with the superintendent has been difficult from the outset. Part of the problem is simply personalities. The superintendent is 60 years old and has come up through the ranks of carpenter to foreman to superintendent. This is the largest job he has had under his control. He is generally competent in dealing with subordinates and subcontractor foremen, but seems self-conscious about his communications skills in dealing with superiors. Also, he seems to have an inherent suspicion of architects.

On the other hand, you and the contractor's project manager have developed good relations. You are both about the same age, late thirties, both college educated, and both facile with computers and other electronic media. The project manager is primarily office based, and you deal with him whenever possible, usually by phone, fax, or e-mail. That relationship exacerbates the problem with the superintendent, who feels that the two of you are making deals behind his back.

You believe that the superintendent is overwhelmed and needs assistance, and you have expressed this to the project manager. The superintendent seems unreceptive to all of your statements, so you have resorted to sending written directives to him, with copies to the project manager. There are four documented disputes to date. You have sent reports on all of them to the project manager. He has not responded yet in writing. The disputes are:

○ The finish on one large section of exposed foundation wall is not acceptable in finished appearance.

○ The deformations in two sections of interior slab on grade exceed specified tolerances.

○ A 200-square-foot section of brick exterior wall does not match the approved sample panel.

○ Several architectural precast panels are inadequately anchored.

You have denied payment for all items, and the contractor has filed claims on each. Their resolution process is pending.

The situation reached a crisis point yesterday when the masonry contractor threatened to leave the job because of slow payment by the general contractor. The superintendent, knowing that you were within hearing range, heaped blame on you for all the problems on the job. Your anger nearly erupted, but you contained yourself. Shortly thereafter you met with the masonry foreman and determined that he really wished to stay and complete a good project, but was being urged by his boss to press for payment. You believe that it is time for you to take drastic action as agent to the owner—but what action to take?

Remember that your firm has no contract with the construction company (Figure 9-3). Your relationship with the contractor is administrative, as is your role on the job. Likewise, neither your firm nor the owner has a contract with the masonry subcontractor. Further, you have no responsibility for means or methods of execution. Obviously this situation calls for highly diplomatic leadership. As the agent of the owner, you have a responsibility to exert efforts to ensure that the project is carried out to meet the contract documents.

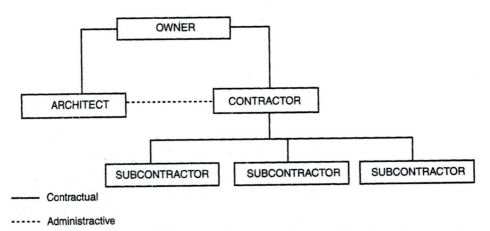

─── Contractual

----- Administractive

Figure 9-3   Contractual and administrative relationships in construction. Contractual relationships are binding; administrative relationships are flexible.

Amplification of Issues to Enhance Understanding of This Case

Contractual relationships in construction are spelled out in standard forms developed by the AIA, AGC, and others, all of which have evolved over time to develop interlocking responsibilities to get projects built while providing the bases of dispute resolution. Parties periodically test the contract clauses by placing demands on others, or by posturing toward actions that may be interpreted as violations of one or more of the agreements. One old saying in construction is that the parties first read the contract "carefully" when a dispute arises.

Discussion Questions

○ How does an architect most appropriately exercise positive influence on a project in the field?

○ Compare an agency relationship with an administrative relation—do they overlap? What are the significant differences?

○ Can a subcontractor leave a project of his or her own accord? What are the consequences?

Assignment

In the role of the architect responsible for contract administration, you must take actions to protect the owner's interests. Devise a strategy that recognizes contractual obligations, agency relationships, administrative relationships, and personal interaction. Then outline step-by-step tactics—with options—to arrive at a satisfactory conclusion. Remember that the central issue is leadership. Resources should include:

○ AIA A101, standard form of Agreement Between Owner and Contractor where the basis of payment is a Stipulated Sum

○ AIA A201, General Conditions of the Contract for Construction

○ AIA B141, Standard Form of Agreement Between Architect and Owner

○ AIA A401, Standard Form of Agreement Between Contractor and Subcontractor

○ Statement of Ethics, American Institute of Architects

Also, research construction company organizations to determine typical relationships between project managers and superintendents. Determine the appropriateness of discussing the project problems with the construction company executives, or whether it would be better to have one of your firm's principals approach a construction executive. Clarify the protocol of an architect talking directly to a subcontractor. Work through to a "leadership solution" that will not violate contractual relationships. Outline and explain the solution with a statement of expected outcomes.

C H A P T E R   1 0

Summary

"Life is an ongoing drama made up a series of episodes—or cases."

All eras are exciting, but as we move briskly into the information revolution, the prospects for change are breathtaking—and scary. Never before has continuing education been as important as it is now. Formal education must focus on learning to keep on learning. Case studies are as appropriate for ongoing professional development as they are for college-level education. All leaders can create case studies for team exercises. Both the creation and the responses will focus efforts on continuous improvement.

Learning From Real-Life Cases

Obviously, not all facets of design and construction have been covered by the foregoing case studies. However, patterns should have emerged. Life is full of "lessons learned," and success in any field depends on accumulating knowledge and skills from ongoing, dynamic learning. It is well established that no more than one-third of the competencies necessary for career success in any field can be achieved in a regular school setting (based on research by this author and others). The other two-thirds involve a mix of, and learning from, experience and semistructured continuing education. Most professional bodies now require some type of continuing education for continued licensure or competence status. The most effective continuing education is that consciously generated by oneself, ideally in collaboration with others. Continuous learning from experiences can involve self-constructed case studies—that is, adapting problems at hand as cases to be deliberately analyzed and solved. Procedures may include the following, which will be most beneficial when written guidelines are prepared and shared by the salient parties:

○ Careful early planning of all projects or major activities—knowing the elements of the "case at hand":
  1. Identify the actors in the drama, their roles, agendas, and probable biases. (*Note:* There are no unbiased people; the honest ones identify their biases.)
  2. Know the probable allies and the possible adversaries; strengthen the former and be aware of the latter—while considering ways to reduce the adversity. (*Note:* Construction, more than most industries, seems to "thrive on adversity," but of course it is not really thriving. Far too much energy is spent on posturing, accusations, and taking defensive positions. More energy should be spent on collaboration, problem solving—and getting the projects built!)
  3. Understand precedents; know what happened before the current act in the drama and what needs to be accomplished prior to subsequent acts.
  4. Know the resources available, where they are located, and who has control over them.
  5. Determine where to expend energies, and where expenditure will go unrewarded.
  6. Identify all the potential hurdles, from government regulations to erratic cash flow.
  7. Set clear, realistic goals and objectives; do not practice self-delusion or mislead others—a malady endemic to design and construction, particularly in regard to cost and time projections.
○ Continuous evaluation of activities:
  1. Be completely honest with yourself.
  2. Seek advice from others: peers, superiors, and subordinates.
  3. Remember that while positive feedback is good for one's well-being, negative feedback is more valuable if delivered in a respectful manner.

4. Have periodic checkpoints for detailed evaluation.
5. Develop checklists for evaluation, to establish criteria for measuring project success in regard to safety, quality, time, and costs.
○ Development of trusting alliances:
   1. In this complex world, individuals become ever less able to accomplish much by themselves in the fields of design and construction; collaborations are essential.
   2. Cultivate collaborative skills.
   3. Become a trustworthy ally.
   4. Seek other trustworthy allies (this could mean a change in employment).
○ Continuous self-improvement:
   1. Maintain good mental and physical health.
   2. Maintain healthy interpersonal relationships.
   3. Select from the voluminous continuing education opportunities available.
   4. Participate in professional and trade associations.
○ Maintenance of records of progress:
   1. Many architects keep graphic and written journals of activity.
   2. Constructors routinely keep job logs.
   3. Shape these ongoing efforts around capturing the salient pieces of learning each day.
○ Scope (outline) problems as case studies, and then deliberately seek solutions.
○ Celebrate successes!

Celebrating Accomplishments

It is crucial to feel good about your work, while always seeking to improve. Displaying enthusiasm about progress and celebrating accomplishments are treasured outcomes! There are few experiences more rewarding than enjoying the success that comes with completing a building to which you have contributed tangible value. The inevitable problems are ultimately solved—and become lessons to build on during the next project.

Architects celebrate accomplishments through awards for design (usually through the AIA local, state, and national components), specifications (through the Construction Specifications Institute), and academic recognition (by alma maters). Contractors historically have measured success in monetary terms, such as annual dollar volume of built work and net profit.

More recently, however, contractors have sought other recognition through their own honors (AGC Build America Awards) and increased civic activity, the latter perhaps linked to increased marketing and direct services to owners.

MINI–CASE STUDY
CELEBRATION OF CONSTRUCTION

In 1995 several construction associations collaborated with the University of Cincinnati Department of Construction Science to establish the Spirit of Construction Foundation of Greater Cincinnati, Inc., with the goals of:

- Celebrating construction
- Elevating and enhancing the image of the construction industry
- Participating in, and contributing to, cultural and educational activity that improves the industry

The success to date has been beyond expectations. Annual Celebrations of Construction are black-tie gala events, attended by hundreds, at which career achievers are honored with Spirit of Construction awards, distinctive pieces of sculpture designed specifically for the honor. The foundation has 70 contributing organizations, has helped to establish a construction exhibit at the local Children's Museum, and assists in attracting young people to the industry—and it is still in the beginning stages!

The United States has historically been a future-oriented nation—tomorrow always appears to be full of opportunity. This is definitely the case with design and construction. The information revolution has just begun to influence building design—in high-technology factories, communications centers, and intelligent buildings. Dramatic evolution will continue in the 21st century.

Also, collaboration among the parties is becoming more refined with increased use of sophisticated project delivery, using advanced versions of design-build and CM. The past adverse relations between designers and constructors have not evaporated, but have taken on new dimensions, a combination of competing for leadership in project delivery and learning new ways to collaboratively serve owners.

Owners are becoming more sophisticated as they recognize the criticality of productive facilities to profitable operations. The roles of facilities managers have become more important than ever, and those roles are filled with well-educated persons skilled in both technical and management operations. Facilities managers are taking primary activity in programming new buildings and then working with designers and constructors to fulfill the design/construct/maintain continuum. Owners seek the right balance between in-house responsibility and outsourcing of duties. Designers and constructors must stay carefully tuned to the fluctuating environment.

A way of staying tuned is through the case-study method. By scoping a project as a case to be explored and solved, and listing all the influencing factors and variables, a deliberated solution can be sought that leads to a successful conclusion. Indeed, the future is bright for the well prepared.

> **A good way for design and construction entities to practice continuing education is to create case studies relevant to current and future operations, for solutions to be sought by different levels of leadership.**

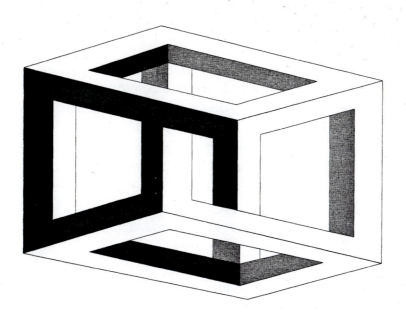

References

American Institute of Architects. Various forms of agreement and guidance documents. Washington, DC, various dates.

American Institute of Architects, Associated General Contractors of America. *AIA/AGC Recommended Guidelines for Procurement of Design-Build Projects in the Public Sector.* Washington, DC: American Institute of Architects, 1995.

Associated General Contractors of America. *Partnering: A Concept for Success.* Washington, DC: Associated General Contractors of America, 1992.

Associated General Contractors of America. Various forms of agreement and guidance documents. Washington, DC, various dates.

Bockrath, Joseph T. *Contracts and the Legal Environment for Architects and Engineers.* 5th ed. New York: McGraw-Hill, 1995.

Chase, G. W. *Implementing TQM in a Construction Company.* Washington, DC: Associated General Contractors of America, 1993.

Collier, Keith. *Managing Construction: The Contractual Viewpoint.* Albany, NY: Delmar, 1994.

Dorsey, Robert W. *Acquisition of Skills and Traits for Success in Managing Construction*. Austin, TX: Construction Industry Institute, 1990.

Dorsey, Robert W. *Project Delivery Systems for Building Construction*. Washington, DC: Associated General Contractors of America, 1997.

Glavinich, Thomas E., and Stella, Paul J. *Construction Planning and Scheduling*. Washington, DC: Associated General Contractors of America, 1994.

Harris, Cyril M. *Dictionary of Architecture and Construction*. New York: McGraw-Hill, 1975.

Hendrickson, Chris, and Au, Tung. *Project Management for Construction*. Englewood Cliffs, NJ: Prentice Hall, 1981.

Hinze, Jimmie. *Construction Contracts*. New York: McGraw-Hill, 1993.

Laudon, Kenneth C., Traver, Carol Guercio, and Laudon, Jane Price. *Information Technology and Society*. Belmont, CA: Wadsworth, 1994.

MacLeod, S. Scott. "Traditional Construction and Models for Future Organizations." *Construction Business Review,* March/April, 1995.

Pena, William. *Problem Seeking*. Washington, DC: AIA Press, 1987.

Surety Association of America. *Contract Bonds: The Unseen Services of a Surety*. Iselin, NJ: Surety Association of America, 1991.

Surety Association of America. *Glossary of Fidelity and Surety*. Iselin, NJ: Surety Association of America, 1991.